Honey-Mad Women

GENDER AND CULTURE
Carolyn G. Heilbrun and Nancy K. Miller, editors

GENDER AND CULTURE
A Series of Columbia University Press
Edited by
Carolyn G. Heilbrun
and
Nancy K. Miller

In Dora's Case: Freud, Hysteria, Feminism
Edited by Charles Bernheimer and Claire Kahane
Breaking the Chain: Women, Theory, and French Realist Fiction
Naomi Schor
Between Men: English Literature and Male Homosocial Desire
Eve Kosovsky Sedgwick
Romantic Imprisonment: Women and Other Glorified Outcasts
Nina Auerbach
The Poetics of Gender
Edited by Nancy K. Miller
Reading Woman: Essays in Feminist Criticism
Mary Jacobus
Honey-Mad Women: Emancipatory Strategies in Women's Writing
Patricia Yaeger

Honey-Mad Women

Emancipatory Strategies in Women's Writing

PATRICIA YAEGER

New York

Columbia University Press

1988

In memory of my grandmothers,
Aurora Maie Bearden Gaddis
and
Lacy Hill Smith

Contents

Acknowledgments

This book would never have been happened if it were not for Carolyn Heilbrun's 1982 NEH Summer Seminar on "The Woman as Hero in Nineteenth and Twentieth Century Literature." I want to express my gratitude to everyone in this seminar, but especially to Anne Howells and Deborah Sitter, whose comments and suggestions on this and other projects have been invaluable. As for Carolyn's presence both in and out of the classroom, I cannot say enough. She changed our lives, and made me, a reprobate Romanticist, into a feminist scholar.

Two other scholar-teachers influenced this book: Drusilla Cornell and Maire Jaanus. To Maire I owe what acumen I have as a literary theorist. It was in her classroom that I woke up to the rigors of philosophy; her intellectual presence has been important in conceiving this text. Dru Cornell introduced me to Habermas in a course on "Jurisprudence" at the University of Pennsylvania Law School; in her classroom I first became interested in questions of emancipation.

Other friends have made memorable contributions to this project. Nancy Miller's editorial comments were splendid, and helped to transform several unruly chapters. Eve Sedgwick helped me around a pugnacious writing block by explaining that my book needn't pursue a single narrative: it could be dialogic. Harriet Chessman shared her best wisdom and many good times, while Claudia Waszkis gave me my first book of Mary Oliver's poetry. I want to thank Joe Boone, Mary Carpenter, Susan Fraiman, Suzanne Graver, Margaret Homans, Annie Janowitz, Gail Reimer, Carolyn Williams, and Bryan Wolf for their advice and encouragement. I'm also grateful to the members of I.D. 450, a feminist collective, for the pleasure and turmoil we've shared over the last few years as each of us searched for a voice.

I should also say a word about the feminist writers whose work I emulate and critique in *Honey-Mad Women*. Nina Auerbach, Rachel Brownstein, Hélène Cixous, Teresa de Lauretis, Jane Gallop, Sandra Gilbert, Susan Gubar, Mary Jacobus, Myra Jehlen, Toril Moi, Tillie Olsen, Kaja Silverman, and Elaine Showalter have been inestimably important in sheltering my voice and bolstering my thoughts about feminist criticism. Although some of my chapters take impetus from disagreements with these critics, this book would not have been possible without their provocative theories and dedication to feminist debate.

Finally, I would like to thank Richard Miller for his sweetness and light, my parents for actually reading the essays I sent them, and David, Nancy, and Kathy for being my best siblings.

A version of chapter 2 appeared in *Browning Institute Studies*, 14 (1987), and some of the material in chapter 8 appeared in a review in *Contemporary Literature* (Summer 1986). I thank the editors of these journals for their willingness to allow me to reprint.

ONE

Honey-Mad Women

The secrecy surrounding sexual activity has been, for me, the price
all women paid for femininity. We were not to speak of our desires.

Paula Webster, *Heresies*

How do women speak about their desires? For male writers and critics there is a long-standing tradition of speaking about pleasure, a tradition C. L. Barber and Mikhail Bakhtin describe in their books on Shakespeare and Rabelais, a tradition Roland Barthes reinvents in *The Pleasure of the Text*. But women, as Paula Webster reminds us, do not possess a tradition that permits us to speak openly about our desires, that permits the woman writer to take her pleasures seriously. "In Western societies, (sexual) pleasure (the advent of non-sense which multiplies sense) is granted to women provided it isn't discussed," says Julia Kristeva in an interview with Xavière Gauthier. "Estranged from language, women are visionaries, dancers who suffer as they speak."[1]

Are there other ways of describing women's relation to speech? Much of feminist criticism suggests that there is not. We have grown accustomed to discovering moments in literary texts when women fail to describe their desires, when women are made into objects of "masculine" language. In William Dean Howells' *A Modern Instance,* to cite a single example, the novel's "hero," Bartley Hubbard, asks the young woman he is courting to go out for a sleigh ride. Playfully eloquent, he writes his invitation on a piece of her stationery. But when Marcia Gaylord tries—laughingly—to tear up his request, Bartley seizes her hands and threatens her,

offering to let go only when Marcia promises not to damage his
words:

> She hesitated long, letting him hold her wrists. At last she said, "Well,"
> and he released her wrists on whose whiteness his clasp left red circles.
> She wrote a single word on the paper, and pushed it across the table
> to him. He rose with it, and went around to her side.[2]

The feminist critic who analyzes this passage will be in
familiar territory. First, the violence, the aggressive demand for
complicity damages both woman's will and her body; Marcia's white
wrists become a blank page—they are made into a writing tablet
for Bartley Hubbard's desires. Second, after Hubbard has deposited
these "red circles" of pain on Marcia's body, he assumes ownership
of her body, so that when Marcia writes a reply that displeases
him, he seizes her hand to guide the pen:

> "No, no!" she protested.
> "Yes, yes! Dear Mr. Hubbard. There, that will do. Now the signature.
> Yours—"
> "I *won't* write that. I won't indeed!"
> "Oh, yes, you will. You only think you won't. Yours gratefully, Marcia
> Gaylord. That's right. The Gaylord is not very legible, on account of a
> slight tremor in the writer's arm, resulting from a constrained posture,
> perhaps. Thanks, Miss Gaylord, I will be here promptly at the hour
> indicated—"[3]

I do not wish to deny Marcia Gaylord's helplessness,
nor should we deny that her story at least partially confirms Kristeva's
perception that women are "estranged from language . . . dancers
who suffer as they speak." This is not, however, the only relationship
to language that women—as writers or heroines—know. In the
chapters that follow I will challenge the validity that Kristeva's image
has for the feminist critic, and explore why this image has achieved
such prominence in our descriptions of women's texts. In addition,
I want to begin to define a countertradition within women's writing,
a tradition that involves the reinvention and reclamation of a body
of speech women have found exclusive and alienating. The goal of
this study is not to dispute the discovery that language is dangerous
for women, but to ask whether we can identify contexts in which

women find language empowering, in which women speak of their pleasure and find pleasure in speech.

In "August," a poem from Mary Oliver's *American Primitive,* we encounter another suffering female speaker—one who has devised an alternative relation to her oral and verbal needs. This blackberry picker is not among the hunted; she has become a gatherer.

> When the blackberries hang
> swollen in the woods, in the brambles
> nobody owns, I spend
>
> all day among the high
> branches reaching
> my ripped arms, thinking
>
> of nothing, cramming
> the black honey of summer
> into my mouth.[4]

The poet's "ripped arms" remind us that woman's attempt to find pleasure in the text, to establish her own contented orality is difficult, even among the "brambles / nobody owns." And yet the poet who risks this danger is productive; the blackberry picker's, the word picker's ecstatic eating leads to other pleasures:

> In the dark
> creeks that run by there is
> this thick paw of my life darting among
>
> the black bells, the leaves; there is
> this happy tongue.   (p. 3)

"This happy tongue" has been left out of our analysis of women's writing. We see the ways in which the woman writer is terrorized by the texts of others, the ways in which her arms, lips, throat are ripped by men's words. But in focusing on these terrifying moments we neglect the woman writer's ecstatic espionage, her expropriation of the language she needs, her own invention of a "terrorist text."[5] In the chapters that follow I want to reconstruct this terrorist text and define an alternate mythology of feminine speech. I have already begun this process of definition by substituting for Kristeva's image of women who suffer as they speak an archetype drawn from Oliver's poems: the archetype of the writer as honey-mad woman, as someone mad for the honey of speech.

Honey is a substance that stands in peculiar relation to human society. Unrefined, it is also manufactured; raw, it is also "cooked"; natural, it is cultural. As liminal substance, honey underlines the liminal character of orality itself—an orality I want to consider through the metaphor of the feast. Because the mouth is the site where that which is alien to the self is incorporated, the feast, according to Mikhail Bakhtin, is a time of "free interplay between the body and outside world," a time of victory over fear, for the feast celebrates the destruction of what the self encounters as threatening. Food "crowns" our relation to work: "the struggle of people against a hostile nature is crowned with food. . . . People 'swallow that which they have defeated.' "[6] The images that dominate feminist critical practice do not always invite us to consider the woman writer's oral victories. There are, of course, good textual reasons for this reticence. In Kate Chopin's *The Awakening,* for example, when Edna Pontellier visits the Ratignolles, she not only finds Madame Ratignole's verbal acumen severely limited by her husband, but Monsieur Ratignolle suggests an oral cure for Edna as well:

> Monsieur Ratignolle was delighted to see her, though he found her looking not so well as at Grand Isle, and he advised a tonic. He talked a good deal on various topics, a little politics, some city news and neighborhood gossip. He spoke with an animation and earnestness that gave an exaggerated importance to every syllable he uttered. His wife was keenly interested in everything he said, laying down her fork the better to listen, chiming in, taking the words out of his mouth.[7]

This passage from *The Awakening* helps to explain why many of the metaphors feminist critics use to describe women's relation to masculine speech stress women's alienation from her own powers of metaphor. But while the usual power that food and drink have to liberate human speech and to loosen the tongue is nullified by Monsieur Ratignolle's presence, the feast is traditionally—in literature and in social life—a time of empowerment. Edna not only pities Madame Ratignolle for the "colorless existence" in which she could never have "the taste of life's delusions" (p. 57), but Edna's own tongue begins to taste these desires at a particularly festive dinner party:

> The dinner was excellent. The claret was warm and the champagne was cold, and under their beneficent influence the threatened unpleasantness melted and vanished with the fumes of the wine. . . .
>
> . . . [Edna] had [a story] of her own to tell, of a woman who paddled away with her lover one night in a pirogue and never came back. They were lost amid the Baratarian Islands, and no one ever heard of them or found trace of them from that day to this. It was pure invention. . . . But every glowing word seemed real to those who listened. They could feel the hot breath of the Southern night; they could hear the long sweep of the pirogue through the glistening moonlit water, the beating of birds' wings, rising startled from among the reeds in the saltwater pools; they could see the faces of the lovers, pale, close together, rapt in oblivious forgetfulness, drifting into the unknown. (p. 70)

In *Rabelais and His World* Bakhtin tells us that "next to the bowels and the genital organs is the mouth, through which enters the world to be swallowed up. . . . All these convexities and orifices have a common characteristic; it is with them that the borders between one's own and other bodies and between the body and the world are breached."[8] In our preoccupation with the male writer's phallic power of "breaching" we tend to ignore the woman writer's double orality—her capacity for transforming boundaries, for defining her own loci of power.[9] This breaching can be glorious, as in Oliver's "Bluefish," in which the speaker identifies with

> The angels
> I have seen
> coming up
> out of the water!
> There I was,
> drifting,
> not far from shore,
> when they appeared,

flying
. . . . .
open-mouthed,
charging
like small blue
tigers after
some schooling
minnows, darkening
the water, ripping it
to shreds.   (p. 79)

In Oliver's poem the angel of the house rises out of the depths of the sea to consume the world with pleasure, with glee:

They poured
like fire over the minnows,
they fell back through the waves
like messengers
filled with good news
and the sea
held them in its silken folds
quietly,
those gatherers,
those eaters,
those powerfully leaping
immaculate
meat-eaters.   (pp. 79–80)

In Oliver's poem suffering is not the issue. These hungry bluefish are fed "with good news" and gently held by the "silken folds" of the sea, and we are invited to take special pleasure in the similitude between the speaker who drifts in this silky medium and her hungry cousins.

As we define a countertradition in women's writing and set beside the metaphors that tell us that language is the medium of woman's oppression and suffering, images of women who seize words and use them for their own purposes, these new images can help us focus on those pleasurable, powerful aspects of women's orality we have hitherto neglected. We need to allow our critical practices to foreground the woman writer's ability to redefine her own marginality—to revise her banishment to the borders of culture—a power at work in Oliver's "The Honey Tree."

> And so at last I climbed
> the honey tree, ate
> chunks of pure light, ate
> the bodies of bees that could not
> get out of my way, ate
> the dark hair of the leaves,
> the rippling bark,
> the heartwood. Such
> frenzy! But joy does that,
> I'm told, in the beginning.   (p. 81)

As Oliver's speaker goes honey-mad, climbing the honey tree becomes an act of pure bodily joy, of visionary excess, of consummate play between desire and the fulfillment of desire. The tree filled with honey becomes the site of vision and of liberation for the woman writer—a bodily liberation that releases the tree energy, the honey energy into the "rippling bark" of her poem.

Before arguing for the empirical validity of an alternate mythology of women's writing, we must first look at the prevailing myths of women's orality, to see why other explanations are in need of revision. Since French feminist writers have come closest to inventing a theory of woman's "linguisticality," and since this theory has become a kind of touchstone American feminists use to discuss women's writing as well, I will preface this analysis of the writer as "honey-mad woman" by coming to terms with some of the writers who have been labeled "French feminists." My goal will be to take what is nourishing from these theories to help shape my own project, while reserving the right to question ideas I consider unsound.

How do "French feminists" define women's relation to speech? Male writers in France have little trouble appropriating the speech they desire. In *The Pleasure of the Text* Roland Barthes explains that his pleasure in language occurs in the "moment when my body pursues its own ideas—for my body does not have the same ideas I do."[10] At home with the old dualities, comfortable negotiating the illusive residues left by Descartes's mind/body split, Barthes is at ease with his own medium of analysis; he defines speech as his "body" of pleasure. "Does the text have a human form, is it a figure, an anagram of the body? Yes, but of our erotic body. The pleasure of the text is irreducible to physiological need" (p. 17). Barthes' pleasure may be irreducible to physiology, but for him it is characterized by a leisurely turn from mind to body, by an exploitation of the erotic connections between mother and son. "The writer is someone who plays with his mother's body . . . in order to glorify it, to embellish it, or in order to dismember it," Barthes says, "to take it to the limit of what can be known about the body" (p. 37).

French feminist writers also focus on the special pleasure of seizing words, the pleasure of speaking itself. "If we don't invent a language, if we don't find our body's language," Luce Irigaray says in "When Our Lips Speak Together," "its gestures will be too few to accompany our story. When we become tired of the same ones, we'll keep our desires secret, unrealized. Asleep again, dissatisfied, we will be turned over to the words of men—who have claimed to 'know' for a long time. But *not our body.*"[11] Irigaray's strategy seems reckless; her need to discover a new body and a new body of speech represents a strange antidote to women's aphasia, a flight to linguistic extremes. Our body, their body, his body, hers—does it matter whose body is speaking? Irigaray assures us that it does. In claiming her own "mother tongue" the woman writer is liable to inherit Barthes' casual dismemberment of the mother's body. "If we continue to speak this sameness, if we speak to each other as men have spoken for centuries, as they taught us to speak, we will fail each other. Again. . . . Words will pass through our bodies, above our heads, disappear, make us disappear" (p. 69). For Irigaray the act of expropriating the male writer's speech is not sufficient. Women can only lay claim to a language from which patriarchy and pain—terms which for her are synonymous— have been excised. "Absent from ourselves, we become machines that are spoken, machines that speak. . . . We have fled into proper names. . . . Get out of their language. Go back through all the

names they gave you. I'm waiting for you, I'm waiting for myself"
(pp. 69–70).

But why should women "get out" of a language we
have spoken for centuries? In "Archimedes and the Paradox of
Feminist Criticism" Myra Jehlen explains that while the woman
writer always writes against her dependence upon men's words, she
must also confront the fact that "the structural formulation" of her
work is prescribed by its "relationship to the inherently formally
patriarchal language which is the only language we have."[12] But
Emile Benveniste says that what is admirable about our system of
speech is precisely its permissiveness, its freedom, its democratic
versatility. Language, according to Benveniste, is "organized in such
a way that it allows each speaker to appropriate the entire language
by designating himself as the 'I.' "[13] This "I" has access not only
to all the words in our cultural lexicon, but to the power of syntax
as well.

In *Cartesian Linguistics* Noam Chomsky echoes Benveniste's beliefs. Since human language is "free from the control
of independently identifiable external stimuli or internal states," at
least in normal usage, and since it is not restricted like the "pseudo
language of animals" to a "practical communicative function," it
is therefore "free to serve as an instrument of free thought and
self-expression."[14] These male writers share a view of language
without anguish, of speech without tragedy and without limitation:
"the fundamental property of a language must be its capacity to
use its finitely specifiable mechanisms for an unbounded and unpredictable set of contingencies."[15] From this point of view a female
subject is as free to claim that "I" as a male one; language is
perfectly malleable and adapts to an "unbounded" set of speakers
and contingencies. Before challenging this Cartesian linguistics from
a feminist perspective, we need to look at the problems with what
Benveniste and Chomsky say from the point of view of the deconstructive philosophy recently propounded in France in order to
see how both views are challenged and expropriated by French
women writers themselves.

French psychiatrists, philosophers, and social critics insist on the restrictive nature of speech. The "I" Benveniste designates

as the proprietor of language, the "I" who claims sovereign power over the letter, is actually made helpless by the flight of his or her lexicon. Words and the syntactic structures mediating our relation to them are elusive, overpowering, dangerous; we live in perilous relation to the words that we speak. In Jacques Derrida's view the "I" is never the unified "self" we imagine. While it seems to represent a self that is internally consistent and persists over time, the "I" is a construct of madness:

As soon as I speak, the words I have found (as soon as they are words) no longer belong to me. . . . As soon as I am heard, as soon as I hear myself, the I who hears *itself*, who hears *me*, becomes the I who speaks and takes speech from the I who thinks that he speaks and is heard in his own name; and becomes the I who takes speech *without ever cutting off* the I who thinks that he speaks.[16]

Derrida's discovery that the "I" is a fleeting and diachronic construction is a simple extension of Hegel's parsing of sense-certainty at the beginning of the *Phenomenology,* but while Hegel remains cheerful about the thoughtful surplus of negativity that the mind's preoccupation with "otherness" insures, Derrida is skeptical:

What is called the speaking subject is no longer the person himself, or the person alone, who speaks. The speaking subject discovers his irreducible secondarity, his origin that is always already eluded; for the origin is always already eluded on the basis of an organized field of speech in which the speaking subject vainly seeks a place that is always missing. (p. 178)

Speech is prior to the subject; it preconstitutes the arena from which we take our syntactical and lexical coordinates. Language is not free to operate as the instrument of liberated thought and unmitigated self-expression as Chomsky and Benveniste imagine, for to mean something is not to "make" meaning, but to draw a particular meaning from a preexisting epistemological field. Thus the subject always relates to language as a beggar or thief to what is coveted:

The *letter,* inscribed or propounded speech, is always stolen. Always stolen because it is always *open.* It never belongs to its author or to its addressee, and by nature, it never follows the trajectory that leads from subject to subject. . . . before me, the signifier on its own says more than I believe that I mean to say, and in relation to it, my meaning-to-say is submissive rather than active. (p. 178)

For Derrida speech is "open" in the sense that it belongs to no one in particular but haunts everyone with the specter of ownership. Words are constantly "preventing, but calling upon each other, provoking each other . . . in a kind of autonomous over-assemblage of meanings, a power of pure equivocality that makes the creativity of the classical God appear all too poor." In the attempt to write or speak words cancel one another out; they exacerbate each other on their journey toward mouth or pen, where the restless desire for possession of meaning is halted by the narrow "passageway of speech against which all possible meanings push each other, preventing each other's emergence."[17] The writer can only send out long or short strings of words which may not say anything at all; writing is always uncertain of itself. "To write is to know that what has not yet been produced within literality has no other dwelling place, does not await us as prescription in some *topos ouranios,* or some divine understanding. Meaning must await being said or written in order to inhabit itself."[18] For Chomsky, language must be adequate for an infinite set of contingencies. For Derrida, it cannot be; language has neither divine nor formal adequacy to reconcile us to the things of this world.

French women writers like Cixous and Irigaray share Derrida's conviction that our roles as speakers involve submission to a speech which means too much and too little, which controls us and is out of control, a speech in which, abysmally, "the speaking subject is always missing." But while these writers echo Derrida's insistence that it is the "cultural field" from which sentences and meanings emerge, for them the absence of the speaking subject is not a narrow academic point but a sinister reality. It is woman as speaker who is most absent from the discursive field: woman who, like Marcia Gaylord, has been banished from even the negative anguish of the masculine writer. The meanings that women imbibe from their cultural matrix are not simply disorienting; as Wittig insists in a famous passage from *Les Guérillères,* they are debilitating, destructive, malevolent.

The women say, unhappy one, men have expelled you from the world of symbols and yet they have given you names, they have called you slave, you unhappy slave. Masters, they have exercised their rights as masters. They write, of their authority to accord names, that it goes back so far that the origin of language itself may be considered an act of authority emanating from those who dominate. Thus they say that they have said, this is such or such a thing, they have attached a particular word to an object or a fact and thereby consider themselves to have appropriated it. The women say, so doing the men have bawled, shouted with all their might to reduce you to silence.[19]

The letter is not as "open" as Derrida imagines. While access to the "narrow passageway of speech" may be limited for men, for women, Monique Wittig insists, it is even more restricted. Put simply, the problem with Derrida's analysis is that he has managed to avoid deconstructing the gender bias of his own narrative; although Derrida himself speaks with candor ("Speaking frightens me because, by never saying enough, I also say too much"), rebel patriarchs like Artaud or Bataille or Edmond Jabès' epigrammatic character Reb Stein are the demigods of Derrida's pantheon.

The masculine name may neither guarantee the ownership of language, nor guarantee that writing will bring freedom, but it is nevertheless a material origin for the book, a designated place for wielding whatever power the letter can wield. "As a child, when I wrote my name for the first time, I / felt that I was starting a book," says Jabès' Reb Stein.[20] Although Derrida applauds Jabès' suggestion that "I am not this man / for this man writes and the writer is no one" (p. 28), Derrida's writer is a *masculine* "no one" whose gendered nonentity gains him access to the agonistic kingdom of inscription.[21] Each speaker may not be able to "appropriate the entire language by designating himself as the I," but we now see that Benveniste has it partly right, that it is the author "himself" who appropriates what he can of the mobile "I am," and that women who write confront an added dilemma. The woman writer also finds that language is prior; that a set of cultural meanings and practices precede her. But French feminist writers have argued that this field is not open to women's voices in the same way that it is open to men's. When women write—the "enlightened," liberated women of the last few centuries who have demanded and gained access to men's discursive field—they experience themselves not as secondary, but tertiary. As Xavière Gauthier suggests in "Is There Such a Thing as Women's Writing?":

Women are, in fact, caught in a very real contradiction. Throughout the course of history, they have been mute, and it is doubtless by virtue of this mutism that men have been able to speak and write. As long as women remain silent, they will be outside the historical process. But, if they begin to speak and write *as men do,* they will enter history subdued and alienated; it is a history that, logically speaking, their speech should disrupt.[22]

The answer to this predicament is startling. Writers like Gauthier or Cixous or Irigaray describe—in euphoric terms—the invention of *another* language system that will redress women's exclusion, that will mime the rhythms of women's bodies, permit feminine excess, express women's needs. "To invent a language that is not oppressive, a language that does not leave speechless but that loosens the tongue," says Annie Leclerc in *Parole de femme.*[23] Hélène Cixous seconds this motion; she tells us that the woman writer "lets the other language speak, the language of 1,000 tongues which knows neither enclosure nor death. To life she refuses nothing. Her language does not contain, it carries; it does not hold back, it makes possible."[24] For Chantal Chawaf the goal is also a redeemed feminine orality:

We need languages that regenerate us, warm us, give birth to us, that lead us to act and not to flee. . . . For me the most important thing is to work on orality. . . . If a music of femininity is arising out of its own oppression, it materializes through the rediscovered body.[25]

Here we find a renewed faith in language, a new "hope of the name"—but only insofar as that name is transgressive and resonates within a nonpatriarchal system. As Cixous insists in "The Laugh of the Medusa":

If woman has always functioned "within" the discourse of man, a signifier that has always referred back to the opposite signifier which annihilates its specific energy and diminishes or stifles its very different sound, it is time for her to dislocate this "within," to explode it, turn it around, and seize it; to make it hers, containing it, taking it in her own mouth, biting that tongue with her very own teeth to invent for herself a language to get inside of. (p. 257)

In *Les Guérillères,* Wittig also asks women to invent their own system of speaking:

This is apparent precisely in the intervals that your masters have not been able to fill with their words of proprietors and possessors, this can be found in the gaps, in all that which is not a continuation of their discourse, in the zero, the O, the perfect circle that you invent to imprison them and to overthrow them. (p. 114)

We will return to Wittig's insistence that women's writing must be nonrepresentational, that it occurs in the interval, but we need, first, to note that American feminists have met this demand for an *écriture féminine,* this demand that we enter the spaces between words and invent a language of our own, with understandable skepticism. In a delightful and witty conversation in *Yale French Studies* Sandra Gilbert and Elizabeth Abel describe their problems with contemporary French theory:

SANDRA GILBERT: But there is another problem for me with a lot of French feminist theoreticians. My sense of their "otherness" has something to do with a way in which their theory is detached from what we have to struggle with. It has to be said that people like Irigaray and Cixous in particular are anti-empirical. They are involved in a kind of word play: interrogating absences in Freud often becomes a sort of wistful fantasy which leaves me faint with desire.

ELIZABETH ABEL: As a feminist I'm still, perhaps in a very naive way, looking for answers about female identity, and I don't want it all to be word play. I feel that's a male privilege. It isn't what I want to do

with texts. I want to figure out what the forms
of female experience are.[26]

But perhaps the reason we find French feminist texts so stunning,
so inviting to read, the reason their texts leave us "faint with desire,"
is that these French writers do touch on the forms of women's
experience: especially upon our need, as women, to invent language
games that challenge and change linguistic codes, our need to write
new possibilities into the language.[27] This is to suggest that what
French feminists are doing *and* talking about is precisely a form
of female experience, that this "word play" Gilbert and Abel hesitate
to affirm is not only healing, but has a specific heuristic function:
it has the capacity to draw our attention to the role of emancipatory
strategies as they help to enact our liberation from a "father
tongue."[28]

    Since the issues these French women writers raise are
so appealing, and since their very strategies of writing resonate with
older responses to women's oppression—why not borrow their word
play to describe the emancipatory strategies that will be the focus
of this study? Why not use the ecstatic prose of a Cixous or an
Irigaray to help us describe the woman writer's pleasure in language?
My reasons for going beyond French feminist metaphors of "writing
the body" and choosing new symbols to describe women's jubilation
in inventing new language games are twofold. First, the French
feminist assertion that language is "masculine" is simplistic; we
need a more capacious model for understanding the woman writer's
relation to speech. Second, the French writers I have been considering do not look to the writing of the past for an understanding
of the struggles that are either ongoing or have been won in women's
texts; they are not interested in the ways women writers of the
past have provided resources which make possible the language
games women now play. In their utopian modeling of woman's
relation to language, Cixous and Irigaray ignore the dialectical forces
within women's speech that have already helped us move in the
direction of a new *écriture*.[29]

    My own quarrel with these French writers takes, then,
a different direction from Abel's and Gilbert's informal critique. I

am pleased that French feminists are attempting to mystify feminine writing, to do something men have done for centuries—that is, to participate in sacralizing and carnivalizing their own gender's speech. French feminists' texts are not just attempts to challenge the patriarchal tradition; they want to devise a mode of feminine *"Sondersprache,"* to discover a tradition that will allow us to read feminine speech as divine speech, as mystified writing. But while I find the French feminists' emphasis on a redeemed orality breathtaking, I want to insist that Wittig, Cixous, Irigaray, and the other writers quoted here *do not go far enough* in defining this orality. *"Ecriture féminine"* names the writing of the future—but to claim it as our own we must be permitted to see its features in the writing of the past.

   "Ecriture féminine," as Elaine Showalter says in "Feminist Criticism in the Wilderness," "describes a Utopian possibility rather than a literary practice."[30] This futuristic conception of women's writing invites us to ignore the radical structures women have invented in the past to protest and to remake a patriarchal discourse their own. "Until now, far more extensively and repressively than is ever suspected or admitted, writing has been run by a libidinal and cultural—hence political, typically masculine—economy," Cixous says in "The Laugh of the Medusa," and "this is a locus where the repression of women has been perpetuated . . . where woman has never *her* turn to speak" (p. 249).

   How is it that woman has not spoken when, for Cixous, "writing is precisely *the very possibility of change,* the space that can serve as a springboard for subversive thought, the precursory movement of a transformation of social and cultural structures" (p. 249)? Perhaps the word play Gilbert and Abel object to when they read Cixous consists of an objection to this hide-and-seek within Cixous' own thematics, or—more seriously—of their sense that the effects of Cixous' assertions can be repressive; her millenarianism asks us to turn our gaze from the struggle that has already gone on in women's writing. She asks us to abandon our sense that the discourse of our foremothers was also in process—was also a discourse of inscriptive social change.

Cixous' brashness is deliberate, strategic—she wants to release the libidinal potential we all feel at the prospect of beginning:

It is time to liberate the New Woman from the Old by coming to know her—by loving her for getting by, for getting beyond the Old without delay, by going out ahead of what the New Woman will be, as an arrow quits the bow with a movement that gathers and separates the vibrations musically, in order to be more than her self.

I say that we must, for, with a few rare exceptions, there has not yet been any writing that inscribes femininity; exceptions so rare, in fact, that, after plowing through literature across languages, cultures, and ages, one can only be startled at this vain scouting mission. (p. 248)

This exclusion of feminine precursors is all the more startling because Cixous is so vehement in her condemnation of "the old Apartheid routine" in which women are taught "that their territory is black: because you are Africa, you are black. Your continent is dark. Dark is dangerous . . . in the dark, you're afraid . . . don't go into the forest. And so we have internalized this horror of the dark" (pp. 247–48). And yet her marginalization of earlier women writers is equally divisive. Cixous forces the women writers of the past toward this dark continent—she excludes them from the collective and honey-mad voice her own essay discovers with bliss: "our lovely mouths gagged with pollen, our wind knocked out of us, we the labyrinths, the ladders, the trampled spaces, the bevies—we are black and we are beautiful" (p. 248).

But since this beauty, this tempestuous struggle is also at work in the writing of those dark and excluded women writers of the past, they are also part of the continent we must labor to reclaim. American feminists have begun this work of reclamation by reformulating the canon and discovering women writers whose works have been ignored by publishers and departments of literature alike. In addition, American feminist critics have reformulated the ways the academy analyzed this canon by proving that questions of genre and periodization inevitably include questions of gender. But what has, until recently, been left out of the revisionary activity of American feminists is the sense of the inventiveness, the playfulness that French feminist writers want to affirm.[31] We may say, then, that the sense of woman's dispossession in the realm of language leads, in the case of French feminists, to a startling word play, to the description and invention of new language games, of abnormal discourses that set the heart spinning, and that this activity should—but does not—lead to an awareness of the word play, the abnormal discourse invented by women writers of the past. American feminists, on the other hand, have excavated the writing of the past, have devoted themselves to the task of canon formation in which new texts are discovered and old texts made to yield up a feminist content. But this content tends to emphasize and reinvent the patterns of victimization that haunted heroines like Marcia Gaylord. Rather than inviting us to see the woman writer's powers of protest and change, we have kept active our sense of the inevitability of women's disempowerment; we have focused on women's discursive limitations rather than exploring the language games women have invented in the past.[32]

I use a phrase like "language games" deliberately because I want to suggest, pace Gilbert and Abel, that playfulness and word play are very much at issue in the woman writer's reinvention of her culture. We need to devise a feminist aesthetic of "play" if we are to understand how women have been able to transform and restructure a literary tradition that forbade them the right to speak. In chapter 7 I will suggest—with Marcuse—that play itself is a form of aesthetic activity in which, for the woman writer, "reality loses its seriousness" and what has been burdensome becomes—at least momentarily—weightless, transformable, transformative.[33] As women play with old texts, the burden of the tradition is lightened and shifted; it has the potential for being remade.

Why are we so uneasy with the concept of play, so reluctant, as feminist critics, to equate the practices of the woman writer with delight, with ludic freedom, with pleasure?[34] In sounding this note, I do not mean to imply that this distrust is uniform. In "It Jus Be's Dat Way Sometime: The Sexual Politics of Women's Blues," Hazel Carby celebrates the playful and empowered self-creation that black women discover in writing or singing the blues.

In fact American feminists themselves are quite playful: think of the witty exchange between Abel and Gilbert cited above, or the wry ending of Nancy Miller's "The Text's Heroine: A Feminist Critic and Her Fictions," in which Miller concludes with a comical aside about American feminists speaking in tropes and wearing sensible shoes.[35] Still, there is a danger in our inability to recognize the woman writer's "play" as a form of work and of struggle. For example, although *Alice Doesn't,* Teresa de Lauretis' study of "feminism, semiotics, and cinema," gives us a wonderfully utopian reading of women's powers of self-creation, de Lauretis also suggests that, for the woman writer, playfulness is not a transformative activity, that women's possibilities have been "played out" by their culture. De Lauretis concludes that the most we can do is subject ourselves to the rigors of consciousness raising, an activity that works because it is weighty, deliberate, freighted with careful self-scrutiny.

As a form of political critique or critical politics, feminism has not only "invented" new strategies, new semiotic contents and new signs, but more importantly it has effected a habit-change in readers, spectators, speakers, etc. And with that habit-change it has produced a new social subject, women. The practice of self consciousness, in short, has a constitutiveness as well as a constituency.[36]

For de Lauretis, consciousness raising, or self consciousness (as she wants us to call it in order to mute the popular associations of consciousness raising with an "excessive preoccupation with one's manner or looks") has not only provided women with the capacity to be "self-analyzing" in a way that allows us to step outside of negative social practices—this activity has also permitted women to move beyond "experimentation in the inner world" to reform their outer world as well; this is what de Lauretis means when she says self-consciousness "has a constitutiveness as well as a constituency."[37] But despite this celebration of transformed and transformable praxis, despite feminism's invention of "new strategies" and "new semiotic contents," de Lauretis leaves us with a sense that it is only through the high seriousness, through the deep-thinking endeavor of self-attentiveness and self-scrutiny, that women's liberation occurs. Word play, irony, aesthetic self-pleasuring do not seem to take a part in this "constitutiveness," and de Lauretis' book ends on this ambivalent note:

From a city built to represent woman, but where no women live, we have come to the gravel path of the academic campus. We have learned that one becomes a woman in the very practice of signs by which we live, write, speak, see. . . . This is neither an illusion nor a paradox. It is a real contradiction—women continue to become woman. The essays collected here have attempted to work through and with the subtle, shifting, duplicitous terms of that contradiction, but not to reconcile them. For it seems to me that only by knowingly enacting and representing them, by knowing us to be both woman and women, does a woman today become a subject. In this 1984, it is the signifier who plays and wins before Alice does, even when she's aware of it. But to what end, if Alice doesn't?" (p. 186)

Not only is Alice excluded from play, but de Lauretis implies that since words have a prior, masculine authority, Alice will not, cannot "play" with them; she only has the option of saying "no" to them, of refusing to invent games someone else might control. After de Lauretis' hopefulness about woman's self-consciousness, a power that presumably involves the play of the signifier, her conclusion seems oddly flat; de Lauretis remains stuck in a negative reading of women's linguistic powers. Language as such remains an anathema to the woman speaker—"it is the signifier which plays and wins before Alice does." The French feminist writers whose utopian projects I have outlined make a similar mistake; in omitting the practices of real, historical women from their analysis of women's writing they remain blind to what has actually happened in women's texts—to the seriously playful, emancipatory strategies that women writers have invented to challenge and change the tradition.

I want, then, to combine these two strategies, to call upon the archaeological know-how of American feminists—with an eye toward the plenitude, the emancipatory pleasure, the redemptive language games French feminists have begun to play. I am intrigued by the ways in which women writers in the last two centuries have made use of abnormal discourse, of word play, of language as

Sondersprache, to say new things, and even more intrigued by
the fact that, while Cixous' dark continent is still around us and in
us, we have found new ways to write ourselves into and out of
this continent at will.

> she was looking
> for the secret bin of sweetness—
> honey, that the bees store
> in the trees' soft caves.
> Black block of gloom, she climbed down
> tree after tree and shuffled on
> through the woods. And then
> she found it! The honey-house deep
> as heartwood, and dipped into it
> among the swarming bees—honey and comb
> she lipped and tongued and scooped out
> in her black nails.　　(*American Primitive,* p. 71)

In Oliver's "Happiness" we meditate upon the female
poet's good appetite; her possession of language is equated with
the possession of a delicious excess of meaning that is forbidden,
but therefore twice delicious. Once found, it lightens the speaker's
clamorous burden of feeling:

> maybe she grew full, or sleepy, or maybe
> a little drunk, and sticky
> down the rugs of her arms,
> and began to hum and sway
> I saw her let go of the branches,
> I saw her lift her honeyed muzzle
> into the leaves, and her thick arms,
> as though she would fly—
> an enormous bee
> all sweetness and wings.　　(p. 71)

The "she-bear" who stands in for the female writer of "Happiness"
drifts toward the meditative meadows Keats describes as the source
of inspiration in "Sleep and Poetry": "to float and sleep in the
sheer nets / swaying from flower to flower / day after shining day."
The heaviness of her body contrasts with the lightness of this

exuberant flying—a contrast that emphasizes the woman writer's capacity to lighten the burden of the tradition she has already begun to transform, to swallow what was meant to swallow her.

The scenes Mary Oliver depicts in her poems are such scenes of theft: we may recall Derrida's insistence that the "*letter*, inscribed or propounded speech, is always stolen. . . . It never belongs to its author or to its addressee." Oliver reproduces the female writer's pleasure in discovering this ownerlessness, in lightening the fictions that weigh her down, in stealing and incorporating the languages that, until she claimed them, did not belong to her.[38]

That this theft is possible implies an alternative view of the woman writer's relation to language and brings me to my second argument with French feminist thinkers: their restricted view of women's capacities as speakers of "male" language. In a much-quoted passage from *Les Guérillères*, Wittig describes language as malevolent, as poisonous:

The women say, the language you speak poisons your glottis tongue palate lips. They say, the language you speak is made up of words that are killing you. They say, the language you speak is made up of signs that rightly speaking designate what men have appropriated. Whatever they have not laid hands on, whatever they have not pounced on like many-eyed birds of prey, does not appear in the language you speak. (p. 114)

Not only has Wittig composed an eloquent injunction requiring women to "get out of [male] language," but her phrase making has been appropriated by feminist writers in America and France— even those who have their reservations about such "French feminisms"—to describe women's relation to language. Why is it fashionable to dramatize "male" language as the chief source of our danger rather than as an opportunity for dialogue and revision? This time, rather than defending or debating the logic of this practice, I want to consider its function. Why might it be useful for the woman writer to symbolize "male" language as a dangerous substance, as poison?

In a chapter from *Negative Dialectics* called "Idealism as Rage" Adorno talks about the relation between idealism and orality; his ideas will help us understand the intellectual and somatic benefits of considering language itself as one's enemy. For Adorno, "the system is belly turned mind, and rage is the mark of each and every idealism."[39] We are never, even in our most profound moments of theorizing, far from our animal being: "The system in which the sovereign mind imagined itself transfigured, has its primal history in the pre-mental, the animal life of the species. Predators get hungry, but pouncing on their prey is difficult and often dangerous; additional impulses may be needed for the beast to dare it" (p. 22). These impulses allow us to act, but they must also be rationalized. The " 'rational animal' with an appetite for his opponent is already fortunate enough to have a superego and must find a reason." The reason most productive of appetite emerges when "the animal to be devoured [is] evil." Combined with "the unpleasantness of hunger," this sense of the opponent's evil fuses "into rage at the victim, a rage whose expression in turn serves the end of frightening and paralyzing the victim. In the advance to humanity this is rationalized by projection" (p. 22). The hungry animal not only wants to eat, it also knows that to attack is dangerous and that danger can—by itself—lead to paralyzing terror. Hunger, then, may be supplemented by rage at the hunger itself, which compounds into rage at the victim.

"Idealism . . . gives unconscious sway to the ideology that the not-I, *l'autrui* . . . is inferior, so the unity of the self-preserving thought may devour it without misgivings" (pp. 22–23). To say that such a psychology of projection is at work in French feminist writings is neither to suggest their pathology nor intimate that the language we speak lacks terrorist qualities. It is simply to suggest that their dramatization of language is itself strategic, that it gives women writers the opportunity to theatricalize danger in order to begin to appropriate the language they need.

Since this reading of French feminist rhetoric is bound to be controversial, let me come at this argument in another way. That the danger of using masculine language is frequently cited by feminist writers cannot be denied. Xavière Gauthier cites an anecdote about Marguerite Duras, who chose her own pseudonym rather than writing in the shadow of her father. "When I asked her if a woman could write if she kept her father's name, she told me: 'That's something which never seemed possible, not for one second. Like many women I find this name so horrible that I barely manage to say it.' "[40] To reverse the direction of this discourse and to speak of male texts as "victims" and women writers as devourers of male language may be going too far, for I am speaking against a mythology that is powerful, desirable, and has the kinesthetic potential all theories of oppression lend to the oppressed. In addition, I am setting my own dialectic against the idea that devouring the father's speech means an inevitable return to phallogocentrism, to patriarchal dominance.[41]

There is another, more positive way to consider this activity of incorporating and going beyond masculine discourse, however. As Adorno explains in *Negative Dialectics*, "no matter how hard we try for linguistic expression of such a history congealed in things, the words we use will remain concepts. Their precision substitutes for the thing itself, without quite bringing its selfhood to mind; there is a gap between words and the thing they conjure" (pp. 52–53). Hence the need to keep writing, and the writer's impetus to move out from the inadequacy of any words that attempt to posit identity. For while "the concept" is inevitably flawed, it is the concept alone (and here Adorno also means the abstracting power of language) that "can achieve what the concept prevents. . . . The determinable flaw in every concept makes it necessary to cite others; this is the font of the only constellations which inherited some of the hope of the name." What is at stake in devouring, erasing, exorcising the father's word is precisely "the hope of the name," the emancipatory, utopian desire that we will find some new name that cherishes us; that will give an "outwardness" to our "inwardness." This moment is an "inalienable one," says Adorno, for "to be known, the inwardness to which cognition clings in expression always needs its own outwardness as well" (p. 53). Hungry for words that will speak our desires in some inexorable way, these French women writers both refuse and insist "upon a single word and concept as the iron gate to be unlocked."

If we do not consider the continuity between this incorporative rage, and the woman writer's courage in trying to invent new names, how else are we to make sense of the gap between the themes and the actual practices of French feminist writers? When Irigaray insists that women must get out of male language, isn't this at once a bold subterfuge that allows her to imbibe, attack, engulf what men have said, a posture permitting her to go "honey-mad," to devour language in even greater abundance, and a utopian seizure of "the hope of the name"? In her commentary on Irigaray's *Speculum of the Other Woman* de Lauretis notes that "when Luce Irigaray rewrites Freud's essay on 'Femininity,' inscribing her own critical voice into his tightly woven argumentation and creating an effect of distance, like a discordant echo, which ruptures the coherence of address and dislocates meaning, she is performing, enacting, the division of women in discourse" (*Alice Doesn't*, p. 7). While de Lauretis emphasizes Irigaray's ability to write in the intervals of Freud's text and decenter his primary meaning, she also celebrates the transformative power of Irigaray's writing. "When others after her—writers, critics, filmmakers—turn back the question on itself and remake the story of Dora, *Bohème*, Rebecca, or Oedipus, opening up a space of contradiction in which to demonstrate the noncoincidence of woman and women, they also destabilize and finally alter the meaning of those representations" (p. 7). If we extend Adorno's notion to feminist theory and suggest that feminist idealism can give "unconscious sway to the ideology that the not-I" is simultaneously inferior and dangerous and therefore must be changed, then we can make sense of the gap between Irigaray's claims and her practice. She does not, in fact, get out of language, but insinuates herself more deeply into its dangerous spaces and unearths her own concepts; she begins to separate Freud's words from their original context and makes them resonate with other meanings.

I can imagine one other objection to this reading of French feminist practice. In talking about speech as an extension of our "animal being" do we demean the woman writer? I think not, although Cixous' insistence that woman is "more body, hence more writing" troubles even those feminist critics who applaud her bold deconstructive schemes. In theorizing women's emancipatory practices we must admit the body—as social construct, as fluid biological entity—into our lexicon. When Dorothy Dinnerstein says in *The Mermaid and the Minotaur* that "what the double standard hurts in women (to the extent that they genuinely, inwardly, bow to it) is the animal center of self-respect: the brute sense of bodily prerogative, of having a right to one's bodily feelings," her words should also be applied to the feminist critic.[42] Insofar as we describe men's speech as empowered speech and women's as disempowered, we perpetuate a double standard that hurts our own "animal center of self-respect." It is this "animal center" that French feminists attempt to address, for as Dinnerstein suggests, a "conviction that physical urges which one cannot help having are unjustified, undignified, presumptuous, undercuts the deepest, oldest basis for a sense of worth; it contaminates the original wellspring of subjective autonomy."[43] In putting forward the image of the honey-mad woman I also want to appeal to this "animal center of self-respect." We need to acknowledge our own "animality" as a form of dignity operant in the material act of writing itself.[44]

If the French feminist idea of inventing another, a "feminine," language also appeals to this "animal center" then, as Gilbert says, this discourse may make us "faint with desire" precisely because the French feminists I have cited here envision, for all women who seize the pen, a realm of fulfilled orality. "To touch upon feminine writing frees, liberates language, word usage," Cixous says in an interview with Verena Conley. "One cannot imagine a political liberation without a linguistic liberation. . . . It is not by chance that all the regional movements grab on to their language. It is in order to escape, if you would like, the language of the father. It is in order to take something from language which would be less authoritarian. It is a lot of work."[45] The freedom Cixous postulates remains a future practice, a metaphor that both points to and blocks our recognition of women's powers of speech. But the "linguistic liberation" Cixous praises is a force already operant in women's writing, and in putting forward an alternate image of woman's orality, we can begin to encounter and analyze an unrecognized process of liberation at work in women's texts. Let us return, then, to our opening metaphor and to the task of inventing an alternate mythology, a more powerful set of assumptions that will allow us to describe women's emancipatory relation to speech.

In explaining the South American tale of the honey-mad woman, Lévi-Strauss suggests that it is woman's capacity to act out her hunger, to go stir crazy, sweet crazy, to eat too much honey, that provokes the need, in cultures where this tale is repeatedly told, for imposed social order: table manners, cooking rituals, and birthing rites are designed to introduce "order into a menacing disorder that has women at its center."[46] Lévi-Strauss adds, however, that this systematic control of women's minds and bodies never quite works, since woman remains, like honey itself, both natural and unnatural, "raw" and "cooked"—something that does not fit on either side of the constructed division between nature and culture. Thus the honey-mad woman's consumption of honey is especially threatening to her culture because it reminds other members of her society that classificatory systems do not work, that these systems mask a fundamental ambivalence about the role of ideology in legislating our relation to nature and to one another. Society's very attempt to initiate a permanent order is disorderly, doomed; only "myth, with its endless transformations," can help a particular society to "express such contradictions and to provide ritual or religious ways of settling them." The "endless transformations" of myth work toward producing an "ordering of the world in which men and women can act."[47] By telling tales about how the honey-mad woman should be punished for her oral excess, the societies Lévi-Strauss analyzes can endlessly enact and reinforce desired gender boundaries.

However, when Mary Oliver rewrites Lévi-Strauss' myth and makes the honey-mad woman a hungry visionary, free, savvy, invulnerable to social closure, when she invents a honey-mad woman who locates herself at the "secret rip" of her own cultural system, the power repressed by the older mythos—by the ideology that makes woman the site of exchange and consumption—begins to change shape. In Oliver's poetry women become appetitive, sexual, aggressive, joyous, exotic beings who steal language happily, who take on and shake off the roles of Satan or Adam or Eve at will, who unlimit the language by placing themselves at the point of commerce where old social practices change.

> Later, maybe,
> I'll come here only
> sometimes and with a
> middling hunger. But now
> I climb like a snake,
> I clamber like a bear to
> the nuzzling place, to the light
> salvaged by the thighs
> of bees and racked up
> in the body of the tree.   (p. 81)

To go honey mad is the equivalent of going language mad. Coming down from the honey tree, coming down from the mountains where the writer has spent the day blackberry picking—"cramming the black honey of summer into my mouth"—the berry picker's lips are "streaked / black," her "fingers purple," while the she-bear who eats too much sweetness is also stained with honeyed ink: "honey and comb / she lipped and tongued and scooped out / in her black nails." The "honey-mad" poet finds, within language, the goods that she needs.

> Oh, anyone can see
> how I love myself at last!
> how I love the world! climbing
> by day or night
> in the wind, in the leaves, kneeling
> at the secret rip, the cords
> of my body stretching
> and singing in the
> heaven of appetite.   (p. 81)

The honey-mad woman offers herself as totem, as ancestress, as an explorer who gives us a map for defining a countertradition within women's writing, a tradition in which the woman writer appropriates the language "racked up" in her own body and starts to sing. A blissful consumer and purveyor of language, the honey-mad writer is a symbol of verbal plenitude, of woman's capacity to rewrite her culture.

However, my foregrounding of an alternative image to describe women's relation to speech is, at this point, no more than a metaphor, and playing with metaphors, however delightful, is not enough to estabish their descriptive validity. A whole series of assumptions that go into our analysis of women's writing have to be challenged before we can allow this as yet hypothetical countertradition to alter our sense of how women's texts work. I want to take on and to challenge these assumptions systematically in the chapters that follow.

What are the assumptions that keep us from seeing woman's capacious use of speech, her pleasure in language? First, we are still dazzled by the assumption that men's writing is empowered writing—that women must struggle, with varying degrees of success—against the shades of powerful male precursors. "Women's literature is still haunted by the ghosts of repressed language," Elaine Showalter says in "Feminist Criticism in the Wilderness." "The problem is not that language is insufficient to express women's consciousness but that women have been denied the full resources of language and have been forced into silence, euphemism, or circumlocution."[48] The purpose of my next chapter is to challenge the notion that women's lexicon has been so completely restricted by male writers, by masculine culture. I want to show that women have shattered male plots, have successfully called upon verbal resources that are unavailable to their male contemporaries. This second chapter will end with a brief manifesto to other feminist critics—a call to abandon our commitment to the concept of "text" as Roland Barthes defines it and begin to consider women's writings as "works," as "texts" that do the work of reinventing culture.

The second set of assumptions we must challenge are those telling us that language has an absolute power to restrict women's identities and that words have this power of restriction because language itself is masculine. In chapter 3 I will set forth an alternative framework for describing women's relation to language based on Hannah Arendt's descriptions of the word's natality, its capacity to begin things again. Arendt will allow us to speak more confidently and more theoretically about the letter's volatility, about its role in allowing the writer to transform the limits of speech, to punctuate the order of words with practices that are not only emancipatory, but feminocentric.

The third assumption that inhibits our investigation of women's powers of speech is the assumption that women have a single relation to language—a relation we can analyze synchronically, or even define over the course of a century. In chapter 4 I want to analyze the images of language that appear in texts by four women writers to show that each writer constructs for herself and for her characters a different relation to language; we must allow the woman writer her heterogeneity in relation to speech, to other women, and to her own culture if we are to avoid making all feminine speech the same.

The fourth assumption I want to examine is the notion that emancipatory strategies are not available to the woman writer: that language—whether it is defined as masculine or feminine—is so overpowering in its representations of reigning ideologies that the woman writer must resort to unusual textual distortions to have her say, that she can only disrupt the dominant discourse by employing deliberately avant-garde practices. Thus in chapters 5 and 6 I will look at specific emancipatory strategies in the writings of Mary Wollstonecraft and Emily Brontë—especially the roles played by dialogue and by novelization in reformulating women's experience. My thesis in chapter 5 is that we need, at this point in our conversation, to pay less attention to women's silences and more attention to the ways women address men's silences and get them to speak. We need especially to attend to the ways in which women writers have ended these silences, have persuaded male writers to speak in women's direction by a peculiar subterfuge: women writers have incorporated men's texts in their own and entered into dialogues with these texts that these male writers have refused to initiate. In chapter 6 I want to explore dialogue generically, to examine the novel as a dialogic and emancipatory form useful to the woman writer because of its multivoicedness. I will challenge Virginia Woolf's suggestion that the novel is a form women choose because it lends itself to thoughts so amorphous and mundane that the woman writer at work can be interrupted. Instead, the novel is a form women choose because its multivoicedness allows the interruption and interrogation of the dominant culture. The novel's polyvocality gives the writer an opportunity to interrupt the speech practices, the ordinary patriarchal assumptions of everyday life. It is, first and foremost, a genre that asks from its writers a commitment to exploration and change.

Having focused in chapters 1 through 6 on the "work" that women writers do in their texts, in chapter 7 I will outline a theory of play—explaining why we need to recognize playfulness as an emancipatory strategy in women's writing, and describing some of the forces that allow the woman writer to go honey mad, to lighten the weight of the tradition and continue her important work of cultural revision.

Chapter 8 will be devoted to analyzing and adding a feminist perspective to several Marxian theories of textuality. These theories will help us to examine the following question: how can we talk about women as victims of language and, at the same time, describe the ways in which language adds a dimension of freedom to our lives? This discussion will touch on the theories of Bakhtin, Kristeva, Macherey, Eagleton, Jameson, and Habermas, and it will conclude with an affirmation of the philosophy of Hannah Arendt, but we will see that no single theory—however well elaborated—is sufficient to account for the complex strategies at work in women's texts.

Finally, a word about my reason for orienting this project around a metaphor, about why I have chosen the "honey-mad woman" as rubric for my book. When there are already so many rich themes and terms for describing the woman writer's relation to culture and language, why is it necessary to construct a new set of metaphors to describe the woman writer's relation to speech? Why not ground this analysis in an ordained theory or visionary epistemology?

Let me begin by answering this last question first—why turn to a metaphor instead of a theory? Max Black distinguishes between metaphors and scientific models in the following way. Within logical models "the maker must have prior control of a well-knit theory if he is to do more than hang an attractive picture on an algebraic formula. Systematic complexity of the source of the model and capacity for analogical development are of the essence."[49] In contrast, the implications a metaphor brings to a discussion are not meta-logical, but proverbial or commonplace. One does not require technical or specialized information for the metaphor to go to work, for it to be understood. It is this workaday character of metaphor that I am seeking, this capacity to offer us ordinary access to extraordinary thinking we may not yet have tried.

Thus a new metaphor can prove useful in engendering new forms of speculation. The iconoclastic combination of familiar and unfamiliar features in metaphor can "provoke" us "into thought," Victor Turner explains. When a new metaphor "provides us with new perspectives, one can be excited by them; the implications, suggestions, and supporting values entwined with their literal use enable us to see a new subject matter in a new way."[50] The goal of my study is not to provide a single theory of women's writing, but to begin to establish a matrix of images that will emphasize women writers' empowerment.

Metaphors are not linguistically inert; they are "metamorphic, transformative," and can bring separate spheres of knowledge together, collapsing them into enlightening, encompassing icons. Since metaphors guide our thinking in ways we may not be aware of, influencing thought as a form of "tacit knowledge," we need, as feminist critics, to examine our own metaphors closely— not only those we have inherited from the tradition, but those we have invented. I am not suggesting that we "police" our language and choose to act the part of repressors, but that we should be aware of the potency of our figures of speech. In seeing women writers as "prisoners of their gender," in describing them as "madwomen in the attic," or "abandoned women," or in foregrounding women's silence, we are emphasizing some aspects of women's literary experience and ignoring others.

The central danger of such "root" metaphors resides in their unconscious appeal, their "aura." "The danger is, of course, that the more persuasive the root metaphor or archetype, the more chance it has of becoming a self-certifying myth, sealed off from empirical disproof." This speaks to both the active nature of metaphors, their capacities to engender thought and activity, and to a metaphor's capacity to select, emphasize, suppress, or organize "features of the principle subject by implying statements about it that normally apply to the subsidiary subject."[51] As women writers and critics, we may wish to employ a wide range of metaphors that evoke and awaken the diversity of women's writing, while at the same time recognizing that these metaphors work in two ways. First, they function as a limit that restricts what we see. Second, as "conceptual archetypes" (as images in search of an organized and a euphoric way to think about women's writing), the best metaphors give access to a "systematic repertoire of ideas by means of which a given thinker describes, by *analogical extension,* some domain to which those ideas do not immediately and literally apply."[52] Thus metaphors have a performative dimension that not only deforms lives but enriches them; the archetypes feminist critics have chosen, when rich enough in descriptive details, have become "useful speculative instruments" which have engendered epistemologies that simultaneously limit us and set us free.

My own contribution to this project will be to unearth a set of metaphors that focus on women's pleasure and productivity in language. These metaphors should help us to recover a community of women writers who, like the hungry beings in Mary Oliver's "Moles," make optimistic, productive use of their lexicons:

> Field after field
> you can see the traceries
> of their long
> lonely walks, then
> the rains blur
> even this frail
> hint of them—
> so excitable,
> so plush,
> so willing to continue
> generation after generation
> . . . . .
> pushing and shoving

with their stubborn muzzles against
the whole earth,
finding it
delicious.   (pp. 10–11)

TWO

The Bilingual Heroine:
From "Text" to "Work"

In *Mythologiques* Lévi-Strauss describes an exotically defiant figure—the "honey-mad woman"—who eats honey in bizarre amounts, who feeds on it wildly and to excess. She consumes honey rather than plantain or meat because honey, as Lévi-Strauss explains, delineates the ambiguous border between culture and nature, the border where—in primitive societies—woman herself is asked to reside. As a pre-articulated, predigested substance, honey is at once raw and cooked, processed and unprocessed, and in consuming it in great quantities the honey-mad woman becomes an archetype of sexual as well as gustatory defiance. Breaking the rules of politic eating she covertly defies the system in which women are exchanged by men for the ostensible purpose of containing women's "natural" disorder and fecundity. An inhabitant, then, of the agonistic border between nature and culture that societies erect to protect themselves from ideological collapse, woman is the unwitting dupe, the strange symbol, the wild card in a primitive metaphysic. But in consuming honey so avidly the honey-mad woman preempts this symbolization, for by consuming a substance like herself she usurps her society's right to consume her.

In this chapter I will suggest that the bilingual heroines in the novels of Charlotte Brontë are also honey-mad women: women who consume, to an excess, the languages designed to consume them. Mad for the honey of speech, Brontë's heroines not only challenge the communal norms of their society but are of special interest to the feminist critic because, in their multivoicedness, they refuse to comply with critical ordinances which limit our understanding of woman's relation to speech. Modern feminist theories have insisted on women's impotence in the presence of "masculine" language. As Teresa de Lauretis explains in *Alice Doesn't:*

woman . . . has no access to the codes of the invisible city which represents her and absents her; she is not in the place of Eco's "subject of semiosis"—*homo faber,* the city builder, the producer of signs. Nor is she in the representation which inscribes her as absent. The woman cannot transform the codes; she can only transgress them, make trouble, provoke, pervert, turn the representation into a trap.[1]

This positing of female powerlessness is tempting to the feminist critic for real textual reasons. To be transgressive, to cause trouble seems, at first glance, to be all that the honey-mad woman can do.

Though now the place of the female subject in language, in discourse, and in the social may be understood another way, it is an equally impossible position. She now finds herself in the empty space between the signs, in a void of meaning, where no demand is possible and no code available; or, going back to the cinema, she finds herself in the place of the female spectator, between the look of the camera (the masculine representation) and the image on the screen (the specular fixity of the feminine representation), not one or the other but both and neither. (p. 35)

I will suggest that when we look at women's relation to language more closely we see that women writers have devised alternate means to put masculine sign systems into crisis, that the woman writer's relation to and transformative power over cultural codes is more complex than de Lauretis admits. By consuming not language, but languages, Brontë's bilingual heroines have discovered an alternative method of placing previously unsymbolized emotions and ideas in practice. The second language serves an emancipatory function in Brontë's texts, enacting a moment in which the novel's primary language is put into process, a moment of possible transformation when the writer forces her speech to break out of old representations of the feminine and to posit something new.

We need at the outset to distinguish two different ways in which the writer can bring a subversive multivoicedness into her text. First, the second language can operate as a form of interruption, as a way of dispelling the power of the myth systems represented by the text's primary language. This practice is not limited to women's texts. In *Vanity Fair* Thackeray makes Becky Sharp speak derisively to her headmistress in French just before she tosses Dr. Johnson's dictionary out the window. Thackeray is using Becky's salacious speech, her witty thrust against English lettters, to challenge the propriety and verbal hypocrisy of his own society. But what does not occur in Thackeray's novel is the second function of novelistic multilanguagedness. Thackeray does not use Becky's dazzling knowledge of French as a space to project what is unspoken into speech; he does not use Becky's other language to signalize what is repressed as a signifiable content in women's lives. The attack on the word "slattern" in *Jane Eyre* and Jane's concomitant learning of French provides an example of both these practices. As in *Vanity Fair,* French becomes the language of disruption, calling into question the accusing word which has been attached to Helen Burns' forehead. "Slattern" is, of course, a word that denigrates women, that calls attention to some slackness of spirit or body not shared by men. When this word is applied directly to Helen Burns' body, bound "like a phylactery round Helen's large, mild, intelligent, and benign-looking forehead," Jane responds by tearing off the defamatory image and tossing it into the fire.[2] In thus destroying a good English word, she seems to be in imminent danger of rebuke, but instead Jane is cleared of an earlier accusation of lying; her attack on the word is obliquely condoned. What emerges is a new relation to language: "In a few weeks I was promoted to a higher class; in less than two months I was allowed to commence French and drawing. I learned the first two tenses of the verb *Etre,* and sketched my first cottage" (p. 106).

This is a moment of textual radiance, of beautiful play with "the hope of the name," as the derogatory word is burnt and replaced by the verb *être*—evoking sonority in Jane's own name, revealing "Eyre" as a cognate for the verb "to be." This utopian moment is extended in Jane's juxtaposition of this new language with a sketch of her "first cottage." To read this image I suggest we pass over the uterine theories of Erickson and consider instead

Heidegger's notion of what is "sheltered" in the work of art. According to Heidegger, the work of art is something that sets up a world and keeps it "abidingly in force"; it opens a space that is "more fully in being than the tangible and perceptible realm in which we believe ourselves to be at home."[3] The work of art, then, "holds open the Open of the world" (p. 45). Here "all things gain their lingering and hastening . . . their scope and limits"; they are called into a "nearness" (p. 45). In *Jane Eyre* the word *être* calls out to, holds open a new possibility in Jane's world: it offers a space within language which had not been there before. This space could be as ephemeral as the word Jane burns, but Brontë extends its moment by coupling it with another metaphor. She posits within her text the possibility of structuring and sheltering this openness with Jane's "first cottage."

"To make space for," as Heidegger suggests, means that we "liberate the Open and establish it in its structure" (p. 45). I am suggesting that this cottage shelters, symbolically, Jane's growing linguistic confidence, and gives her the freedom, in the next few sentences, to play the part of a honey-mad woman who is at home with her own obstreperousness, who feasts on words without feeling a honey-mad frenzy:.

That night, on going to bed, I forgot to prepare in imagination the Barmecide supper, of hot roast potatoes, or white bread and new milk, with which I was wont to amuse my inward cravings. I feasted instead on the spectacle of ideal drawings, which I saw in the dark—all the work of my own hands; freely pencilled houses and trees, picturesque rocks and ruins, Cuyp-like groups of cattle, sweet paintings of butterflies hovering over unblown roses, of birds picking at ripe cherries, of wren's nests enclosing pearl-like eggs, wreathed about with young ivy sprays. I examined, too, in thought, the possibility of my ever being able to translate currently a certain little French story-book which Madame Pierrot had that day shown me; nor was that problem solved to my satisfaction ere I fell sweetly asleep. (p. 106)

According to Kaja Silverman, "the structuration of the female subject begins not with her entry into language, or her subordination to a field of cultural desire, but with organization of her body" through a language that speaks for her.[4] De Lauretis adds that it is only when women's desire has "been made congruent with the desire of the Other" that the female, who has now become "woman," can gain access to speech (p. 150). Jane, however, attacks the zoning of Helen's body, the way in which it is primed to accept a misogynous meaning; she preempts this discursive program and gains access to a speech that allows her to organize her own body, her own orality in new ways. What is called into the "open" of Jane's novel by her new double-languagedness is another body of sound—one that affirms her own being and introduces the terrifying disruptiveness of the madwoman's laughter which erupts from the house where Jane has been summoned to speak French with Adele. At Thornfield, of course, Jane's appropriation of French is challenged by Rochester's bilingual fluency (for him it is the language of seduction). But his prison house of language, in turn, is destroyed by the madwoman's fierce semiosis, and what emerges in the text is the possibility of a new house of language in which Jane will possess a larger share of dialogic power. As Rochester says near the end of the novel: "What, Janet! Are you an independent woman? A rich woman?" She replies, "Quite rich, sir. If you won't let me live with you, I can build a house of my own close up to your door, and you may come and sit in my parlour when you want company of an evening" (p. 459).

When representations of a foreign-language system appear in Brontë's novels (with the interesting exception of *Shirley*), we do not find an image of the word as limit—something feminist theory has taught us to expect—but of the word as vector, as harbinger of an abnormal way of thinking which is capable, in its strangeness, of bringing the heroine into dialogue with something new.[5] In novels by male writers a second language can also serve an iconic function, but the iconicity operates differently. In *Jude the Obscure,* for example, Jude returns from visiting Arabella and finds his Greek text "open, just as he had left it, and the capital letters on the title-page regarded him with fixed reproach in the grey starlight, like the unclosed eyes of a dead man."[6] These letters stare out bleakly at us from Hardy's page as well. But rather than symbolizing an undisclosed possibility in Jude's life, a linguistic equivalent for something that Jude can only name or locate outside normative speech, in Hardy's novel Greek and Latin represent Jude's dream of ascending through the class structure; his interest in these dead languages is ultimately conservative. Greek and Latin become the empty signifiers of a dying English culture, a stultifying way of life that Jude aspires "backwards" to reach. For Jude what seems "open" is in fact already closed; Latin does not offer him a route to alternative stories but an even greater sense of class consciousness and personal limitation. I am suggesting that in women's writing the incorporation of a second language can function, instead, as a subversive gesture representing an alternative form of speech which can both disrupt the repressions of authoritative discourse and still welcome or shelter themes that have not yet found a voice in the text's primary language.

While feminist critics do not agree that the only expressive solution for the woman writer is to get out of masculine language, even American feminists have argued that we find in women's texts a critique of language's adequacy and that the only self-descriptive function women's language can serve is a negative one: to represent women's absence from speech, her unrepresentability.[7] I have begun to argue, in contrast, that the incorporation of an alien language within Brontë's texts represents something more than this brief negativity. Jane's discovery of the word être not only represents a carnivalesque moment of release, a momentary dispersal of the dominant discourse, but a sudden openness of the text to strangeness, a new gathering of meaning—of calling women's desires into a nearness which is structured through Jane's desire not for a room, but for a house of her own—a house promising the institution of a new dialectical possiblity for women in speech. Brontë explores this possibility more fully in the multivoiced houses of Villette: "I looked, I read—printed in fair characters—'Externat de demoiselles. Numéro 7, Faubourg Clotilde. Directrice, Mademoiselle Lucy Snowe.' "[8]

While the inclusion of French phrases in Brontë's novels emerges from her conviction that ordinary language is restrictive, Brontë also manages to seize upon a form of abnormal discourse which will disrupt and enter into dialogue with the text's primary language; she begins to construct an alternate system of representation. Richard Rorty says that such need arises whenever ordinary language is insufficient for a speaker's needs. "Abnormal discourse is what happens when someone joins in the discourse who is ignorant of these conventions or who sets them aside," taking us out of ourselves by the power of its strangeness.[9] Clearly male writers invent "abnormal" discourses as well; we find such an attempt at defamiliarization in Wordsworth's *Lyrical Ballads*. But what I am defining in Brontë's text is not this local variety of protest or change, but an interest, an investment in inventing a discourse that will put the hegemonic structure of the primary language entirely into question. The point is to make the dominant discourse into one among many possible modes of speech. By placing this discourse in contradiction the woman writer begins to rescript her available language games, to locate multivocality as one site of transformation for women's own writing and productivity.

Another way to go about stressing this difference is to return to my opening image, to ask: what is the literary status of the honey-mad man? Keats opens "The Fall of Hyperion" expressing faith that any poet who feeds at the sources of language is capable of writing good verse: "Since every man whose soul is not a clod / Hath visions, and would speak, if he had lov'd / And been well nurtured in his mother tongue."[10] This nurturing takes place in Keats' poem when his speaker enters a fragrant summer arbor and discovers a half-finished feast that "seemed refuse of a meal / By angel tasted or our Mother Eve," (ll. 30–31). This feast is an objective correlative for the "mother tongue" the poet needs for his poetry, and even though the feast has been diminished by the epic appetites of earlier poets, he eats

deliciously;
And, after not long, thirsted; for thereby
Stood a cool vessel of transparent juice,
Sipp'd by the wander'd bee, the which I took,
And, pledging all the mortals of the world,
And all the dead whose names are in our lips
Drank. That full draught is parent of my theme.   (ll. 40–47)

Sipping where the bee sips, the poet drifts asleep to wake up in an "old sanctuary" piled high with odd fragments of poetry. Here we have all the wonderful claptrap the blocked writer cannot spin together: "imageries from a sombre loom / All in a mingled heap confus'd there lay / Robes, golden tongs, censer and chafing-dish, / Girdles, and chains, and holy jewelries" (ll. 77–80). The reader of Keats will recognize these images from "Ode to Psyche"—allowing us to locate Hyperion's geography in an internal landscape, within the "wreathed trellis of a working brain." But unlike the "Ode to Psyche," these images resist, in multivoiced collusion, any attempt at poetic unity. The word heap will not nourish the poet; he barely manages to climb the stairs where his poetic destiny awaits him:

> I strove hard to escape
> The numbness, strove to gain the lowest step.
> Slow, heavy, deadly was my pace: the cold
> Grew stifling, suffocating, at the heart;
> And when I clasp'd my hands I felt them not.
> One minute before death, my iced foot touch'd
> The lowest stair; and, as it touch'd, life seem'd
> To pour in at the toes; I mounted up. . . .   (ll. 127–34)

This fetishism gives way to feverish images which are both static and overpowering: "Without stay or prop, / But my own weak mortality, I bore / The load of this eternal quietude, / The unchanging gloom and the three fixed shapes / Ponderous upon my senses . . ." (ll. 388–92). As he struggles to make this visionary world come to life, the poet is vampirized by his own speech; he waits "a whole moon" for the heavy figures of Saturn and Cybele to come to life: "For by my burning brain I measured sure / Her silver seasons shedded on the night, / And every day by day methought I grew / More gaunt and ghostly" (ll. 393–96). The night receives the moon's benisons, while the poet receives nothing. Language, for all its promised honey, refuses to deliver the requisite identity the poet needs. The honey-mad man, then, is depleted by his own desires for linguistic ecstasy, and yet—and this is the surprise–he does not construct an antithetical relation to the words and images that disable him. Is this because the male

Romantic's own identity, his self-naming, is dependent on the very language that consumes him? (The poet, after all, is participating in a form of self-cannibalism, drinking a liquid resonant with names that are already "in" his lips.) In fact, when Keats does give up the Hyperions, he looks for an even purer version of the "mother tongue":

I always somehow associate Chatterton with Autumn. He is the purest writer in the English language. He has no French idiom, or particles like Chaucer—'tis genuine English idiom in English words. I have given up Hyperion . . . English ought to be kept up. (Sept. 19, 1819)[11]

I want to hypothesize that one of the verbal practices making women's writing of this period different from men's is an emancipatory interest directed toward language itself, a sense, precisely, that English must not be "kept up," that it is harmful to women. While this idea has only gained recent currency in feminist and in postmodernist thought, I am suggesting that this concept has been available as metaphor for some time. I would add that the images of language we see in the poetry of Wordsworth, Coleridge, and Keats suggest that the word represents for them not only a means of communication, not only a vehicle through which divinity passes into humanity, but it also delineates a metaphysical border defining a sharp epistemological limit. "Forlorn! the very word is like a bell / To toll me back from thee to my sole self!" Keat's speaker exclaims in "Ode to a Nightingale," allowing the consciousness of syntactic limits to turn his verse from its gorgeous plurality to mere binary possibility: "Do I wake or sleep?" We can contrast Keats' foregrounding of this limiting word, which closes his poem's conversation, with Brontë's representation of the word être which opens a new conversational place in Jane Eyre. For both Keats and Wordsworth the moment of ripping the word from its context, of challenging syntactic structures, is greeted by anxiety, and a turn toward the fiction of the "sole self" or the pontificating self who can create poems that end in elegant theses. Keats and Wordsworth dramatize—and may also experience—an anxiety about words that are torn from their roots, fragmented, ripped out of place, and an anxiety about multilanguagedness, while Brontë evinces a fierce interest in words, especially foreign words, that are out of place, disjunct, fragmented, uprooted from their "order" in the sentence, and she frequently locates her own moments of textual freedom at sites of a liberating multilanguagedness.[12]

I am not suggesting that these male Romantics never instigate revolutions in diction or question their normative status as language users. The speaker of Coleridge's "Nightingale," for example, wants to escape not just the heavy burden of Milton's verse, but the "imitative lisp" of all speech, for language has the power to distance men from nature's blessing. "I deem it wise / To make him Natures's play-mate," Coleridge says of his child. "He knows well / The evening-star" implies that this child knows the universe in ways that the deified poet cannot, for the child is prelinguistic; his eyes catch the moonlight in a vision unmediated by language.[13] And yet, paradoxically, Coleridge is happy to seize for himself the nominative function, the deific power of creating others through speech. In Coleridge's "Nightingale" the primary sign system is revealed in its limitations, but neither language itself nor the social order it upholds come under attack because the unspoken is also the unspeakable; it is that which disappears the moment it is contained in a language. Charlotte Brontë, on the other hand, brings to our awareness the ways in which the limitation language imposes on our lives is not so much ontological as it is cultural and in need of repair. Her novels both point to the social closure of speech, and preserve what Adorno calls "the hope of the name," the hope of making new use of that empty, delectable space between the name and that which we ask the name to delineate.[14] For Brontë what is "unspoken" does not indicate the metaphysical, but the cultural limits of speech, and I have begun to suggest that Brontë chooses to symbolize this socially excluded zone of representation through her incorporation of an alien language system that reveals how much what is unspoken asks for a language. Brontë brings an abnormal lexicon into her novels to symbolize what should be sayable in words but remains unexpressed; in Villette, for example, she uses French to introduce the possibility of interrupting the dominant discourse and holding new possibilities in discourse open to view:

"And where are you going now?" I inquired.

"Oh! at—*chose,*" said she.

Now, Miss Ginevra Fanshawe . . . only substituted this word "chose" in temporary oblivion of the real name. It was a habit she had: "chose" came in at every turn in her conversation—the convenient substitute for any missing word in any language she might chance at the time to be speaking. (p. 46)

We have seen that making gaps in one's language and filling in these spaces with other words, with abnormal speech, is a productive praxis for the woman writer; it opens within her text a register of extralinguistic metaphors that nonetheless speak. In *Villette* this revolutionary practice is normalized, domesticated, made a daily possibility, and Lucy herself will make use of the gaps in language to get the better of Monsieur Paul (by calling him "my friend" rather than *"mon ami"*), while in the chapter "Cloud" she will use a gap in the fence paling to gain ownership of the "moonlit, midnight park." But at this point Ginevra's carelessness is both a revelation and a disorderly chaos Lucy wants to correct: " 'Chose,' however, I found in this instance, stood for Villette—the great capital of the great kingdom of Labassecour" (p. 46). Lucy judges Ginevra from within a tradition of elevated, respectful diction which, as we will see, is similar to Wordsworth's treatment of the blasphemous woman's speech in Book 7 of *The Prelude.* But while Wordsworth silences those urban interlocutors who are deaf to Nature's blithe music, Lucy lets Ginevra keep talking.

If, early and late in *Villette,* Polly Home represents Lucy's sweet, immature, male-obsessed double, and Miss Marchmont the double as passive, self-pitying invalid, Ginevra Fanshawe represents the double as giddy romantic, as dialogic playmate. "I am quite an ignoramus, I know nothing—nothing in the world—I assure you; except that I play and dance beautifully—and French and German of course I know, to speak; but I can't read or write them very well. Do you know they wanted me to translate a page of an easy German book into English the other day, and I couldn't do it. Papa was so mortified" (p. 45). Carelessly multilingual, Ginevra is, at first, Lucy's verbal opposite. Her giddiness is not, however, without terrorism, without useful blasphemy. The refusal to translate, to make one language the equivalent of another is, as Ginevra explains, enough to "mortify" her father, and *Villette* begins to thematize this mortification, to stir up discomfort in the patriarchal order. From the beginning of her friendship with Ginevra Lucy Snowe begins to allow herself to experience the limits of language, to be riven, put into practice, changed. However, in delineating this process of growth and rebellion through the metaphoric use of another language, through Lucy's increasing bilingualism, Brontë keeps her heroine within the shelter of an order of words: in attacking the thetic security of her original language Lucy's subjectivity is still permitted a verbal location, a place that prevents her complete disfigurement and psychosis.

Silly, but surreptitiously dangerous, Ginevra tells Lucy that her school is "horrid: but I go out every Sunday . . . and send lessons *au diable* (one daren't say that in English, you know, but it sounds quite right in French)" (p. 76). French is established from the very beginning of Villette as the language of transgression, of anger, and of gaiety, and Ginevra'a last phrase in this scene is wonderfully devilish: "and won't I order about that fat odious stewardess! Heureusement je sais faire aller mon monde" (p. 47) ("Fortunately, I know how to get my way"). Lucy refuses this irrepressibility; when Ginevra goes below she quotes somber poetry to herself and repeats comforting maxims. But at the same time, her desires have grown oral and more honey mad: "deep was the pleasure I drank in with the sea breeze; divine the delight I drew from the heaving Channel waves" (p. 47). Although this inky delight makes Lucy quite seasick, the pattern for the novel is set. Lucy will go to Labassecour to gather a double orality, a new power to interrupt or to "mortify" what she describes when she arrives in Labassecour as "the Fatherland accents."

With this in mind, let us begin to complicate our picture of the way in which French functions metaphorically in *Villette* by exploring Brontë's simultaneous play with multilanguagedness and with motifs from Keats' "Fall of Hyperion." Whereas Keats feels challenged by his vatic role and makes it up the steps to the poetic altar despite great personal sacrifice, Lucy Snowe falters completely. Low-spirited, friendless, caught in a storm in the "Long Vacation,"

Lucy desires, like any good Romantic, to have "wings" that could "ascend the gale, spread and repose my pinions on its strength, career in its course, sweep where it swept." She feels a "wild longing" for power, but is stopped on a gargantuan stair—a replica of Keats' epic machinery in the second "Hyperion":

I suddenly felt colder where before I was cold, and more powerless where before I was weak. I tried to reach the porch of a great building near, but the mass of frontage and the giant-spire turned black and vanished from my eyes. Instead of sinking on the steps as I intended, I seemed to pitch headlong down an abyss. I remember no more. (p. 147)

The references to Shelley's "Ode to the West Wind" and to Keats are unmistakable, as is Lucy's exclusion from their form of plotting. She has, like Keats, been involved on a quest—for her, the construction of a new identity through the medium of a second language. But Lucy's story seems to move backwards: she does not wake up in the temple of poetry, but in the homier space she loved as a child—by the good English fireside of Mrs. Bretton. It is as if Brontë's text suddenly capitulates to Lucy's need to be grounded in a single language, as if Brontë, panicking for her heroine, is saying "English ought to be kept up." This abrupt jump from the French world of Labassecour to the Britain of the Brettons is stranger than Keats' change of voice when he abandons the Hyperions and writes the dense English verse of "To Autumn." Waking up in a new room Lucy confronts the uncanny as the furniture, including a scroll couch with "autumn tinted foliage," and two tiny footstools brilliant with embroidered flowers "grow familiar" (p. 149). Initially stuck in his epic, Keats is finally swept from the alien world of Hyperion to the hearty English countryside and English diction of "To Autumn." But Brontë creates a situation in which this warm English world is inserted *within* the epic and alien French world of Labassecour where Lucy is making her destiny. Keats feels he must choose one kind of language or another, and he chooses to house himself in the harvest world of the Brettons (with their English bees whose "honey hath o'er brimmed their clammy cells").

But Brontë feels that her heroine must have access to several linguistic worlds, several registers of syntactic difficulty—

that she must have a diversity of ways to become honey mad—
and Brontë therefore creates a drama in which English and French
remain in conflict and in dialogue with one another. Intriguingly,
English has become the momentary language of sheltering and
French the language of self-emptiness and coercion. Brontë has
created a novelistic structure in which each of these languages helps
to emancipate the heroine from the other's repressive incursions.
As if in confirmation of this new turn in her linguistic drama, Lucy
is at first greeted at the Brettons' by a native *bonne* who "spoke
neither French nor English" and gives her a "dark-tinged" liquid
which puts her to sleep, making Lucy into a nearer equivalent of
the passive Snow White than the honey-mad women of Lévi-Strauss'
tales.

      This honey-mad moment comes later in the novel when
Lucy drinks another potion which—once more—is designed to put
her to sleep. This time the drug gives her the alarming powers
Keats longs for, and more, because Lucy has, by this point in the
novel, already "swallowed" the antidote—she has consumed the
languages designed to consume her—has learned to play in the
space between words, to decenter and demythologize both her
primary language and her secondary one. This potion not only
awakens her, but gives her access to the poetic relics Keats' speaker
could not string together. She finds herself "in a land of enchantment,
a garden most gorgeous, a plain sprinkled with coloured meteors,
a forest with sparks of purple and ruby and golden fire gemming
the foliage" (p. 412). The altar and temple that Keats struggled so
hard to reach are here, along with "pyramid, obelisk, sphinx"—
"the wonders and the symbols of Egypt teemed throughout the
park of Villette"; an explosion of codes, symbols, and systems are
at Lucy's disposal, and she revels in their variety. "Safe I passed
down the avenues—safe I mixed with the crowd where it was
deepest. . . . I took revel of the scene; I drank the elastic night
air" (p. 413). Honey-mad, bewildered by her own imaginative beauty,
Lucy wants to consume more; she feels a passionate thirst and
runs toward

the stone basin, with its clear depth and green lining: of that coolness and verdure I thought, with the passionate thirst of unconscious fever. Amidst the glare, and hurry, and throng, and noise, I still secretly and chiefly longed to come on that circular mirror of crystal, and surprise the moon glassing therein her pearly front. (p. 414)

What she longs to drink is not water in its elemental liquidity, but pure imagination, a thirst-quenching sense of her own creative powers. What she imbibes instead is a rhapsodic multi-voicedness:

The song, the sweet music, rose afar, but rushing swiftly on fast-strengthening pinions—there swept through these shades so full a storm of harmonies that, had no tree been near against which to lean, I think I must have dropped. (p. 414)

Once more Brontë opens the possibility of imaginative collapse; but Lucy is held up by a stunning polyvocality:

Voices were there, it seemed to me, unnumbered; instruments varied and countless—bugle, horn, and trumpet I knew. The effect was as a sea breaking into song with all its waves. . . .

. . . that host-like chorus, with its greatly-gathering sound, sundered the air above them. (p. 414)

Lucy's earlier desire for wings that "could ascend the gale" is here fulfilled, and finally, Lucy is free, as Keats is not, to be antithetical, iconoclastic, to "defy spectra," to destroy the image of the nun which has daunted her. Keats holds aloft in private agony "the frozen God still bending to the earth / and the sad Goddess weeping at his feet," but Lucy dashes her nemesis to the floor:

I tore her up—the, incubus! I held her on high—the goblin! I shook her loose—the mystery! And down, she fell—down all around me—down in shreds and fragments—and I trode upon her. (p. 429)

According to Gilbert and Gubar, woman writers like Brontë cannot

fully participate in the Romantic conventions of what amounted by her time to a fully developed literary tradition. . . . Thus, where the male Romantics glorified the "buried life" to an ontology, Brontë explores the mundane facts of homelessness, poverty, physical unattractiveness, and sexual discrimination or stereotyping that impose self-burial on women. While male poets like Arnold express their desire to experience an inner and more valid self, Brontë describes the pain of women who are restricted to just this private realm . . . [who] long, instead, for actualization in the world.[15]

It is my suggestion that rather than feeling excluded from the Romantic tradition, Brontë has discovered a duplicitous, double-voiced way to consume it; she has begun to reshape the Romantic tradition for her own purposes—splitting and fragmenting its plots just as Lucy has splintered the goblin nun.

Brontë's playful capacity to surmount and shatter the male Romantic poet's plots has been thus far ignored by feminist critics. Writing about *Villette* in "The Buried Letter: Feminism and Romanticism in *Villette*," Mary Jacobus suggests that

the divorce of the Romantic Imagination from its revolutionary impulse poses special problems for Victorian Romantics. Where vision had once meant a prophetic denunciation of the *status quo* and the imagining of radical alternatives, it comes to threaten madness or mob-violence. Losing its socially transforming role, it can only turn inward to self-destructive solipsism.[16]

So Keats in "The Fall of Hyperion" turns to "self-destructive solipsism." His language feeds on itself. But Brontë takes his plot and splits it; she takes her heroine up his epic stairs and lets her fall from the difficult world where she is building an identity in a second language into a second world where she is sheltered, where she can be momentarily nourished by both mother and father tongue because she has established a linguistic world elsewhere, a bilingual identity. When Lucy leaves the Brettons and returns to this identity, she enters into a fiercer dialogue with English letters than before and in a series of splittings and doublings gathers for herself a language that is, intermittently, as fiery as Vashti's—"Yes, I have a tongue aflame, and rightly," she lashes out in French at Monsieur Paul (p. 290). Brontë then gives Lucy the full-voiced vision that Keats denied his speaker—a vision allowing a radical denunciation of the status quo and glimpses of what are, for the novelistic heroine, the radical option of going language mad, of consuming the honey of language for the sake of the ego and gaining a revisionary and Romantic capacity for self-delight.

Honey-mad men, the Romantic poets speak again and again of a failure to achieve their own visionary victories. "Kubla Khan" ends, for example, halfway between euphoria and despair:

> I would build that dome in air,
> That sunny dome! those caves of ice!
> And all who heard should see them there,
> And all should cry, Beware! Beware!
> His flashing eyes, his floating hair!
> Weave a circle round him thrice,
> And close your eyes with holy dread,
> For he on honey-dew hath fed,
> And drunk the milk of Paradise.[17]

The desire for honey, is, in the case of Coleridge's speaker, quite dangerous. This vision represents a wish for self-transcendence, for revolutionary ecstasy that threatens to tear him apart. In *Villette*, however, a concomitant visionary moment is preceded by a moment not of self-, but of language-splintering: "the strange speech of the cabmen . . . seemed strange to me as a foreign tongue," Lucy says, arriving in London for the first time. "I had never before heard the English language chopped up in that way" (p. 38). After English is so chopped the heroine is not only free to become multilingual, but she begins to steal visions from honey-mad men and to use them for her own purposes, and Kubla's dome rises again in the middle of London: "THE DOME. While I looked, my inner self moved; my spirit shook its always-fettered wings half loose; I had a sudden feeling as if I, who never yet truly lived, were at last about to taste life. In that morning my soul grew as fast as Jonah's gourd" (p. 39).

This discovery of Charlotte Brontë's multivocality may come as a surprise, since nineteenth-century women novelists can still be found—for the purposes of many critical discussions—

languishing in the shadow of their Romantic precursors. One of my concerns in this chapter has been to contrast the images of language that appear in Brontë's texts with the speech habits of the male Romantics, focusing on those moments in *men's* texts in which language becomes an object of contemplation. In this discussion I have neither considered men's writing as an arena of prior and therefore absolute or intractable literary practice, nor have I presented men's writing as a region of power disabling the feminine writer and enforcing her voicelessness or her anxiety of authorship. Simply, I have begun to consider men's writing as speech partially limited by the author's time and his gender. As Myra Jehlen suggests in "Archimedes and the Paradox of Feminist Criticism," we need to begin to deny "the normative universality of men's writing," and thus to historicize it, "rendering it precisely as 'men's writing' "[18] Within this framework I have suggested that male poets like Keats, Wordsworth, and Coleridge do not express their emancipatory needs in relation to language in the same ways that women writers do.

For example, if we consider the ending of Keats' "Nightingale" in closer detail, we may notice that conventional readings explain the poem's finale in moral terms: the poet must return to his identity within the human (the masculine?) world, and his discovery of the "limits" of language insures the separation of self from unbounded nature. I want to linger over these images because our usual understanding of Keats' poem should help to reveal critical biases and explain why some feminist critics may persist in understanding men's as empowered and women's as disempowered writing.

Keats' most provocative reader, Thomas Weiskel, upholds the "truth" of Keats' discovery that the word functions as an absolute limit; he suggests that Keats' return to the "forlorn" world is inevitable. The end of "Ode to a Nightingale" satisfies us, says Weiskel, because the poetic "I" recognizes the fictionality of the image it has advanced and "desublimates": " 'forlorn' is reduced back out of the fiction to the 'sole self' where it originated."[19] But of course Keats' invocation of the limits of language does not return us to an origin; instead, the word allows the poet to traverse a path from one fiction to another. Thus in "Nightingale" Keats explores language's dual functions—its pluralizing capacity, its ability to multiply, to divide, to become the stuff of extraordinary fictions—but he ends by affirming the word's function of isolating and insuring identity. It is this thetic function—with its authentication of the "sole self"—that Keats "Nightingale" finally upholds.

Keats, of course, protests the need for this or any other form of identitarian closure in his letter on the chameleon poet: a letter frequently cited to explain that the impulses expressed in men's and women's writing are one and the same. The poet, Keats says, is continually "filling in for some other Body—the Sun, the Moon, the Sea and Men and Women who are creatures of impulse who . . . have about them an unchangeable attribute—the poet has none; no identity—he is certainly the most unpoetical of all God's creatures."[20] Keats may go the farthest of all his fellow poets in dissolving his own belief in identity, but he finally asks the images of language that appear in his texts to serve a normative or conservative function. We go to a poem like Keats' "Nightingale" not to be revolutionized, not to challenge our belief in that dominant discourse which eulogizes a unified masculine cogito, but in search of epistemological solace—to give ourselves over to high verbal madness, knowing that the egocentric boundaries the poem so pleasurably assaults will be reestablished. So while the conclusion of Keats' "Nightingale" is generally celebrated as the acme of openness, of negative capability, we could also look at this verse as the epitome of a form of binary thinking that envisions thought as a series of oppositions rather than a productive cacophony of socially dangerous music.

In contrast, I have suggested that when writers like Brontë are caught in the lower terms of the binary subordination that language imposes on women, one of their strategies of disentanglement is to develop a liberatory interest in language that, in this case, involves working with the metaphoric capacities provided by a second language system—a system that can enter into dialogue with the first and help to revise or to divert its misogyny. In order to broaden the scope of this analysis and show that these strategies are not at work in Brontë's fiction alone, I want to examine a similar strategy in George Eliot's *Mill on the Floss*, and to compare

Eliot's use of bilingualism both with Charlotte Brontë's and with Thomas Hardy's in *Jude the Obscure.*

In *The Mill on the Floss* Eliot emphasizes the second language's capacity to interrupt her text's primary language in Maggie's decision to do away with conventional grammatical structures, to pursue the words in her brother's Latin text by using her own set of rules: "she delighted in new words, and quickly found that there was an English Key at the end, which would make her very wise about Latin, at slight expense." Maggie not only makes up her mind to skip the rules in the syntax, since "the examples became so absorbing," but these examples lead to a procession of floral and faunal images similar to the explosion of metaphors we see in *Jane Eyre:*

The mysterious sentences, snatched from an unknown context—like strange horns of beasts, and leaves of unknown plants, brought from some far-off region,—gave boundless scope to her imagination, and were all the more fascinating because they were in a peculiar tongue of their own, which she could learn to interpret.[21]

These meditative moments in Eliot and Brontë are reminiscent of moments in masculine texts—specifically the "voyage of conception" that Keats describes in a letter to John Hamilton Reynolds. I want to make a distinction, however, between the "voyage of conception" as Keats imagines it and the meditative euphoria young women like Jane or Maggie experience. For Keats, reflection upon any text seems productive: "When Man has arrived at a certain ripeness in intellect any one grand and spiritual passage serves him as a starting post towards all 'the two-and-thirty Pallaces,' " Keats says. "How happy is such a 'voyage of conception.' "[22] For Jane and Maggie "any grand and spiritual passage" will not serve. They require, first, a text in an alien tongue, a text outside the environs of ordinary discourse, and, second, a text that is splintered and fragmented—words that have been hauled from their roots, mauled, maligned, disassociated from their context—a language liberated from thetic fixity. Jane meets these conditions by attacking her primary language and replacing its misogynous terms with "the work of my own hands." Maggie finds a gustatory pleasure in Latin words because they exist in an interpretable "tongue of their own" and because they have already been split off from their syntactic context—they are already fractional:

The most fragmentary examples were her favourites. *Mors omnibus est communis* would have been jejune, only she liked to know the Latin; but the fortunate gentleman whom every one congratulated because he had a son "endowed with *such* a disposition" afforded her a great deal of pleasant conjecture, and she was quite lost in the "thick grove penetrable by no star," when Tom called out,

"Now, then, Magsie, give us the Grammar!" (p. 218)

Tom's familiar imperative stops Maggie's "voyage of conception," and when she protests to his schoolmaster, Mr. Stelling replies that girls shouldn't do math or Latin because "they've a great deal of superficial cleverness; but they couldn't go far into anything. They're quick and shallow" (pp. 220–21). It is just such an interruption or appropriation of speech for male ends that has encouraged feminist theorists to insist on women's exclusion from language. Although these theories have a wide-ranging textual justice, we need to see that these textual appropriations may work dialectically, and that Tom's appropriation of Maggie's speech is only part of the story: the moment of male interruption can also represent a moment when the dominant structure itself is placed in contradiction. In fact, when Tom tries to control Maggie's access to Latin by asking her to coach him, to mend his still shaky possession of these strange-sounding locutions, Maggie starts using the Latin text again for her own purposes: "Tom sailed along pretty well for three lines; and Maggie was beginning to forget her office of prompter in speculating as to what *mas* could mean, which came twice over, when he stuck fast at *Sunt etiam volucrum*" (p. 218).

We may say that within Eliot's novel this second language has, for Maggie, an emancipatory and for Tom, a regulative function. Maggie is beginning to contemplate what *mas* or masculine might mean, beginning another dangerous "voyage of conception," while Tom, despite his "superior" gender, has smaller access to this playfulness. As he tries unsuccessfully to check Maggie's imaginative meanderings, he gets stuck at a crucial Latin phrase—

"Sunt etiam volucrum"—"there are also names." He "sticks at" Latin names in much the same way that the hero of Keats' "Nightingale" sticks fast at the word "forlorn." Tom is stopped by an alien language—its rules represent a limit for his imagination, while Maggie's imagination starts at the very point where conventional linguistic rules end. Does this mean that language itself can serve a blocking function for men and at the same time be liberating for women? Feminist critics have stated the reverse; they claim that men employ language for their own ends while women are contained by the "masculine" word's authority. We should question such hypotheses and begin to inquire whether the practice of "sticking at names" occurs elsewhere in the word habits of male writers. Is Tom Tulliver's reaction anomolous, or does his predicament tell us something about an upwardly mobile nineteenth-century Englishman's relation to language? Let us compare Maggie's perusal of her brother's Latin text with Jude's passion for Latin in *Jude the Obscure.*

As a child, Jude experiences a bitter need to posses a Latin grammar, and he goes to great lengths to procure this text, only to discover that "the charm he had supposed in store for him was really a labour like that of Israel in Egypt" (p. 27). Hardy makes us feel that the weight of civilization inheres in this little text; we find none of the orality, the glad animal spirits, the profusion of self-renovating metaphors associated with learning a foreign language in *Mill on the Floss* or *Jane Eyre.*

To acquire languages, departed or living, in spite of such obstinacies as he now knew them inherently to possess, was a herculean performance which gradually led him on to a greater interest in it than in the presupposed patent process. The mountain-weight of material under which the ideas lay in those dusty volumes called the classics piqued him into a dogged, mouselike subtlety of attempt to move it piecemeal. (p. 27)

Unlike Maggie, Jude is unable to use the interim space in the Latin text for liberation or private pleasure. Skipping over the syntax, Maggie uses the gap between the text and the English key at the end; Jude "conscientiously covered up the marginal readings, and

used them merely on points of construction, as he would have used
a comrade or tutor who should have happened to be passing by."
This is Jude's way of "getting into the groove he wished to follow."
Maggie avoids this "groove" and gets purposefully lost in the "thick
grove penetratable by no star"; her discovery of an alternative
language serves as a means of calling an unnamed euphoria into
the open.

For Jude sexual and textual pleasure are at odds with
one another, but if we compare Hardy's representations of the
"bilingual hero" with the creations of other male novelists, Hardy's
response does not seem anomolous. In nineteenth-century novels
in which the male writer gives his hero a second language and this
second language itself appears in the text, the incorporation of
French or Latin functions much as it functions in *Jude,* though
not so ominously. In *Henry Esmond,* for example, French or Latin
phrases allow us to measure a character's (or sometimes the narrator's) good breeding, while in James' *The American* the hero's
desire to learn French comes from the same emotional region as
his desire to do well in business; he would acquire extra ways of
speaking in the same way he acquires additional business partners.[23]
(Among twentieth-century male writers the play between two languages takes a slightly different form. The chapter in French in
The Magic Mountain opens up that text in an exciting way, but
even though, say, Jake's Spanish in *The Sun Also Rises* has the
luster of alterity, of setting up an alternative discourse to represent
what cannot be represented in his primary language, his knowledge
of Spanish does not represent Jake's exploration of forbidden
impulses, of impulses his culture denies him, but becomes a badge
of Jake's deeper, more spiritual machismo.) In *The Mill on the
Floss,* by way of contrast, the Latin text functions as French does
in *Jane Eyre.* The discovery of a language one can "interpret"
rather than learn by rote, as Jude does, or "acquire" as Christopher
Newman does in *The American,* leads to a cascade of images
which represents, for Maggie as for Jane Eyre, unspoken possibilities
which her brother's appropriation of the Latin text closes down. To
cite a final nineteenth-century example, in *Sartor Resartus* German
is inserted liberally in Carlyle's text so that it operates as a formal

device of comedy and estrangement. The ironic juxtapositions of English and German allow Carlyle to experiment with his own form of "abnormal discourse"—but German does not operate as a form of liberatory discourse available for the projection of Carlyle's, or his character's, unspoken reveries. In Brontë's texts and in Eliot's *Mill on the Floss,* however, the incorporation of a second language functions subversively, as an alternative form of speech which disrupts the repressions of authoritative discourse and welcomes or shelters themes that have not yet found a voice in the text's primary language.

I have dwelt at length on the differences between textual bilingualism in writing by women and men in order to support the argument that we must no longer assume that male writers, simply by virtue of their affiliation with a male literary tradition, produce an empowered writing that disables the woman writer. In this chapter I have begun to produce evidence for this argument in two different areas. First, by exploring textual bilingualism as a capacity the woman writer uses to explore extradiscursive zones, I have located a language game in which women have surpassed their male contemporaries in ingenuity and in the invention of emancipatory strategies. Second, in extending this analysis to an examination of Brontë's revisions of the male Romantics in *Villette* I have attempted to extend our vision of the structural multilanguagedness women employ in their writing. I want to pursue my analysis of this multilanguagedness through the end of this chapter.

Although a number of critics have described the ways in which Romantic poets have limited the woman writer's capacity to revise the stories she inherits, I have begun to renegotiate the direction of this analysis, to show that revision and cultural production is something the woman writer can do. In her excellent study of Dorothy Wordsworth, Emily Brontë, and Emily Dickinson, *Women Writers and Poetic Identity,* Margaret Homans describes those literary forces that conspire against the nineteenth-century woman writer. As someone caught in her culture's misogynous terms, the writer Homans describes is unable to imitate the rhapsody and verbosity of her male contemporaries:

In Romantic poetry the self and the imagination are primary. During and after the Romantic period it was difficult for women who aspired to become poets to share in this tradition, not for constitutional reasons but for reasons that women readers found within the literature itself. Where the masculine self dominates and internalizes otherness, that other is frequently identified as feminine, whether she is nature, the representation of a human woman, or some phantom of desire. . . . To become a poet, given these conditions, required nothing less than battling a valued and loved literary tradition to forge a self out of the materials of otherness.[24]

Homans focuses on the ways in which this otherness is reinforced in male texts—first, through woman's "association with nature," and second through "her exclusion from a traditional identification of the speaking subject as male" (p. 12). What I want to examine next in *Villette,* however, is the way in which Brontë renegotiates both the meaning of woman's association with nature and the traditional association of visionary speech with male poets. We will see that Brontë not only uses the metaphor of bilingualism but uses the multivocal structure of the novel to combat inimical readings of feminine identity created by her male precursors.

Virginia Woolf has emphasized that the novel is the form the nineteenth-century woman writer adopts because of its adaptability to woman's material conditions, its openness to interruption, to the intrusion of friends or family. I want, however, to suggest that the novel is a form attractive to the woman writer not because it is interruptible but because it is disruptive; the novel's multivoicedness allows the woman writer to interrogate and to challenge the very voices that tell her to conform. I will examine this dynamic at greater length in chapter 6, but for now let me emphasize that the novel's polyphonic structure allows the woman writer to attack and revise the male tradition on several different textual levels; it offers another form of "multilanguagedness" and permits the woman writer's "battle" against "a valued and loved literary tradition" to take place in a space in which women can repudiate, admire, and rework the tradition's own spaciousness. Within the novel a poetic plot that represses "the feminine" or places women in positions of marginality or otherness can be presented, then disrupted and polyphonically splintered: its pieces realigned and shattered again to form constellations of meaning useful for the woman writer's own ends.

This is not the usual reading of women's deployment of the novel as genre. For Homans, as for Woolf, the novel becomes the form that women use because it mirrors, all too accurately, the confinement of the feminine world:

If the novel was more available to women because those portions of society that women experienced formed appropriate subjects for prose fiction, then the novel is more readily available to critics of women's writing because the connections between the work and a measurable, describable "female experience" are so much more demonstrable than in poetry. (p. 7)

We must go part way with this thesis before breaking with it. Clearly *Villette* resounds with echoes from Keats' "Hyperions," Wordsworth's *Prelude,* the Lucy poems, Coleridge's "Kubla Khan," "The Nightingale," and "Dejection: an Ode," and when we first hear these poems infiltrating Brontë's text, we can hear only Lucy's exclusion, her relegation to the status of otherness and helplessness that Homans describes as women's Romantic inheritance. Lucy Snowe seems especially unable, as feminine speaker, to break into a tradition in which the "speaking subject" is traditionally male. In fact the first allusion to Coleridge's "Nightingale" comes early in the novel when Polly Home learns that it is time to leave the Brettons and return to her father. She spends the evening caressing Graham Bretton's foot (the site of Blake's Miltonic inspiration, of Keats' ascent up the prophetic stair), and when Polly is finally forced to go to bed, grief-stricken, Lucy can only attempt to revive her with bitter wisdom: a wisdom so full of lessons in feminine helplessness that Polly grows more depressed. "Paulina, you should not grieve that Graham does not care for you as much as you care for him," Lucy says. "It must be so." Polly, as Lucy says, must accept her lot "because he is a boy and you are a girl; he is sixteen and you are only six; his nature is strong and gay, and yours otherwise." Hearing these words Polly grows quieter. Cold and lonely, she creeps into Lucy's bed:

She came . . . instantly, like a small ghost gliding over the carpet. I took her in. She was chill: I warmed her in my arms. She trembled nervously; I soothed her. Thus tranquillised and cherished she at last slumbered.

"A very unique child," thought I, as I viewed her sleeping countenance by the fitful moonlight, and cautiously and softly wiped her glittering eyelids and her wet cheeks with my handkerchief. "How will she get through this world, or battle with this life? How will she bear the shocks and repulses, the humiliations and desolations, which books, and my own reason tell me are prepared for all flesh?" (pp. 27–28)

At the end of "Nightingale" Coleridge gives us a similar scene between a poet-father who is fond of maxims and who, like Lucy Snowe, wants to comfort his comfortless child.

> and once, when he awoke
> In most distressful mood (some inward pain
> Had made up that strange thing, an infant's dream—)
> I hurried with him to our orchard-plot,
> And he beheld the moon, and hushed at once,
> Suspends his sobs, and laughs most silently,
> While his fair eyes, that swam with undropped tears,
> Did glitter in the yellow moon-beam! Well!—
> It is a father's tale: But if that Heaven
> Should give me life, his childhood shall grow up
> Familiar with these songs, that with the night
> He may associate joy.[25]

Coleridge encourages us to have faith in the power of this "father's tale" to make things come out right, for his poet-father is ambitious to help his son acquire a mode of speech superior to his own that will also help the son construct health-giving patterns of association. Coleridge's poem ends with a vision of possible utopia—through the intervention of his vital male voice the poet-father stage-manages his son's escape from ordinary history.

As Lucy holds her child in the moonlight she can only preach resignation; the father's tale, as the daughter hears it mediated through the words of a surrogate mother, brings torment, not blessing. Nor does the moon stop Polly's tears—it is as "fitful" as Lucy is cautious. Unlike Coleridge's son, Polly does not experience utopian blessing; she is not called upon to experience the continuities between a beneficent feminine voice and nature's power. Instead, the moon's "glitter" marks her fall into history and pain. "She departed the next day; trembling like a leaf when she took leave, but exercising self-command" (p. 28).

At this point in Lucy's story, Homans' thesis seems justified. But if we are not so quick to jump at an analysis of women's victimization, we can see an interesting pattern developing here. Women's alienation from poetic plots (as male Romantics have defined them) seems at first to be absorbed into Brontë's novel and affirmed, but as the novel continues, Lucy's distance from the power Coleridge's male speaker possesses begins to disappear. Brontë's text begins by echoing Coleridge's poem in order to represent those problems of powerlessness the poem poses for the heroine or reader who wants to "enter" its terms. What happens as Brontë continues to write is that the poem is split, riven, put into process, and revised in stages.

Brontë's female protagonists are enrolled in a masculine story at the beginning of *Villette*. Structurally, Polly and Lucy find themselves inserted into the archetectonics of Coleridge's poem and repulsed by this same archetectonics; Brontë's heroines are not allowed to participate in the poem's own happy terms. Brontë's heroines are initially overcome by this difference, but as they try to participate in a structure that rejects them, that is, as Brontë's novel continues, the heroine's counterpresence within the plot that rejects her (her pressence as someone who refuses to be completely contained by male stories) begins to transform the stories themselves. The original structure is split open, its inevitability challenged, and Brontë refuses to allow her heroines to agree to the exclusive election that Coleridge and son have kept for themselves. To include Lucy and Polly in this masculine story, then, does not simply victimize them, or reveal the ways men's stories exclude them. Instead, this inclusion is Brontë's way of lodging a form of protest which the text later expands and explodes. Coleridge's poems are gradually absorbed and finally transformed by the novel's working machinery.

Where does Coleridge's verse appear again? Once Lucy has begun to develop her bilingual identity, to become more self-conscious and capable, Brontë starts to weave together a complex series of images from several Romantic poems and places Lucy at varying degrees of distance from these images. At first, when Lucy describes her visionary experiences in *"l'allée défendue"* behind the *Pensionnat de Demoiselles* where she teaches, she seems no more than a shadowy replica of Wordsworth's "Lucy Gray" ("I made myself the gardner of some tintless flowers," she tells us). Full of meek affection for nature, Lucy contrasts her vestal instincts with the gay life of the city that passes her by. But she is not without Romantic consolation:

A moon was in the sky, not a full moon, but a young crescent. I saw her through a space in the boughs overhead. She and the stars, visible beside her, were no strangers where all else was strange: my childhood knew them. I had seen that golden sign with the dark globe in its curve leaning back on azure beside an old thorn at the top of an old field, in Old England, in long past days, just as it now leaned back beside a stately spire in this continental capital. (pp. 95–96)

Lucy is, quite literally, remembering a time when she "knew well the evening star"; she has already begun to claim the power Coleridge bestows on his child. And in claiming this moment of election for Lucy, Brontë also allows her heroine to interrupt another Coleridgean association. Estranged from the moon's blessings, the Ancient Mariner yearns "in his loneliness and fixedness . . . towards the journeying Moon, and the stars that still sojourn, yet still move onward; and everywhere the blue sky belongs to them, and is their appointed rest, and their native country and their own natural homes, which they enter unannounced, as lords that are certainly expected and yet there is a silent joy at their arrival."[26] The Mariner is excluded from this haven, but Lucy identifies with its kindredness; the sky contains "signs" that speak to Lucy directly and allow Lucy to claim for herself a "Romantic" sense of nature's companionableness and of her own election. But the business of revising male plotting is hardly over. This direct association of woman with nature stirs within Brontë too many unrevised memories of woman's designated "otherness." In confronting Lucy's equation with the forces of nature, the chapter starts to go wild. Anecdote leads to anecdote in an abrupt and disconnected fashion. In the scene where Lucy is invoking the male subject's power of election for herself, she is still sitting—diminutive, alone—by an "old thorn" in England; she resembles no one so much as Martha Raye, the saddest of Wordworth's heroines. Like Coleridge's child, like Lucy, Martha Raye "is known to every star, / And every wind that blows." Her reputation is earned through her sad powers of violence and natality; she is said to have given birth to a baby she has murdered and buried beneath the thorn. Lucy Snowe manages to transcend Martha Raye's helplessness (rather than acquiring the Romantic capacity of Fancy or Imagination, Martha Raye can only mutter crazily: "Oh misery! oh misery! / Oh woe is me! oh misery!"), but Lucy has not transcended Martha Raye's limited association with the uncontrollable cycles of nature.

There is, however, a third pattern of Romantic association that enters Lucy's meditations and moves toward a more powerful feminine praxis. "Dejection: an Ode," Brontë's other poetic source for this chapter, begins with a quotation from the "Ballad of Sir Patrick Spence," a ballad equating the "feminine" with the dangerous forces that can be unleashed within nature:

> Late, late yestreen I saw the new Moon,
> With the old Moon in her arms;
> And I fear, I fear, my Master dear!
> We shall have a deadly storm.[27]

Lucy, of course, sees a similar sign with a more benign meaning: "I had seen that azure sign with the dark globe in its curve, leaning back on azure beside an old thorn at the top of an old field, in Old England." As avatar of Wordsworth's Martha Raye Lucy is not so much bound by Brontë's male precursors as she is wrestling with emblems of her own powerfulness. This is also true of Coleridge in "Dejection," where Coleridge's male speaker quiets the painful voices his own inner storm evokes by giving his mind over to a tamed and feminine spirit; he blesses a female friend, imagining her to posses a half-natural, half-magical power to tame his own catastrophic energies. "Dejection" ends with Coleridge's voicing of her benediction: "And may this storm be but a mountain-birth, / May all the stars hang bright above her dwelling, / Silent as though they watched the sleeping Earth! . . . Joy lift her spirit, joy attune her voice; / To her may all things live, from pole to pole, / Their life the eddying of her living soul!" (ll. 128–36). Thus Coleridge parcels out his misery to a feminine *genius loci* as a way of triangulating and healing his depression; he finds a symbolic means to close whatever in the unconscious remains brutish and open.

Still, "Dejection" ends beautifully; the poet reconciles himself to his own internal oppositions. After stirring up poetic trouble with the opening image of woman as dangerous other, in concluding, Coleridge's speaker closes the self off to agonized negativity via the image of woman as friendly, pacific, uncomplicated "other." In "Dejection" Coleridge can resolve these feelings—at least in literary terms—because he keeps woman in this position of otherness—and can therefore project his own unruly energies onto her alien zone. However, when Brontë revises for Lucy Coleridge's experience of an unbearable psychic storm in "Dejection," Lucy (and for that mater, Brontë) is stuck—in a way Coleridge is not: the storm "stirred up a craving cry I could not satisfy." This thunderstorm shakes the whole school and the Catholic students and teachers respond, as Coleridge does, with a panic redeemable through projection and prayer:

Within the dormitory they gathered round the night-lamp in consternation, praying loud. I could not go in: too resistless was the delight of staying with the wild hour, black and full of thunder, pealing out such an ode as language never delivered to man—too terribly glorious, the spectacle of clouds, split and pierced by white and blinding bolts. (p. 96)

Lucy cannot split off these undesirable energies and project them onto some other, since she is already placed in that position of other. What happens, instead, is that she has to continue to experience the split in herself; she is put into process: "As for me, the tempest took hold of me with tyranny: I was roughly roused and obliged to live." She is forced, then, to continue to experience the internal power she represses externalized in bolts of thunder and delight. Her self-splitting leads to the memory of an evening in the garden when her language once more is riven and changed: an evening when a letter—written in French—is thrown into the garden: "Presently the rude Real burst coarsely in . . . a tree overhead shook, as if struck by a missile; some object dropped prone at my feet." Lucy is thrust into an arena of doubleness in which conflict cannot be resolved by simple projection. As she translates the French letter into English she gets a new reading of herself from a startling perspective. The letter names her as "that dragon, the English teacher—*une véritable bégueule Britannique . . . comme un vieux caporal de grenadiers, et revêche comme une religieuse*" (p. 98). Described as a British monster, as someone sour and tough as a nun, Lucy's quiet persona is suddenly pushed into mystery; the aura of power and crazed holiness that surrounds the dangerous moon at the beginning of "Dejection" is suddenly introjected. Engaging this new twist in her story, she becomes a precursor of the female detectives who take on new enigmas and new personae at will, and in Brontë's next chapter we glimpse Lucy acting out these different roles: at one moment she meekly erases the signs of Dr. John's intrusive footmarks in her little garden world, and at another she rages at the destructive texts inflicted on her pupils: "I would have given two francs for the chance of getting that book once into my hands," she says, eager to destroy the "nightmares of oppression, privation and agony" that these saints' lives ask pupils to emulate (p. 103).

This potentiating doubleness invades Lucy's worst moments of self-effacement. The garden penetrated by Dr. John— who mucks about "trampling flowers and breaking branches in his search" for the letter Lucy herself inadvertently receives—evokes a similar scene from Wordsworth's "Nutting" in which a youth breaks into a forest bower and destroys its innocence. Wordsworth's poem ends with a moment of contrition: "Then, dearest Maiden, move along these shades / In gentleness of heart; with gentle hand / Touch—for there is a spirit in the woods."[28] In effacing Dr. John's footsteps Lucy is playing the role of this dutiful sylvan spirit. Coming back to the bower like a demure nature goddess, Lucy repairs the

Doctor's bad work: "Some plants there were, indeed, trodden down by Dr. John in his search, and his hasty and heedless progress which I wished to prop up, water, and revive; some footmarks, too, he had left on the beds: but these in spite of the strong wind, I found a moment's leisure to efface very early in the morning, ere common eyes had discovered them" (p. 102). Lucy is playing the demanded Romantic role—but with this dementia, this difference— she is simultaneously effacing Dr. John's and Wordsworth's signatures and reasserting her own. Her text, after all, is preparing us for another reading of the heroine's relation to nature and moonlight.

        Brontë has inserted something new—a woman's splintered but self-assertive voice—into the plot of Coleridge's "Dejection," and rather than collapsing under the power of masculine print, that voice begins to speak otherwise—to claim for itself a position of egotistical—and feminine—power:

A gathering call ran among the faculties, their bugles sang, their trumpets rang an untimely summons. Imagination was roused from her rest, and she came forth impetuous and venturous. With scorn she looked on Matter, her mate—
"Rise!" she said; "Sluggard! this night I will have *my* will; nor shalt thou prevail."
"Look forth and view the night!" was her cry; and when I lifted the heavy blind from the casement, close at hand—with her own royal gesture, she shows me a moon supreme in an element deep and splendid. (pp. 409–10)

By the end of *Villette* the feminine moon of "Dejection" has come to represent an imaginative power Lucy has taught herself to identify with and to claim. Nor should this turn in Brontë's revisions of Coleridge's poetry be surprising. As Gilbert and Gubar note in *The Madwoman in the Attic,* the woman writer's dialogue with the male Romantics can prove useful, "for, as Northrop Frye has argued, a revolutionary 'mother-goddess myth' which allows power and dignity to women—a myth which is anti-hierarchical, a myth which would liberate the energy of all living creatures—'gained ground' in the Romantic period" (pp. 98–99). The question is how to initiate this dialogue without being seized by its terms. In this chapter I have tried to suggest one of the answers. The woman writer can open up the language games she is enabled to play, can multiply the very languages her heroine speaks, and we will later see why this may happen more readily within the novel—a form allowing women writers the spaciousness and the multivoicedness they need to seize, splinter, and begin to rewrite the old stories.

For the moment, I will simply draw attention to the fact that Lucy is led by this moon to a gap in the paling that has fenced her in—"a man could not have made his way through that aperture, nor could a stout woman . . . but I thought I might . . . and once within, at this hour the whole park would be mine—the moonlit, midnight park!" (p. 410)—and finally the Romantic equation of woman with the creating, fecundating, destroying power of nature is empowering:

> Leaving the radiant park and well-lit Haute-Ville (still well lit, this it seems was to be a "nuit blanche" in Villette), I sought the dim lower quarter.
>
> Dim I should not say, for the beauty of moonlight—forgotten in the park—here once more flowed in upon perception. High she rode, and calm and stainlessly she shone. . . . The rival lamps were dying: she held her course like a white fate. . . . with pencil-ray she wrote on heaven and on earth records for archives everlasting. She and those stars seemed to me at once the types and witnesses of truth all regnant. The night-sky lit her reign: like its slow-wheeling progress, advanced her victory. (p. 427)

Wordsworth's and Coleridge's depictions of women have gradually been revised by Brontë's "pencil-ray," and their "rival lamps" are now "dying" in Brontë's text. The moon and stars cease to be absolute symbols of feminine trouble—of the stormy power women pour upon men from bitter skies; they become emblematic of woman's power to create a new verbal universe, to invent strategies of self-representation, of dialogue with the tradition, of emancipation that allow us to recognize women's texts not as the site of this victimization, but as a wonderful theater of revision and struggle.

If I have begun to stress within *Villette* utopian moments of polysemy and playfulness, it is because the character of Lucy Snowe is too often read negatively, and the emancipatory moments in Brontë's texts disappear if, in addition to seeing the sober side of Lucy's character, we do not admire the contrapuntal moments of passion and self-creation Brontë also emphasizes. It is my conviction that the feminist critic must do all she can to rescue the emancipatory potential of the texts she reads, and that we should be careful not to elide the playful ecstasies in this or any novel, especially since, in Brontë's experiment with incorporating a second language so fully and so subversively into *Villette's* primary language system, Brontë is inventing a new language game for her heroine— a language game that involves pleasure seeking and play as well as a new form of "mastery."[29] For example, we have seen that Ginevra Fanshawe is one of Lucy's feminine doubles whom critics often fail to recognize as a double because she represents a pleasure-seeking duplicity that we have not learned to associate with either Lucy Snowe or with the woman writer who is embarked on the serious task of reinventing her culture's ideas about femininity. In the remainder of this chapter I want to focus more fully on these moments of play and pleasure in women's writing—on the benefits the woman writer discovers in going honey mad.

I have begun to extract from *Villette* a typology of pleasure, bliss, and playfulness in writing that I want to pursue through one or two other scenes. "Nothing is more depressing than to imagine the Text as an intellectual object (for reflection, analysis, comparison, mirroring, etc.)," says Roland Barthes in *Sade, Fourier, Loyola.* "The text is an object of pleasure."[30] We have already used Brontë's text for "reflection, analysis, comparison, mirroring, etc"—but there is no reason we cannot take on Barthes' project as well. What Barthes listens for when he reads is the text's "transport, not the message," what he hopes to see is "the terrorist text, allowing the received meaning, the (liberal) repressive discourse that constantly attempts to recover it, slough itself off like an old skin" (p. 10). Let us look at these literal moments of transport in *Villette* and contrast Lucy's pleasure in journeying to London and beginning to invent her own "terrorist text" with Wordsworth's devaluation of play and multivoicedness in Bartholomew Fair.

For Wordsworth, the cacophonous spectacle he finds in London is frightening; the violence of Bartholomew Fair destroys his poetry and "lays . . . The whole creative powers of man asleep!" Wordsworth does not place himself among the city's polyglossic voices, but above them: "Upon some showman's platform."[31] Still, Wordsworth is complicitous with this "unnatural" drama; he makes himself part of the spectacle he critiques even as he tries, as high-toned poet, to avoid equivalence "with those that stretch the neck and strain the eyes, / And crack the voice in rivalship" (ll. 696–97). What Wordsworth does not want to discover is "the struggle going on within discourse" that will put his own myth making into crisis, that will reveal the competitive edge, the rivalry with other poets, the "crack" in his own voice. Above all, he does not want to enter into the wrong sort of playful discourse "with chattering monkeys dangling from their poles, / And children whirling in their round-abouts" (ll. 694–95). As Bakhtin explains, such speech diversity is potentially revolutionary—it permits "the fundamental liberation of cultural-semantic and emotional intentions from the hegemony of a single and unitary language."[32] For Wordsworth this "acute feeling for language boundaries" could be too productive; it could shatter the resistance of the "unitary, canonic language" he uses to summarize the meaning of his excursion by exposing the limitations of this language.

We see Wordsworth's careful conservation of his own way of speaking more clearly in an earlier passage of *The Prelude* when he hears

> for the first time in my life,
> The voice of woman utter blasphemy—
> Saw woman as she is, to open shame
> Abandoned, and the pride of public vice;
> I shuddered, for a barrier seemed at once
> Thrown in, that from humanity divorced
> Humanity, splitting the race of man
> In twain, yet leaving the same outward form.
> (ll. 384–91)

Like Helen Burns when she is branded by the word "slattern," Wordsworth is marked by what he sees, and this marking is serious; the cracking of voice Wordsworth fears takes on cosmic proportions as the race of man is split "in twain" by woman's voice. This "splitting" does not lead, however, to a productive sense of the dangerous potential of woman's word or the overt social contradictions in which Wordsworth—the democratic poet of *Lyrical Ballads*—finds himself. Instead, the Wordsworth who revises his memory of this scene begins to temporize, to turn this woman into an object of knowledge:

> Later years
> Brought to such spectacle a milder sadness,
> Feelings of pure commiseration, grief
> For the individual and the overthrow
> Of her soul's beauty; farther I was then
> But seldom led, or wished to go; in truth
> The sorrow of the passion stopped me there.
>
> (ll. 393–99)

It is this quality of being stopped or stuck at one's own nominations that I have begun to associate with Keats and with Wordsworth's writing—the capacity to name can also mean the willingness to go no further than syntactic limits permit; Wordsworth uses the thetic, equating power of the verb "to be" to stop this woman's meaning (he sees woman "as she is") and rename her. Process, productivity are censored and resanctified as structure, as stasis.[33]

By way of contrast, the moment in *Villette* when Lucy Snowe is cursed by a London crowd is enormously productive. As the structure of the language she uses to position herself in the world is attacked, Lucy, as we have already seen, begins to question the sanctity of her own mode of speech: "When I left the coach, the strange speech of the cabmen and others waiting round, seemed to me odd as a foreign tongue. I had never before heard the English language chopped up in that way" (pp. 38–39). This "chopping" of English allows Lucy to change her syntactic location, to place herself in an active, thetic relation to verbs that is unusual for the novelistic heroine, and liberating: "Prodigious was the amount of life I lived that morning. Finding myself before St. Paul's, I went

in; I mounted to the dome: I saw thence London. . . . I got. . . .
I went. . . . I dared," and finally, "I formed a project" (pp. 40–41).
This space of assertion, this positing of arrant selfhood is continually
interrupted in *Villette* by Lucy's self-doubt. But this interruption is
always useful—it not only shakes up the conventional structures
Lucy has inherited but also helps to reposition Lucy in a productive,
emancipatory relation to those structures that might contain her; it
forces a moment of self-contradiction which leads to new praxis.
As Lucy is rowed to the ship that is to take her to Labassecour,
like Wordsworth she is "marked" by a curse. Given the ideas of
de Lauretis and others about woman's inability to work through
the limitations of patriarchal discourse, we might expect this marking
to be disabling. Instead, the results are transformative:

> The watermen commenced a struggle for me and my trunk. Their oaths
> I hear at this moment: they shook my philosophy more than did the
> night, or the isolation, or the strangeness of the scene. One laid hands
> on my trunk. I looked on and waited quietly; but when another laid
> hands on me, I spoke up, shook off his touch, stepped at once into a
> boat, desired austerely that the trunk should be placed beside me—
> "just there." . . . I was rowed off. (pp. 41–42)

For Wordsworth, a woman's frightening oath becomes another
occasion to reiterate his philosophy; just as later, astonished by the
silent words on the blind beggar's placard, Wordsworth forecloses
on the distance between language and matter by making this distance
metaphysical. Wordsworth turns these occasions of being "marked"
by someone else's words into a negative mysticism: what is alien
within the self is projected outward into the otherness of woman
or of the universe. When Lucy Snowe comes up against the limits
of language, however, her philosophy is mercifully shaken, and what
emerges is renewed mobility.

> Black was the river as a torrent of ink; lights glanced on it from the
> piles of building round, ships rocked on its bosom. They rowed me up
> to several vessels; I read by lantern-light their names painted in great,
> white letters on a dark ground; the *Ocean,* the *Phoenix,* the *Consort,*
> the *Dolphin,* were passed in turns; but the *Vivid* was my ship, and it
> seemed she lay further down. (p. 42)

For Wordsworth, London is an "endless stream of men and moving things"—a place of too many voices, too much language, of words which dizzy both ear and eye: "Shop after shop, with symbols, blazoned names . . . / With letters huge inscribed from top to toe; / Stationed above the door, like guardian saints" (ll. 158–62). But while Wordsworth finds nothing but "blank confusion" in London's hectoring crowds, Lucy finds there a world of new writing; the white letters which show up against the dark river of ink bring to mind the fantasies of another woman writer who claims her texts are written in bold black and white: "I write," says Hélène Cixous, "in milk and night."[34] Cixous is a honey-mad woman par excellence; a writer whose fantasies of writing as ecstasy and reading as serene self-engorgement overgo Lucy Snowe's more timid imaginings. "A desire for text. Confusion!" Cixous says in "La Venue à l'écriture." "What is happening to her? A child! Some paper! Drunkenness! I am overflowing. My breasts are overflowing! Milk. Ink. Time to nurse. And me? I too am hungry. The milky taste of ink!"[35] Cixous' aphrodisiac desire for "text" seems a far cry from Lucy's aphasia, but the startling white letters which rock upon the "bosom" of the river on which Lucy travels toward her waiting ship make a promise both violent and playful: " 'The Vivid' started out, white and glaring, from the black night at last." On board this wild ship, Lucy begins to discover a new way of doubling the self and, in her conversations with Ginevra Fanshawe, a new kind of orality.

   In pursuing this analysis I have been following the arc of Barthes' suggestions in *Sade, Fourier, Loyola* that the reader should not master the "fury" of someone else's writing by absorbing its "contexts, convictions, a faith, a cause, nor even images: it is a matter of receiving from the text a kind of phantasmic order" (p. 8). In Brontë's text this phantasmic order is conveyed through her violation of the text's primary language, her experimentation in appropriating and rewriting male images of women, and her playful reversal of the colors of page and text, her desire to write Lucy's story in French and in English, in "milk and night." For Barthes the receiving of such a phantasmic order entails the refusal to "master" an author's secrets, her "contents," her ostensible philosophy. It is not in the text's "moral discourse" (Lucy's maxims), nor in its pattern of "social responsibility" (Lucy's love for Monsieur Paul or her vocation as schoolteacher) that the text touches us, but in its transport, in what we can feel of the author's "happiness of writing" (p. 9).

I have emphasized Charlotte Brontë's particular "happiness of writing" because we rarely examine this aspect of the woman writer's pleasure in her text. Nevertheless, if we adopt Barthes' terms too rigorously, we confront a limitation in our possible discourse about women's texts; we lose sight of the ways the women writer not only plays as she scribbles, but also does "work." For the woman writer these terms must go hand in hand; for Barthes, they do not. In "From Work to Text" Barthes explains that in order to experience the literary text as fully as possible, we need to discard our notions of the text as "work," to forget about the writer's strategems and examine his or her writing in terms of its "textuality," that is, its openness and playfulness, its bizarre volatility.

"The difference is as follows: the work is concrete, occupying a portion of book-space (in a library, for example); the Text, on the other hand, is a methodological field." [36] The difference between "work" and "Text" is, in Barthes' terms, the difference between something inert, structured, finished, and an activity:

While the work is held in the hand, the text is held in language: it exists only as discourse. . . . In other words, *the Text is experienced only in an activity, a production.* It follows that the Text cannot stop at the end of a library shelf, for example; the constitutive movement of the Text is a *traversal [traversée]*: it can cut across a work, several works." (p. 75)

Given Barthes' terms we want at first to describe *Villette* as a "Text"—as signifying material that is subversive, that refuses containment by a single interpretation, but like Barthes' "Text" is always at play and will refuse to stand still. Decentered, the text is always decentering; disclosing, the text always makes plural.

The Text . . . is linked to enjoyment *[jouissance]*, to pleasure without separation. Order of the signifier, the Text participates in a social utopia of its own: prior to history, the Text achieves, if not the transparency of social relations, at least the transparency of language relations. It is the space in which no one language has a hold over any other, in which all languages circulate freely.[37]

If this sounds exhilarating, if this matches my contention that languages are placed into new and subversive circulation in relation to one another in Brontë's text, I must also add that this circulation is not entirely free, since Lucy's "father" tongue, English, is placed in specific dialogue with her "other" tongue, French, so that the hegemonic structures of both languages may be called into question. Brontë's text is not the site of a "free" circulation, but of a specific and deliberately emancipatory activity; her writing does not consist of "free" playfulness, nor does it consist of an entirely restricted grammar. Instead, Brontë's text cultivates an alternative language through which Brontë labors to change the terms of Lucy Snowe's existence; her novel begins to chip away at the problems of woman's imprisonment within language. *Villette,* in other words, is a "text" that *works,* that does work.

I want to end this essay on the honey-mad woman, on the woman who consumes languages playfully and with pleasure, by suggesting that we need to start again to describe women's texts as "works"—to reclaim this word, to use "work" in its active, laborious sense, to refuse to echo Barthes' notion that literary "work" is something fixed and inert. This goes for the productions of the feminist critic as well. As Frank Lentricchia explains in *Criticism and Social Change,* "an active, self-conscious work of interpretation will show the political work that the canonized 'great books' have done and continue to do."[38] He says that the critic's task is to see the "work" "as a product of struggle" and to interrogate it "so as to reproduce it as a social text in the teeth of the usual critical lyricism that would deny the social text power and social specificity in the name of 'literature,' " or, we could add—that would deny the work social power in the name of the "Text."

For the woman writer to go honey- or language-mad is not, then, to allow her language to circulate freely—as woman herself has done for too many years. Her laborious "text" is engaged in the necessary business of stealing and recontextualizing languages, of doing this pleasurably, while recognizing that this pleasure involves muscular activity, involves dangerous, decisive, mind-bending work.

Thus, in climbing "the honey tree" the heroine of Mary Oliver's poems finds all the pleasure she needs. In "smashing yokes and censors" Cixous' heroine finds room in her "text" for the operations of more than one language. As for Brontë's heroines, this quest involves the effort of stealing, of binding the honey text to her mouth, "biting that tongue with her very own teeth," as Cixous says in "The Laugh of the Medusa," "to invent for herself a language to get inside of."[39] This honey-mad eating not only brings pleasure, but offers a transgressive, a blissful way to do much-needed work.

THREE

The Animality of the Letter

In chapter 2 we examined Charlotte Brontë's invention of a bilingual heroine and her use of this heroine's bilingualism to revise the poetic plots of Coleridge, Wordsworth, and Keats. In this chapter I want to pursue the woman writer's capacity for revision a step further. Having advanced an alternative metaphor for describing the woman writer's relation to language, I now want to suggest an alternative metaphor for describing the transformative properties of language itself: properties we will consider through the metaphor of the "animality" of the letter. In addition to focusing on the ways women are limited by language, we need to focus on those linguistic properties that allow women to seize upon and to use the word to their advantage. We will begin this exploration of the letter's "animality" with a look at another revisionary text, a poem that rewrites the themes of Melville's *Moby-Dick*—"Humpbacks," by Mary Oliver.

Moby-Dick is a novel that, despite the irony and the feminization of its hero Ishmael, is unabashedly phallocentric. Oliver's poem depicts the joys of another kind of whaling. The poem's speaker is entranced by the leaping whales she sees on a New England whale watch. Her whales leap joyfully out of the water into the air, and in allowing these whales (which Oliver genders as female) to frolic above the surface of the water, to leap into the empty spaces above their watery boundaries, the poem also addresses the question of how the woman poet can lighten—can play with and alter—the voice of a masculine tradition that wants to keep feminine language subdued and submerged.

In "Humpbacks" Oliver not only takes advantage of the letter's animality; she mimes its mobility in her chosen images. At issue in the poem is a question we have begun to address: how do we describe the woman writer's emancipatory acts and interests, how do women move into unenclosed space when what binds us together—the force of gravity, the convexity of the sentence—holds us so tightly in place?

In Melville's chapter "The Grand Armada," we are in the midst of an epic chase; the whalers are killing scores of whales with their harpoons and the whales—hundreds of them—are going mad, swimming in concentric circles which convey to Ishmael the "delirious throb" of the hunt. The whaling boat containing Ishmael and Queequeg tears "a white gash in the sea"; its passengers are menaced "on all sides . . . as we flew, by the crazed creatures to and fro rushing about us."[1] Suddenly the boat glides "between two whales into the innermost heart of the shoal, as if from some mountain torrent we had slid into a serene valley lake" (p. 496), and the whalers find themselves in a "sleek" produced by whales' bodies, "by the subtle moisture thrown off by the whale in his more quiet moods." This watery arbor enclosing the calving bodies of mothers and the copulating bodies of the younger whales is also enclosed by the concentric circles of hunter and hunted: a series of protective rings have been formed by those whales who, in the midst of their frenzy, still try to keep safe the "small tame cows and calves; the women and children of this routed host" (p 496).

This scene from *Moby-Dick* offers itself as a feminist parable. In *Alice Doesn't* de Lauretis reminds us that women are "all but absent from history and cultural process," and yet, "culture originates from woman and is founded on the dream of her captivity."[2] In *Moby-Dick* women are all but absent from Mellvile's narrative of culture, and yet "the feminine" is contained symbolically—worshipped and constrained—in this jewel-like chapter at the center of the novel. Penetrating to the heart of *Moby-Dick* we find the most domestic, peaceful scene imaginable: whales come sniffing about the whaling vessel "like household dogs" and allow the sailors to pat their heads and scratch their bellies. Here the mysteries of motherhood are unfolded to the sailors: "suspended in those watery vaults, floated the forms of the nursing mothers of the whales, and those that by their enormous girth seemed shortly to become mothers" (p. 497). These infants and mothers participate in a transcendent metaphysic; as Ishmael watches, the infants maintain a dreamy stare—half directed toward the vast deep around them, half directed toward the upper atmosphere. Meanwhile, the umbilical cord connecting mother and infant remains fully visible to the whalers; it floats eerily through the water. The scene is deliberately surreal, visionary: "Some of the subtlest secrets of the seas seemed divulged to us in this enchanted pond. We saw young Leviathan amours in the deep" (p. 498).

Why does this scene need to be rewritten by a woman writer? Ishmael prefers the peace of this feminine world to the ferocity of the chase; these female whales are at the center of the whales' and whalers' worlds. To answer this question precisely we need to ask: what does it mean to be at the center?

The center is not simply the point of the circle's "origin," but the site of its stasis as well. The center is that point where what is structured is also anchored, held in place; it is the site legislating and limiting the "play" of the structure as a whole. According to Derrida the center "closes off the play which it opens up and makes possible. As center, it is the point at which the substitution of contents, elements, or terms is no longer possible."³ As that which escapes structuration, the center is the acme, the epitome, the paradigm of what the surrounding structure desires or needs. As such, the center itself is immobile, fixed, the place where "anxiety can be mastered, for anxiety is invariably the result of a certain mode of being implicated in the game, of being caught by the game" (p. 279). Ishmael and his cohorts take pleasure in resting at this center—the place where they can transcend the anxieties of the chase and contemplate, for a moment, the price of "being caught by the game" while still participating in its folly. At the same time, this male "transcendence" is won at great cost to the representation of feminine energy. The space of "the feminine" is located in Moby-Dick outside the space of play: it is also beyond the space of social transformation and productivity.

Thus Melville's "Grand Armada" presents feminine creatures in the double bind de Lauretis describes. These female whales
become absent from history and from cultural process, and yet
culture itself is founded upon the dream of their capture.[4] In *Moby-
Dick* this female energy remains the source of inspiration, vision,
and capital, but is removed from the realm of praxis—from the
possibility of interrupting the whaler's quest and beginning something
new.

Derrida suggests that the center functions "not only to
orient, balance, and organize the structure—one cannot in fact
conceive of an unorganized structure—but above all to make sure
that the organizing principle of the structure would limit what we
might call the *play* of the structure" (p. 278). The center "closes
off the play which it opens up and makes possible. As center, it
is the point at which the substitution of contents, elements or terms
is no longer possible." In Melville's text, to place this image of "the
feminine" at the center (at the point where the possibility of
transformation or substitution disappears) is also to restrict feminine
"natality"—the power, as Hannah Arendt defines it, of beginning
things again. Melville replaces this natality with a simple-minded
reproductive fecundity. Not only Melville's plot, but his images
restrict woman's capacity to be culturally productive, to begin things
anew.

Mary Oliver's poem begins with the same metaphysical
dilemma Melville poses at the center of *Moby-Dick*. Her narrator
muses about what it means to be at the center; she questions what
holds body and world together:

> There is, all around us,
> this country
> of original fire.
>
> You know what I mean.
>
> The sky, after all, stops at nothing, so something
>   has to be holding
> our bodies
> in its rich and timeless stables or else
> we would fly away.[5]

While in *Moby-Dick* the somnambulent bodies of the nursing whales hold the bodies of the whales and whalers in their concentric circles of fear and productivity, in "Humpbacks" Oliver insists that the mysterious forces holding us to the earth are less nameable. In orienting her reader to this mystery, however, she must first decenter the weightiness, the centripetal energies defining "the feminine" as center.

We can feel the complexity of this decentering at work in Oliver's poem from its beginning, for when the whales rise above the surface of the water the whale watchers can see that their bodies not only look too large to rise, but they are also weighed down with excrescences—layered with barnacles. It is as if these bodies are layered with a substance like language that is heavy with meaning and keeps these creatures in the deeps. But this weight is nothing compared to the whales' desires to breach the surface of the water, to play:

> Off Stellwagen
> off the Cape,
> the humpbacks rise. Carrying their tonnage
>   of barnacles and joy
> they leap through the water, they nuzzle back under it
> like children
> at play.
>
> They sing, too.
> And not for any reason
> you can't imagine.
>
> Three of them
> rise to the surface near the bow
> of the boat,
> then dive
> deeply, their huge scarred flukes
> tipped to the air.   (pp. 60–61)

What separates the whales in Oliver's poem from Melville's is not only a species difference (his text is focused on sperm whales, hers on humpbacks), but the ability these playful animals have to break through the surface of the water in order to agitate the surface of the poem in unexpected ways. As the humpbacks breach, they evoke within the whale watchers—and within the lyric "I" who is composing the poem—a desire to share this transcendent moment, to gain access to a transformative energy that emerges in the form of communal vision:

> We wait, not knowing
> just where it will happen; suddenly
> they smash through the surface, someone begins
> shouting for joy and you realize
> it is yourself as they surge
> upward and you see for the first time
> how huge they are, as they breach,
> and dive, and breach again
> through the shining blue flowers
> of the split water and you see them
> for some unbelievable
> part of a moment against the sky—
> like nothing you've ever imagined.   (p. 61)

When Derrida argues that "the absence of the transcendental signified extends the domain and the play of signification infinitely" (p. 280), his concept seems very abstract. But if we imagine the forces of Oliver's poem rupturing the centrifugal circles of female enclosure in *Moby-Dick*—if we imagine this stretching, this streaking of the whales into sky-space as the abandonment of the "transcendental signified's" absolute space—then we have recognized a moment when the domain of play is literally extended.

As if to confirm this breaching of the signified, the poet herself suddenly finds a new voice. As the whales leap and frolic, defying their heaviness, defying all forces that conspire to keep them beneath the water, the poem's speaker hears someone shouting for joy and realizes that it is herself, that something heavy, intractable, feminine is careening up from under the surface of the water, entering discourse in a new way, as if the laughter of the sky itself were scattering the concentric strategies of Melville's text, or any text that has weighed the woman writer down, kept her from sporting with the tradition.

How is such transformation possible? How is it that Oliver's text can celebrate—so forcefully and so magnanimously—woman's speech, her shouting, her power over the word? To put this another way, why is it that we, as feminist critics, have not begun to theorize this power? What keeps us from recognizing women's texts as "works"—as places where the woman writer is engaged in confronting and appropriating, destroying and reconstructing the sociolect? Why haven't we spoken more freely about those textual sites where women's struggles to unlimit the language, to change discursive formations and enact another variety of "cultural revolution" become visible? My interest in describing the letter's "animality" (a metaphor that already has an objective correlative in the leaping bodies of the humpback whales) will be to suggest a theory of language that will help us claim the woman writer's productive violence more fully. To do this we will need to examine both the constraints language imposes upon women writers and the freedom it offers, for if we understand language as the place where the female subject is constructed, and as no more than that, we can begin to feel at home with a theory that gives language absolute power over the female subject, rather than constructing a theory allowing us to understand the ways in which women have instigated change.

Because so much theoretical attention has been focused on women's experience of constraint, in this chapter I want to stress—in a theoretical as well as a textual dimension—the emancipatory potential language possesses for the woman writer. My purpose, again, is dialectical. To emphasize the woman writer's empowerment alone is as reductive as emphasizing linguistic restrictions alone. These restrictions have been the feminist critic's too-constant theme:

Within the existing social arena the female subject does not participate in the production of the meaning which organizes her outside and gives her an inside, since she is excluded from what Foucault calls "discursive fellowships." While it is no doubt true that all subjects, male and female, are structured through discourse, and are in that respect passive, men enjoy another kind of discursive association as well, which is not available to women—an "active" or "speaking" association.[6]

In "*Histoire d'O:* The Construction of a Female Subject" Kaja Silverman insists that "on the basis of her gender" the female subject is excluded from all hegemonic fellowships "except those like feminism, which have grown up in opposition to the dominant symbolic order. She is consequently deprived of the power and knowledge which those fellowships imply, and is incapable of occupying anything but the position of a spoken subject" (p. 326). In this schema women's only alternative is to write in the silent intervals Wittig discovers in *Les Guérillères:* the caesura becomes the woman writer's only space of proliferation. Julia Kristeva puts this differently in her much-quoted interview in *m/f:* "women cannot *be;* the category woman is even that which does not fit into *being.* From there women's practice can only be negative, in opposition to that which exists, to say that 'this is not it' and 'it is not yet.' "[7] Even Kristeva separates the woman writer's practice from the patterns of cultural appropriation and scriptive violence she describes so passionately as an attribute of writing in *Revolution in Poetic Language.* "What I mean by 'woman,' " she says in *m/f,* "is that which is not represented, that which is unspoken, that which is left out of namings and ideologies."

One of the current goals of feminist criticism is to draw our attention toward the cultural obsession with things masculine, to make us conscious of the ways in which women's desires to participate in the making of history become difficult, almost impossible, in a world where patriarchal obsessions are structured into the very fabric of communication.[8] We have been asked to conclude that there is little women can do within language as it is presently constituted to transform our limited power as speakers.[9] We have seen that even after her canny analysis of women's powers to effect social change in *Alice Doesn't,* de Lauretis is still unwilling to take us past one final, ambivalent note: "In this 1984, it is the signifier who plays and wins before Alice does, even when she's aware of it. But to what end, if Alice doesn't?" (p. 186) Despite her affirmation of "self-consciousness" or consciousness raising at the end of *Alice Doesn't,* de Lauretis is elsewhere in agreement with the Kristevan injunction that women's practice can only be negative, can only set itself in opposition to what already exists. Although this is not my own point of view, it is a powerful argument, and we will find it useful to pursue the insistence of thinkers like Kristeva, Silverman, and de Lauretis that women are consistently disempowered in the realm of language. Let us renew our understanding of how perfidious this immersion in the "discursive formations" of masculine culture can be by looking at Wallace Stevens' "The World as Meditation."[10]

The setting of Stevens' poem is Penelope's bedroom in Ithaca. It is morning, and Penelope is still lying in bed, waiting for her husband's return. Instead of Ulysses' glamorous apotheosis we witness this daily waking: her loving reaction to the sun which climbs over the threshold, her ritualized waiting for Ulysses' return. "Is it Ulysses that approaches from the east, / The interminable adventurer? The trees are mended. / That winter is washed away. Someone is moving / On the horizon and lifting himself up above it." Penelope seems rooted, peaceful, clothed in the permanence of Ulysses' love. But the poem also moves toward a zone of uncertainty in which its characters begin to waver like reflections in water. "But was it Ulysses? Or was it only the warmth of the sun / On her pillow? The thought kept beating in her like her heart. / The two kept beating together. It was only day." This thought, like the sun, has a strong, elemental power—as if this warming presence, and what Penelope's imagination has made of it, are more erotic, more wonderful than what Ulysses has made of himself. Penelope becomes, for Stevens, the meditative center of the poem, the one who composes "the world as meditation." As Stevens describes her, she is the poet whose "barbarous" imaginative "strength . . . would never fail." But for all her barbarity, Penelope's creative powers are focused elsewhere; she is neither interested in her own lyric presence nor in the great world around her, but only in Ulysses' return. "She wanted nothing he could not bring her by coming alone. / She wanted no fetchings. His arms would be her necklace / And her belt, the final fortune of their desire."

What is striking about Stevens' poem is how completely natural and elegiac he makes Penelope's obsession seem: "She would talk a little to herself as she combed her hair, / Repeating his name with its patient syllables, / Never forgetting him that kept coming constantly so near." Penelope, the one most "present" in the poem, is finally most absent. Why? Talking to herself, Penelope recreates Ulysses as absent presence; she co-composes herself into "a self with which to welcome him, / Companion to his self for her, which she imagined, / Two in a deep-founded sheltering, friend and dear friend." The sentiments are beautifully limiting; Stevens' poem does not protest Penelope's reveries but asks us instead to fall in love with her self-abnegation.

According to Michel Foucault we tend to confuse discursive practices—the socially prescribed ways of thinking and speaking that inhabit each human being—with "expressive operations" through which individuals formulate their own desires. In speaking of Penelope's meditative eloquence, Foucault would insist that we read her desires as a preinscribed language game, for individual expression is always the product of "a body of anonymous, historical rules, always determined in the time and space that have defined a given period, and for a given social, economic, geographical, or linguistic area, the conditions of operation of the enunciative function."[11] Desire and its relation to discourse is inscribed by anonymous, historical rules, as are the notions governing the ways a prior discourse—like Homer's epic—can be appropriated.

In shifting our dialogue in the direction of Foucault's diacritic scheme we may well despair. If we accept his terms (as Peggy Kamuf does in her powerful essay, "Replacing Feminist Criticism"), we are left with little more than the negative manifesto Kristeva gives us to describe women's speaking, or with the simple urgency of Irigaray's manifesto in "When Our Lips Speak Together"—that we should get out of "male" language altogether. In chapter 1 we began to see that psychological and rhetorical benefits do result from Kristeva's and Irigaray's positions; their dramatizations of women's need for either a negative verbal practice (writing in the cracks of language—rupturing its totality), or for an *écriture féminine,* are productive. In chapter 2 we began to explore why there are good theoretical and emotional reasons for wanting, as women, to produce a counterlanguage. But for the moment I want to insist that there is a danger in taking up these ideas too quickly, before we have thought in more detail about what really happens in the interaction between women and speech. To this end I want to continue exploring the ways in which women writers have constructed an emancipatory relation to a dominant literary tradition. To do this will require us to look again at our relation to language, this time by asking whether our faith in the word's control over our lives is entirely justified, and whether Foucault's description of the linguistic "regime of truth," his discovery of our subservience to violent discursive practices, tells the whole story.

At the beginning of Jean Anouilh's *Antigone* we are reminded that language is destiny, that our fate as language users makes us unfree. "Antigone is young," says Anouilh. "She would much rather live than die. But there is no help for it. When your name is Antigone, there is only one part you can play; and she will have to play hers through to the end."[12] Anouilh has extended the meaning of Sophocles' tragedy to include not only Antigone's part in a family romance, but her fate as a speaker, as someone who is "spoken" by language.

Why might this foregrounding of the "linguistic romance" in *Antigone* be appealing? As structuralist and poststructuralist readers of texts, we have been captured by the idea that language maims and constrains us. Within this myth of the word's inexorability, we have discovered a new form of fatality; we argue that what is killing about the word is not that self and word are identical— but that the word is always other, that it remains outside the self and yet is responsible for constructing what selfhood we possess. As Karlis Racevskis suggests in *Michel Foucault and the Subversion of Intellect:* "Man exists, then, as an element of discourse. Since this existence is due to a radical change in the epistemological configuration of Western discourse, man is simply to be viewed as the product of a historical contingency."[13] Not surprisingly the term "language" in the index to Racevskis' book takes on wild connotations; it carries cross-references to the terms "death" and "other." Racevskis insists that we will only begin to emancipate ourselves from "humanistic" delusions once we recognize the ways in which "our thinking has been conditioned by forces beyond our conscious control" (p. 58). This recognition is not meant, in itself, to be liberating or empowering, for language operates within his rhetorical system in much the same way that terms like "fate" or "necessity" functioned in an older English. As Racevskis adds, any "illusory mode of producing the truth about ourselves" can only be "a function of the *episteme* that governs our mode of cognition" (p. 58).

In Foucault's schema the "episteme" is that grid of possibilities determining the ways in which knowledge is gathered and disseminated in a particular culture. Since our decisions are limited by this framework of accumulated possibilities, we are blind to its limitations and "believe ourselves bound to a finitude which belongs only to us, and which opens up the truth of the world to us by means of our cognition."[14] We are contained by a discursive formation that we seem to use freely but cannot control: a containment Foucault explicates in "Truth and Power":

Truth is a thing of this world: it is produced only by virtue of multiple forms of constraint. And it induces regular effects of power. Each society had its regime of truth, its "general politics" of truth: that is, the types of discourse which it accepts and makes function as true; the mechanisms and instances which enable one to distinguish true and false statements, the means by which each is sanctioned; the techniques and procedures accorded value in the acquisition of truth; the status of those who are charged with saying what counts as true.[15]

Language represents the chief form of our constraint. Its power is pervasive, corrupting: "there is no prediscursive fate disposing the word in our favour. We must conceive discourse as a violence that we do to things, or, at all events, as a practice we impose upon them; it is in this practice that the events of discourse find the principle of their regularity."[16]

For Foucault, this violence is so pervasive that the only emancipatory activities we can collectively affirm are those negative raids on the sociolect that Kristeva describes as woman's best recourse for social action. In a world where we are blinded by words, the most we can do is to assault the discursive framework as a whole and discount the validity claims of whatever asserts itself within reason. "Instead of seeing, on the great mythical book of history, lines of words that translate in visible characters thoughts that were formed in some other time and place, we have the density of discursive practices, systems that establish statements as events."[17] For Foucault, texts "construct" the world we inhabit; they establish historical characters and conundrums as part of our "archive," as something that exists in our minds simply because it is "enunciable."

According to this view of language, whatever can be said is contaminated by its participation in a "system of enunciability." We are governed by the "law of what can be said, the system that governs the appearance of statements as unique events." A system of enunciability describes "a system of functioning"; there is little room in Foucault's system for the linguistic play affirmed, say, in Bakhtin's descriptions of insult and parody. According to Bakhtin, such transgressive practices allow not only words, but speakers themselves to be released "from the shackles of sense," to define moments within discourse when we are able "to enjoy a period of play and complete freedom and to establish unusual relationships."[18]

The Foucauldian position does not rule out belief in transgression or mobility, but it does militate against the positive discovery of emancipatory moments.[19] If we are part of the "regime of truth" which defines our present moment, we cannot hope to see beyond it. As another of Foucault's disciples, Paule Bové, maintains in "Intellectuals at War: Michel Foucault and the Analytics of Power," the only radically emancipatory act we can conceive as intellectuals is to call the entire structure of knowledge, of jurisprudence, and ethical thinking into question:

How is it established that these criteria are not themselves part of the "regime of truth" whose function in our society leads not only to what one of Foucault's critics calls "unmitigated malignity," but to regulative authority for intellectuals who continually reestablish their identity by exercising the discourses of this regime to reposition themselves in their own interest—namely, to achieve influence and an audience?[20]

The assumption that language always represents high power stakes— that dialogue always implies a quest for domination, and that discourse never succeeds at communicative interaction but only at the dispossession and repositioning of power relations—is a very large assumption indeed.

Curiously, it is Bové who chides Foucault's critics for failing to examine their assumptions. "Charging that Foucault's analytics of power denies the possibility of any revolutionary practice is not critique," Bové says. "It is the assertion of a set of assumptions unexamined by those who hope to lead that revolution—or at least its imaginings" (p 51). Bové's assumptions are equally suspect. That language reflects "the hegemony of the present" seems true, but that an author's attempt to struggle against this "regime and its affiliations is inevitably to reproduce and extend it and the misery it causes" seems less obvious. The enemy is named too easily and the complexity of voices at work in any social formation obviated. While the "old" intellectual was to be the bearer of "universality" in its most rationally elaborated form, Bové insists that progressive academics have moved into a new era of academic responsibility. "The new role of the intellectual requires an unceasing critical concern with the present to detach truth from the current forms of hegemony," says Bové. "This detachment does not, of course, assure that the future will be any better. The negative function of the intellectual in the present moment is to locate and exploit breaks in the very linkage he or she opposes" (p. 53).[21] This politics implies a poetics. Suddenly the only speakerly or writerly act that is valuable is the act of negation, rupture, discontinuity. While for the woman writer such rupture and discontinuity are crucial in beginning to break up a dominant discourse—this deconstructive activity is not the whole story. In chapter eight I will suggest why "negativity" is inadequate as a feminist ideal. But first we need to look at another bilingual heroine: one who seems, in her limited powers of speech, to support Foucault's theories, but who is also surrounded—and ultimately uplifted—by animals, perhaps by the very "animality" of the letter itself.

Near the beginning of *Alice in Wonderland,* Alice is lost and miserable; she is swimming in her own pool of tears and wants to find her way to the shore. Hearing something splashing nearby she swims closer, imagining, from the sounds, that she will find a large walrus or hippopotamus who can carry her to land.

She finds, instead, a large mouse which (since she has grown
smaller) is just about Alice's size. Uncertain how to address this
creature, Alice begins stiffly: "O Mouse, do you know the way out
of this pool? I am very tired of swimming about here, O Mouse!"[22]
As she struggles through this treacherous water, Alice's formality
seems out of place, but, as the narrator explains: "Alice thought
this must be the right way of speaking to a mouse: she had never
done such a thing before, but she remembered having seen in her
brother's Latin Grammar, 'A mouse—of a mouse—to a mouse—
O mouse!' " (p. 18).

Alice's speech is worse than useless; the mouse refuses
to reply until Alice, rarely at a loss for words, speaks in an entirely
new key. " 'Perhaps it doesn't understand English,' thought Alice;
'I dare say it's a French mouse, come over with William the
Conqueror'. . . . So she began again: *Ou est ma chatte?*' "—a
sentence taken directly from the beginning of Alice's French lesson
book. The mouse *does* understand French, and it begins to quiver
and shake in a disconcerting manner. Attempting to be mannerly,
Alice begins to apologize: "I quite forgot you didn't like cats." "Not
like cats!" the mouse replies. "Would *you* like cats if you were
me?" (p. 18). Alice knows, instinctively, that she must use another
language when speaking to this alien creature; she experiments with
Latin locutions and with French in the hope of starting a conversation. But her desire for good talk is continually thwarted; the
grammatical constructions Alice plucks from her Latin book which
had seemed, in the world outside Wonderland, to be filled with
authority, shimmer to nothing in the salt pool of tears, while Alice's
excursion into French is even more excruciating, since the only
words Alice remembers say things hostile to the mouse's existence.
When Alice switches to English, she fares no better. Trying to
change the subject she chooses the safer topic of dogs, and tells
the mouse about "a little bright-eyed terrier" of her acquaintance
who will "fetch things when you throw them, and it'll sit up and
beg for its dinner, and all sorts of things—I can't remember half
of them—and it belongs to a farmer, you know, and he says it's
so useful it's worth a hundred pounds! He says it kills all the rats
and—Oh dear!" (p. 20).

In the *Introduction to Metaphysics* Heidegger explains that the uncanniness of our linguistic power resides in the "seeming familiarity" of words, in their approachability, their malleability. Because of this malleability, "what is fundamentally more remote and overpowering than sea and earth"—that is, language itself—seems "closest of all" to us. While our environment has a dazzling, distracting power to motivate and restrain us, Heidegger insists that the paradoxically impulsive and restrictive power of language is no less extraordinary:

What is now named—language, understanding, sentiment, passion, building—are no less a part of the overpowering power than sea, earth, and animal. The difference is only that the latter, the power that is man's environment, sustains, drives, inflames him, while the former reigns within him as the power which he, as the essent that he himself is, must take upon himself.[23]

In *Alice in Wonderland* this power is externalized in Alice's tears, which mingle with the "overpowering power" of "sea, earth, and animal." Speaking to the mouse, Alice is just as lost as she was before it appeared; her speech only adds to her helplessness. "What is it to speak?" Heidegger asks in his essay on "Language." "What is it to name?" "The naming calls. Calling brings closer what it calls. . . . Where to? Into the distance in which what is called remains, still absent."[24] When Alice names things she calls them as well, and this calling is threatening; the cat and the rat-eating dog enter into such "nearness" that her conversation with the mouse almost ends. Alice's language calls out comically and unmercifully; it brings things into a nearness which frightens the mouse half to death.

The tears in which Alice goes swimming are likened, in William Empson's wonderful reading of *Alice*, to an amniotic sea in which Alice "runs the whole gamut from birth to sexual self-discovery to death." "She is a father in getting down the hole, a foetus at the bottom, and can only be born by becoming a mother and producing her own amniotic fluid."[25] But I am suggesting that these tears serve another symbolic purpose: they signalize

Alice's wandering, lost and ungrounded, in the uncontrollable sea of language itself.

Thus Alice is trapped in a language she appears to use freely but cannot control. Words begin to cloud her situation, to bring in extra amounts of surmise, and that which is absent seems doubly present. In *Alice in Wonderland* Dodgson insists on our shared recognition that speaking is coercive and painful. "Must I suppose that in my discourse I can have no survival?" asks Foucault in *The Archaeology of Knowledge*, "and that in speaking I am not banishing my death, but actually establishing it; or rather that I am abolishing all interiority in that exterior that is so indifferent to my life, and so *neutral*"? According to Foucault, we prefer to repress the discovery that speech "is a complex, differentiated practice, governed by analysable rules and transformations, rather than be deprived of that tender, consoling certainty of being able to change, if not the world, if not life, at least [our] 'meaning,' simply with a fresh word."[26] But in his view of speech there are no verbal strategies we can define, with any certainty, as emancipatory. Our task as political beings is limited; we can, at most, stop treating "discourses as a group of signs"—that is, as "signifying elements" which refer to a set of objectively represented contents— and devote our energies to unmasking discourses as "practices that systematically form the objects of which they speak."[27] Foucault's revelation of the practical dimension of speech, of the force that enables words to "systematically form" the objects they seem to describe, is meant to negate all belief in intention. As modern beings already constructed in Descartes' meditative image, we are suddenly lost in Foucault's universe, swept away by the currents of language and history; we founder in invisible verb-swells, caught in the word's labyrinthine embrace.

Is there another way to read Alice's story without sliding back into Descartes' metaphysic? Despite the persuasive fatality of Foucault's system, despite the enthusiasm his ideas have drawn from feminists and phallocritics alike, and despite the fact that Alice's talk with the mouse fits like a puzzle piece into Foucault's observations, I want to look at Alice's predicament from a different perspective, to examine her relation to language from the point of view of the optimism inherent in Hannah Arendt's philosophy of action.

Arendt's philosophy points toward our ability to perform—in action or speech—what is "infinitely improbable." In *The Human Condition* she describes our capacity for praxis in terms that direct us toward the emancipatory potential in action and speech:

Action . . . no matter what its specific content, always establishes relationships and therefore has an inherent tendency to force open all limitations and cut across all boundaries. Limitations and boundaries exist within the realm of human affairs, but they never offer a framework that can reliably withstand the onslaught with which each new generation must insert itself. The frailty of human institutions and laws and, generally, of all matters pertaining to men's living together, arises from the human condition of natality and is quite independent of the frailty of human nature.[28]

In *The Human Condition* Arendt takes us beyond Foucault's insistence that, since what exists is prestructured, we can never see ourselves, even proleptically, as revolutionary beings. For Arendt, we are born into a world whose possibilities are preordained, but within this prestructured world new actions are possible. "With word and deed we insert ourselves into the human world and this insertion is like a second birth, in which we confirm and take upon ourselves the naked fact of our original physical appearance" (pp. 176–77). Speech has this capacity to initiate, to interrupt and start things anew because speech is more than a function of the social order: the word can always be said or seized differently, can operate as a form of action. "The fact that man is capable of action means," Arendt says, "that the unexpected can be expected from him" (p. 178).

For Arendt action is synonymous with natality, and birth itself becomes an emblem of the human capacity to begin, and to begin again. Arendt does not, however, believe in the easy beginnings and endings that have entranced other philosophers of action. As creaturely beings we are also conditioned beings bound by our historical moment. "Men are conditioned beings because everything they come in contact with turns immediately into a condition of their existence," Arendt says. The world is the product of human hands and minds, and these products "constantly condition their human makers." Arendt agrees with Heidegger that our invented surroundings are often more powerful than the elements themselves.

In addition to the conditions under which life is given to man on earth, and partly out of them, men constantly create their own, self-made conditions, which, their human origin and their variability notwithstanding, possess the same conditioning power as natural things. Whatever touches or enters into a sustained relationship with human life immediately assumes the character of a condition of human existence. This is why men, no matter what they do, are always conditioned beings. (p. 9)

Still, for Arendt, it is essential that we recognize the erratic, spontaneous, "natal" power each human being possesses. To be able to act is to enter the flux and influence its direction. "The conditions of human existence—life itself, natality and mortality, worldliness, plurality, and the earth—can never 'explain' what we are or answer the question of who we are for the simple reason that they never condition us absolutely" (p. 11). For Arendt we have the capacity to insert ourselves "with word and deed . . . into the human world," and "this insertion is not forced upon us by necessity, like labor, and it is not prompted by utility, like work." Our action "may be stimulated by the presence of others whose company we may wish to join, but it is never conditioned by them; its impulse springs from the beginning which came into the world when we were born and to which we respond by beginning something new on our own initiative." Arendt is convinced that "it is in the nature of beginning that something new is started which cannot be expected from whatever may have happened before. This character of startling unexpectedness is inherent in all beginnings and in all origins" (pp. 177–78).

Arendt's insistence that language has "natal" power suggests another reading of Alice's journey through the amniotic sea of words. Each of Alice's verbal initiatives carries with it a history; each word possesses a set of preinscribed meanings Alice cannot avoid. The positions of words that have been foregathered into a sentence, the thetic obstinance of "O Mouse," the persistence of her memory of a dog so hungry for rodents that he is worth a hundred pounds—all these linguistic practices thwart Alice's desire to communicate, to find her way back.

Language does not fail Alice completely, however. We may say instead that it acts unpredictably, that Alice's words have the power to elicit an unexpected dialogue with the mouse which—willy nilly—gets Alice what she wants. Language has, according to Arendt, this capacity to initiate a "second birth"—to instigate something new—precisely because it is unpredictable, because words usher us into the space of dialogue, of debate, or of silliness—into a space where the unexpected can happen.

I want to support Arendt's contention that the word can act, that words possess real emancipatory dignity, by analyzing a word-obsessed fragment from *The Autobiography of Malcolm X*. This is not, of course, a text by a woman, but Malcolm X's autobiography does represent the emancipatory strategies of a member of a disenfranchised minority and offers us instructive parallels with women's texts. The passage we will look at describes another animal and another "bilingual" moment—the moment in which Malcolm X describes his overcoming, in prison, of the powerfulness of "the oppressor's language." Rather than getting out of the dominant language, rather than escaping the speech of the oppressor, Malcolm X wants to get *into* it, to learn to speak the white man's despicable speech.

The chapters of Malcolm X's autobiography describing his life in prison detail his conversion experience to the Muslim religion. In becoming a Black Muslim, Malcolm X experiences unexpected frustrations, for as a man who stopped his schooling in eighth grade and who excelled at "being cool," who learned to speak street jive among the best pimps and panhandlers in New York, Malcolm X is suddenly unable to communicate with his new peers; he feels frustrated at his inability to express himself in the simple English his Muslim brothers and sisters use in their daily preaching. Malcolm X needs to learn English as a "second language" to communicate with Elijah Muhammed and to preach Elijah's word, and while his street jive is rich in the metaphors and colloquialisms that make Black English lively, Malcolm X experiences his own speech as something alien, as a foreign tongue lacking the dignity and clarity a Muslim practitioner needs: "How would I sound writing in slang the way I would *say* it, something such as, 'Look daddy, let me pull your coat about a cat, Elijah Muhammed'?"[29] Regretting his lack of formal schooling Malcolm X describes this "jive talk" as limiting: "every book I picked up had few sentences which didn't contain anywhere from one to nearly all the words that might as well have been in Chinese. When I just skipped those words, of course, I really ended up with little idea of what the book said" (p. 171). Malcolm X finds himself in Alice's position, eager to communicate, but not in command of the language he needs. He sets himself the task of acquiring a new voice by studying the dictionary—not simply by reading it through, but copying it page by page, verbatim, "down to the punctuation marks."

If, as Foucault says, discourse is a violence that we do to ourselves as well as to things, the dangers of making oneself vulnerable, as the member of an oppressed minority, to the structures and tenets of the oppressor's language should be obvious. I should add that neither Foucault's voice, nor Bové's nor Racevskis' is the only voice cautioning us here. In her poem "The Burning of Paper Instead of Children," Adrienne Rich defends the position that words, in and of themselves, are culpable, that an oppressor's speech can only convey an oppressive self concept, and that in speaking the dominant gender's language we hold ourselves open to our culture's bitter "regime of truth." Since Rich's poem speaks directly to the validity of Malcolm X's desire to learn the oppressor's speech, and since it gives a more impassioned argument than we find in Foucault, I want, briefly, to summarize her point of view.

Rich's poem begins with a defense of her son who, together with a friend, has burned a mathematics textbook in the friend's back yard. The friend's father has punished his son and forbidden the boys to play together. Angry, bereaved that his son would destroy a book, this father has written Rich a note explaining why she should punish her son as well. Rich is appalled at this suggestion, but she is not without sympathy for the father's conflict. He is strict because the burning of a book seems tragic to him, unthinkable. As he writes, "The burning of a book . . . arouses terrible sensations in me, memories of Hitler; there are few things that upset me so much as the idea of burning a book."[30] Rich quotes this letter in its full-voiced dignity, but she also responds with healthy outrage. For her books are not inviolable; they contain voices which must be attacked, which must burn with the fiery "knowledge of the oppressor." As she says at the poem's beginning, "this is the oppressor's language / yet I need it to talk to you" (p. 48). To revalue words that have made us their victims, to attempt to communicate with words that have victimized women of all races as well as men of color—is to enter culture complicitously. Since we must fight oppression, but have only the oppressor's weapons to fight with, to use these weapons means, automatically, that the other has won.

　　　　Rich's tactic is to fight these normative structures by wrenching the syntactic patterns of her poem into new shapes. In "The Burning of Paper Instead of Children" she quotes the poignant, ungrammatical prose of one of her writing students and then imitates this student's style in her own prose fragments: "People suffer highly in poverty," Rich's student has written, "Some of the suffering are: a child did not had dinner last night: a child steal because he did not have money to buy it: to hear a mother say she do not have money to buy food for her children and to see a child without cloth it will make tears in your eyes" (p. 48). Rich reads this prose responsively; she does not compete with its poetry, but deepens it:

I am composing on the typewriter late at night, thinking of today. How well we all spoke. A language is a map of our failures. Frederick Douglass wrote an English purer than Milton's. People suffer highly in poverty. There are methods but we do not use them. Joan, who could not read, spoke some peasant form of French. Some of the suffering are: it is hard to tell the truth; this is America; I cannot touch you now. In America we have only the present tense. I am in danger. You are in danger. The burning of a book arouses no sensation in me. I know it hurts to burn. There are flames of napalm in Cantonsville, Maryland. I

know it hurts to burn. The typewriter is overheated, my mouth is burning,
I cannot touch you and this is the oppressor's language. (p. 50)

Unless it is mangled, bent into formlessness, forced into new shapes,
Rich intimates that language is powerless to say what we mean.
Even the poet's language is like napalm; her typewriter heats up,
her mouth is on fire because "it hurts to burn," because the words
she speaks permit the burning of children in Vietnam and Maryland,
encourage poverty, defend patriarchy's vagrant suttees. Language
is the path of a malevolent casuistry directed against Afro-Americans,
against white women, against children. Why, then, does Malcolm
X set out to copy and memorize the words he finds in the white
man's dictionary?

"I believe it took me a day. Then, aloud, I read back,
to myself, everything I'd written on the tablet. Over and over, aloud
to myself, I read my own handwriting" (p. 171). Malcolm X may
need to know this dialect to pursue his political goals, but at what
cost? "Frederick Douglass wrote an English purer than Milton's,"
Rich says, but we live in a world where his dreams have been
undone. Joan of Arc did not speak the oppressor's language, but
a peasant dialect which resembled Malcolm X's street jive. Rich
implies that Joan of Arc's rustic speech was more revolutionary,
more productive than Douglass's complicity. But while we cannot
deny the power of Rich's analysis, what Malcolm X recalls from
his copying and memorizing of that first dictionary page is quite
liberating:

I woke up the next morning, thinking about those words—immensely
proud to realize that not only had I written so much at one time, but
I'd written words that I never knew were in the world. Moreover, with
a little effort, I also could remember what many of these words meant.
I reviewed the words whose meanings I didn't remember. Funny thing,
from the dictionary's first page right now, that "aardvark" springs to
my mind. The dictionary had a picture of it, a long-tailed, long-eared,
burrowing African mammal, which lives off termites caught by sticking
out its tongue as an anteater does for ants. (p. 172)

What Malcolm X remembers, what "springs" to his mind, is completely subversive—the picture of a "burrowing" African animal

with a powerful tongue—an animal that "lives off termites." The pun on "termites" has both wit and bite. This mammal is not only mythically "long-tailed," and "long-eared," but it has the characteristics of a survivor whose very vitality depends on its ability to appropriate with its tongue the terms of a dominant culture which turn living wood to detritus.

Malcolm X's African double eats woodmites, word-mites, termites; it sets out to tongue, to devour every word in the forest, on the veldt, in the dictionary, no matter how white, bourgeois, capitalist, imperialist, or antithetical to its goals. We are back in the territory of Mary Oliver's "Happiness": "And so at last I climbed the honey tree, ate / chunks of pure light, ate / the bodies of bees that could not get out of my way." The message of both works is that it is not necessary to burn the oppressor's words in order to change them. In fact, the central irony of Malcolm X's story is that "aardvark," the term that grabs him so powerfully, is Afrikaans. And yet this word, coined by the "oppressor" himself, has a blunt and revolutionary effect; it immediately begins to deconstruct everything white America and South Africa stand for.

How is this possible? The myth behind Rich's "The Burning of Paper Instead of Children," behind Foucault's insistence that the letter itself is a form of constraint, behind the feminist notion that language is patriarchal, is the myth that books—that dictionaries themselves—are totalizing and repressive tools of social regulation. According to this myth we cannot deconstruct this multiple totality from within since our very tools of deconstruction will only be upheld by the discursive formations that contain us. Despite the authority of this theory we have seen that Malcolm X treats the dictionary as a fragmentable form, a form that is not a totality, but made out of fractions that can be recombined to give voice to other social formations. It is in this context that we can describe the transformability of the word itself—and think about a volatility intrinsic to language which I will describe as "the animality of the letter."

What Malcolm X does, as he deconstructs white culture's text, is to set up a metaphor that allows something outside the dictionary—the subversiveness of Afro-Americans—to appear suddenly inside the dictionary. It is this magical capacity, this unpredictable property that inheres in the word and allows it to refuse an old social formation and to represent a new or emergent order, that interests us here.[31]

In "Outwork" Derrida explains that *"différance"* not only designates the deferment of meaning that occurs whenever we write or speak; he also wants "differance" to designate "that war economy—which brings the radical otherness or the absolute exteriority of the outside into relation with the closed, agonistic, hierarchical field of philosophical oppositions, of 'differends' or 'difference' " that seems to structure the inside.[32] This "war economy" can become visible in a text because the oppositions which seem to constitute the "inside" and "outside" are really false categories:

To claim to do away immediately with previous marks and to cross over, by decree, by a simple leap, into the outside of the classical oppositions is, apart from the risk of engaging in an interminable "negative theology," to forget that these oppositions have never constituted a *given* system, a sort of ahistorical, thoroughly homogeneous table, but rather a dissymmetric, hierarchically ordered space whose closure is constantly being traversed by forces, and worked by the exteriority, that it represses: that is, expels, and, which amounts to the same, internalizes as one of *its* moments.[33]

We have seen that this expulsion of closure operates in Malcolm X's text but we have not yet understood how it operates. In the passage describing Malcolm X's trek through the dictionary, the word is stimulated in a new way: it dances out of its thetic position in the order of words—the order of racist and capitalist thinking—and is liberated into a play of subversive meaning which is nonetheless already there, which haunts the dictionary as its "exteriority."

In his essay on "Edmond Jabès and the Question of the Book" Derrida gives us more information about the ways in which inside and outside come together in the moment of metaphor. First, Derrida asks us to imagine that "the letter lives," that the letter wants to spill over into and make use of the space around it even as it depends on that space for its place in the order of words. Using examples from Jabès' *The Book of Questions,* he describes this "desire" of the letter to spill into new space as its "animality":

The animality of the letter certainly appears, at first, as *one* metaphor among others. (For example, in *Je bâtis ma demeure* the sex is a vowel, etc., or even *"Aided by an accomplice, a word sometimes changes its sex and its soul."* Or, further: *"Vowels, as they are written, resemble the mouths of fish out of water pierced by the hook; consonants resemble dispossessed scales. They live uncomfortably in their acts, in their hovels of ink. Infinity haunts them"*).[34]

Reading Derrida's prose, we may feel as if we are back in the dense linguistic sea of Alice's Wonderland, but for all its withheld lucidity, Derrida's essay moves toward this instructive point:

Above all, it is metaphor *itself,* the origin of language as metaphor in which Being and Nothing, the conditions of metaphor, the beyond-metaphor of metaphor, never say themselves. Metaphor, or the animality of the letter, is the primary and infinite equivocality of the signifier as Life. The *psychic* subversion of inert literality, that is to say, of nature, or of speech returned to nature. This overpowerfulness as the life of the signifier is produced within the anxiety and the wandering of the language always richer than knowledge, the language always capable of the movement which takes it further than peaceful and sedentary certitude.[35]

How is such movement possible? Derrida argues that new meaning can only emerge because a "lapse" occurs between words and significations. "To allege that one reduces the lapse through narration, philosophical discourse, or the order of reasons or deduction, is to misconstrue language, to misconstrue that language is the *rupture* with totality itself. The fragment is neither a determined style nor a failure, but the form of that which is written" (p. 71). When Malcolm X fractions the dictionary in a way that makes this lapse visible, he makes use of the "animality of the letter," of the "generous distance between signs" and thus places his aardvark at the "beginning" of another order of speech.

We can get a surer glimpse of what Derrida describes as the playfulness of the letter by turning to Roland Barthes' essay on "The Spirit of the Letter." According to Barthes we will never understand our position in speech until we acknowledge that the letter leads a double life. If the letter is a noisy cipher which endlessly "decrees that Law in whose name every extravagance can be reduced ('Keep, I pray you, to the letter of the text')," at the same time the letter "tirelessly releases a profusion of symbols"; it is complicitous in releasing "an imagery vast as a cosmography."[36] Insofar as it upholds the law, the letter gives us the extreme of censorship, but insofar as it offers a path for wandering away from the law, the letter gives us an extreme pleasure.

To dramatize the letter's volatility, Barthes describes a book by Massin called *Letter and Image* in which all twenty-six letters of the alphabet are collocated with animated drawings done by artists from different historical periods. Under the artist's pen each of these letters becomes wild and delightful. Its "animality" is revealed as each letter is

put in a metaphoric relation with *something other* than the letter: animals (birds, fish, serpents, rabbits, some devouring others in order to form a D, and E, a K, an L, etc.), men (silhouettes, limbs, postures), monsters, vegetal structures (flowers, tendrils, trunks), instruments (scissors, sickles, tripods, etc.): a whole catalogue of natural and human products comes to double the alphabet's brief list: the entire world is incorporated into the letters, the letter becomes an image in the tapestry of the world. (p. 100)

We are reminded of the fluctuating floral and animal metaphors that proliferate in *Jane Eyre* and in *The Mill on the Floss* when Jane and Maggie open their French and Latin books. In these works, as in the text of Massin, the letter is revealed in its transformability, its volatility; for Jane and for Maggie, terms that had been misogynous or deliberately neutral in meaning suddenly turn and address the heroine with her own verbal potency. For Massin this volatility acts within a context that is less political: the letter can become the trunk or body or voice of anything and everything.

Thus it is that the letter, as Barthes remonstrates, lives in Massin's texts in a "baroque region where meaning is destroyed beneath symbol" (p. 100). When the letter ceases to be the origin of the image, when it suddenly is recognized as no more than a "floating term" which attaches itself to various meanings, its readers are enabled to recognize that "the letter, after all, is only a paradigmatic, arbitrary bridgehead, since discourse must begin . . . but this bridgehead can also be an exit, if we conceive, for instance, as the poets and mystagogues do, that the letter (writing) institutes the world" (p. 101). Paradoxically, the letter becomes the unpredictable point of exit from the formal closure provided by the letter, and the text the site where "floating chains of signifiers . . . pass and intersect each other: writing it in the air." We may say that what Malcolm X does in plucking new metaphors from the dictionary is to make them light, to return the letter to the air, to catch words in midflight. And in that motion we recognize, if only for a moment, the arbitrariness of the configurations that bind us. This "air" is not vacant of meaning—it is the space of excluded discourse itself.

We are now ready to come back to Mary Oliver's "Humpbacks" and to Hannah Arendt's *The Human Condition* and see them in a new light. While Arendt insists that we are conditioned by whatever surrounds us—including our own words and the words of others, she adds that

the life span of man running toward death would inevitably carry everything human to ruin and destruction if it were not for the faculty of interrupting it and beginning something new, a faculty which is inherent in action like an ever-present reminder that men, though they must die, are not born in order to die but in order to begin. (p. 246)

Action, in Arendt's schema, becomes "the one miracle-working faculty of man." "Seen from the viewpoint of the automatic processes which seem to determine the course of the world," action "looks like a miracle" (p. 246), as does Malcolm X's discovery and renegotiation of the dictionary's oppressive wisdom. For Arendt, "the miracle that saves the world, the realm of human affairs, from its normal, 'natural' ruin is ultimately the fact of natality, in which the faculty of action is ontologically rooted. It is, in other words, the birth of new men and the new beginning, the action they are capable of by virtue of being born" (p. 247). What Derrida describes in terms of animality, Arendt describes as natality, for she wants to emphasize that no matter how improbable the appearance of a new event might seem, there is always pressure toward re-creation.

Derrida does not develop his metaphor of "animality" much further since he is less interested in developing a politics than in dramatizing a potential space within metaphysics that will allow the philosopher to focus on the gap or aperture between terms. Derrida does not want the letter to posit "something"; he wants to mark the verbal acrobatics that the space between letters, between "outside" and "inside," makes possible. But Arendt *is* interested in the moment of positing: for her culture is founded— covertly, unexpectedly, fitfully, hopefully—on the articulation of emancipatory interests:

In this sense of initiative, an element of action, and therefore of natality, is inherent in all human activities. Moreover, since action is the political activity par excellence, natality, and not mortality, may be the central category of political, as distinguished from metaphysical, thought. (p. 9)

Arendt can celebrate this moment of positing as Derrida cannot because for her "logocentrism" is not the ultimate problem. "The limitations of the law are never entirely reliable safeguards against action from within the body politic," she says. "The boundlessness of action is only the other side of its tremendous capacity for establishing relationships, that is, its specific productivity" (p. 191). Every body politic, perhaps every discursive formation, tries to protect itself against "the inherent boundlessness of action"—but these institutions, discursive formations, and practices "are altogether helpless" to counteract the second "outstanding" characteristic of action—"its inherent unpredictability." This unpredictability of outcome is closely related to the revelatory character of action and speech, in which we disclose ourselves "without ever either knowing . . . or being able to calculate beforehand" whom we reveal (p. 192). Action—of word and deed—is the "infinite improbability which occurs regularly" (p. 300).

Arendt is not optimistic that such change will occur. "The new always happens against the overwhelming odds of statistical laws and their probability, which for all practical, everyday purposes amounts to certainty; the new therefore always appears in the guise of a miracle." Still, in the chapters that follow I will point out that these "miracles" happen regularly in women's writing—and happen with a constancy that, while it may not be predictable, is analyzable.

The idea that only what I am going to make will be real—perfectly true and legitimate in the realm of fabrication—is forever defeated by the actual course of events, where nothing happens more frequently than the totally unexpected. To act in the form of making, to reason in the form of "reckoning with consequences," means to leave out the unexpected, the event itself, since it would be unreasonable or irrational to expect what is not more than an "infinite improbability." (p. 300)

Arendt's ideas are useful in initiating our search for a theory more valuable to the feminist theorist than the simplified notion that women are repressed by language. In reading *Alice in Wonderland* I have suggested that Alice is not only swimming in her own natal sea, that Dodgson's book is not only reproducing our prelinguistic, pre-oedipal experiences and our anxieties about those experiences (as it depicts Alice's trip down the rabbit hole, her entrapment in the rabbit's womblike house, her erratic control over her changing size), but he is reproducing the natality, the fundamental improbabilities acted out in our life within language. I have added that we also witness this "natality" or animality of the letter—its unpredictability, its capacity to spill over into the empty spaces dividing word from word—in Malcolm X's subversive recovery of the word "aardvark" in his autobiography. Here Malcolm X recreates that colonial script into a term with deeply personal and revolutionary meanings for the colonized. And in a text I will analyze in the next chapter, Eudora Welty's "A Piece of News," we are privy to just this sort of volatility in a woman's text—a volatility depicted through "natal" metaphors which describe a young woman's discovery of the productive power of language:

Presently she stirred and reached under her back for the newspaper. Then she squatted there, touching the printed page as if it were fragile. She did not merely look at it—she watched it, as if it were unpredictable, like a young girl watching a baby. The paper was still wet in places where her body had lain.[37]

Like Arendt, Welty refers to this woman's discovery of the word's productive power as a natal moment, a discovery of the word as a deed which might allow this heroine to enter the world in a new way: "Crouching tensely and patting the creases away with small cracked red fingers, she frowned now and then at the blotched drawing of something and big letters that spelled a word underneath. Her lips trembled, as if looking and spelling so slowly had stirred her heart."[38] The newspaper, despite its representations of the status quo, also has the potential to act as the site of "a second birth": its neat lines are as full of difficult potential as a baby.

Arendt helps us to define several of the characteristics of the language games women play—characteristics I will investigate in the following chapters.[39] First, she gives us a way of describing the ways in which writing as such is unpredictable, since even ordinary speech or writing—even complicitous forms like dialogue—can lead to an unexpected category change, to a new form of emancipation or abnormal discourse. Second, Arendt gives us a theory that helps us to organize our perception that the woman writer has the capacity to interrupt the primary discourse, to shatter its meaning, and that this disruptive capacity is a power to be reckoned with, for it means the potential for dismantling old social forms and writing new ones. The "episteme" is not so intractable as Foucault (or, more accurately, as Foucault's followers) imagine. Finally, I will pay close attention to Arendt's idea that emancipatory language games "occur regularly," that even though the unpredictable, liberatory moments in women's writing "look like a miracle" when measured against the weight of the "oppressor's language," these transformative, productive moments occur in women's texts with sufficient regularity and legibility that we can begin to name them, to analyze them, and even devote a book to them.

All three of these characteristics occur in Oliver's "Humpbacks," with its emphasis on the unpredictable emergence of the speaker's word, on this word's capacity to interrupt masculine discourse, and on the promise of its emancipatory recurrence and irrepressibility. And yet, although the lines separating human and inhuman, spirit and matter, masculine and feminine are broken in

Oliver's text, still the whales, like the poet's words themselves, must fall back into the sea of language:

> they crash back under those black silks
> and we all fall back
> together into that wet fire, you
> know what I mean.   (p. 61)

We return to the salt pool of tears, of language, to the sea which is, for all its boundedness, still the sea of potential natality, of the animality of the letter. But these female whales who fall back into this wordy sea do not lose the capacity for play, for productivity, for transformation:

> I know a captain who has seen them
> playing with seaweed, tossing
> the slippery lengths of it into the air.
>
> I know a whale that will come to the boat whenever
> she can, and nudge it gently along the bow
> with her long flipper.   (p. 62)

The seaweed, like so many slippery sentences, entrances the captain, invites his play, his peacefulness, and Oliver's text begins to replicate the peaceful scene in *Moby-Dick* where the sailors play with the puppylike whales. Only here the female whale is in control; she is nudging the boat along and changing its course. In "Humpbacks" the whale has a shaping power Melville withholds. And this playfulness, this happiness and lightening of everything heavy and intractable, is a capacity Oliver wants the reader to recognize as her or his own:

> Listen, whatever it is you try
> to do with your life, nothing will ever dazzle you
> like the dreams of your body,
>
> its spirit
> longing to fly while the dead-weight bones
>
> toss their dark mane and hurry
> back into the fields of glittering fire

where everything,
even the great whale,
throbs with song.   (p. 62)

The letter's animality is everywhere. The heavy bones, the verbs, the verse of the whale begin to touch upon themes we have been considering—the ways in which women are limited by a body of speech which weighs them down with its "dead-weight bones." And yet in Oliver's poem, these bones "toss their dark mane and hurry / back into the fields of glittering fire." The repressive themes and verbosities of patriarchy may seem improvident for the woman writer, and yet they can still succor new themes, can still be made to speak for the woman writer who is throbbing with song.

FOUR

Alice Can

The title of this chapter should be read playfully for the games it yields can be played on several levels. First, "Alice Can" is meant to offer a revision of and homage to Teresa de Lauretis' *Alice Doesn't,* a text filled with brilliant analyses of women's absences in literary and cinematic scripts. Still, for all the pleasure it gives, in *Alice Doesn't* de Lauretis locates the impetus of women's empowerment somewhere between the poles of a Kristevan negativity and a Deweyan self-consciousness; despite her affirmation of consciousness raising, de Lauretis refuses to affirm women's aesthetic powers of being able to, of positing. Second, "Alice Can" reflects (as, of course, the title *Alice Doesn't* does for de Lauretis) my pleasure in the unpredictable linguistic practices we find in Lewis Carroll's Alice, who learns to negotiate the world's disarming nonsense as she journeys through Wonderland. Finally, "Alice Can" is an affirmation of all the Alices I have known, and of Alice Jardine's fine books and essays: not my intended subject (in fact, these are not texts I refer to in this chapter), but in naming an "Alice" who "can" this meaning slips in, willy nilly, as the words hit the page.

This slippage, and the beautiful systematization of this slippage in women's writing, will be the subject of this chapter. I will focus on the reasons that feminist critics need to talk about two aspects of language at once. We need to examine language both as constraint and as means of emancipation or action. Although words enact the repressions of the dominant culture, language can also deflect and begin to reconstruct the dominant culture's direction, especially in those moments when words themselves become the objects of representation.

Let us begin by asking how far we have come in describing a countertradition that would allow us to measure the woman writer's pleasure in her own orality, to savor women's pleasures in speech. My dramatization of the "animality of the letter" in chapter 3 opened new possibilities for such an analysis. But something still limits our capacity to describe women's relation to language as an emancipatory relationship, even after we have discovered the usefulness of Hannah Arendt's philosophy of action or hypothesized the playful freedom a poem like "Humpbacks" holds open for us. What holds us back? A number of strong voices among feminist theorists still deny that women can use language productively. These same voices are capable of affirming the letter's volatility, of explaining that the word can be the site of new praxis for male writers, but they deny that the letter's unpredictability is available for the woman writer.

In *Alice Doesn't,* after a thoughtful critique of the limitations of Lévi-Strauss' and Lacan's analyses of woman's roles within patriarchal economy, de Lauretis dismisses those aspects of Lévi-Strauss' and Lacan's theories that propose the sign as absolute site of cultural fixity. She explains that, Foucault to the contrary, we can allow ourselves to wax theoretical about the "author" as creative source for literary or cinematic texts. That is, we can talk about an individual subject's creativity once we stop dwelling on the limitations of sign systems and consider instead the productivity of "codes" as they interact in heterogeneous social systems.

Codes are, for de Lauretis, those "socially established, operational rules that *generate* signs." As generative structures, codes are practices that are volatile, that admit their own transformations and can change according to the diverging pressures brought to bear upon them by various "semantic fields."[1] Thus "any new practice of discourse" can set up "a different configuration of content," or introduce "other cultural meanings that in turn transform the codes and rearrange the semantic universe of the society that produces it" (p. 34). If we consider the transformations of codes that are possible because sign systems are in conflict with one another, we can also talk about creativity "from the perspective of the maker, the speaker, the artist, the *producer* of signs" (p. 35), since the subject is the place of these sign systems' relation, their coming together. And therefore we can talk about the artist as "maker," despite the inhibiting force of his or her social order. De Lauretis offers, then, a sophisticated theory of aesthetic production that neither ignores the social constraints under which the artist labors, nor denies the artist's capacity to disrupt and to transform these constraints.

In the present critical climate, such a theory is welcome and especially useful for the feminist critic involved in "gynocriticism."[2] It is surprising, then, that women do not figure in de Lauretis' discussion of such aesthetic practices—except as its objects. Woman, she says, has no place within this heterogeneous culture as a maker of signs, as social creatrix:

For me, historical woman, discourse does not cohere; there is no specific term of reference, no certain point of enunciation. Like the female reader of Calvino's text, who, reading, desiring, building the city, both excludes and imprisons herself, our questioning of the representations of woman in cinema and langue is itself a re-presentation of an irreducible contradiction for women in discourse. (pp. 35–36)

De Lauretis' critique obscures the ways in which women's writing has been politically productive; she ignores the ways in which women writers have used the letter's volatility to rewrite their relation to society and to discourse itself. My hypothesis about bilingualism in *Villette,* for example, emphasizes the liberating language games Brontë plays, as Lucy Snowe's second language becomes a space for interrupting her culture's primary myth system and providing a symbolic arena for projecting the as yet unexpressed.

In *Alice Doesn't* de Lauretis does allow for a single degree of emancipatory interaction between women and texts. In speaking of feminist criticism as praxis she explains that "a critical feminist reading of the text, of all the texts of culture, instates the awareness of that contradiction and the knowledge of its terms; it thus changes the representation into a performance which exceeds the text" (p. 36). But while this text of excess (which includes, either implicitly or explicitly, a critique of women's exclusion from social struggle) does, occasionally, wait on the performance of twentieth-century feminists whose consciousness has been raised, nevertheless we must recognize that numerous women's "texts" have done similar work without the perspective offered by feminist critical theory. I have suggested that as feminist critics interested in rescuing the emancipatory potential of the texts that we must read, we must cease to designate these texts "Texts"—in the Barthesian sense—and begin to focus upon their power as "works" in which the writer's performance starts to challenge and change the biases of her inherited culture.

To make this argument explicit, I want to look at Eudora Welty's "A Piece of News," a work that seems to be about women's impotence within language, about one woman's victimization by masculine culture and texts. I will suggest that while Welty's story presents such victimization, it also presents its heroine's real and potential pleasure in speech, her sense of discovering a verbal possibility that is submerged, repressed, embattled—but cherished by the narrator all the same.

"A Piece of News" is a story about a woman named Ruby Fisher who reads in the newspaper about another woman, also named Ruby Fisher, whose husband has shot her in the leg. While this story begins as a comedy of errors, its tone is finally closer to elegy than comedy. As the first Ruby Fisher feels pleasure in seeing her own name in print, a new fire starts to burn in her mind; we sense something writhing within her. I will suggest that she glimpses the animality, the volatility and transformative capacity, of the letter itself. Her husband disrupts this pleasure; sensing the exoticism and power she finds in the word, he burns the newspaper story that gives her such joy, but not before Welty has used Ruby Fisher's own paradoxical relation to this misogynous text to give us a sense of Ruby's powerful inner life, of her desire for a continuum between her eccentric habit of talking to herself and her desire to speak within the *polis*—to discover an avenue to the public world of talk where her pleasure in the word will be permissible and resonant.

"A Piece of News" seems, in its opening paragraphs, to portray nothing very remarkable. The tone is quiet, the exposition simple; the only interesting event is suggested by the heroine's dampness: she has been out in the rain—we do not even think to ask, "with whom?" Nor are we invited, particularly, to invest in the woman herself. "She stood in front of the cabin fireplace, her legs wide apart, bending over, shaking her wet yellow head crossly, like a cat reproaching itself for not knowing better." Soaked to the skin, cross as a lynx, this young woman is not, at first, given a name, nor is she strong-voiced or articulate. We overhear her "talking to herself—only a small fluttering sound, hard to lay hold of in the sparsity of the room." Even the narrator has difficulty catching her words: " 'The pouring-down rain, the pouring-down rain'—was that what she was saying over and over, like a song?" Although water streams over her body, and words stream out of it, nothing happens; this anonymous woman is absorbed in the simple acts of retrieving bodily warmth and domestic orderliness. "She was holding her skirt primly out to draw the warmth in."[3] But while the opening actions are minimal, Welty gradually warms up to her protagonist. Colors spill into the text, the language takes on a somatic grace: "quite rosy, she walked over to the table and picked up a little bundle. It was a sack of coffee, marked 'Sample' in red letters, which she unwrapped from a wet newspaper. But she handled it tenderly." As she caresses the newspaper, the girl's "fluttering" words grow distinct: "Why, how come he wrapped it in a newspaper!" she asks (pp. 21–22). The coffee is a gift from a traveling salesman she picked up in the morning; it is a small object given in exchange for larger sexual favors. Curiously, Welty chooses to focus her story on this gift itself. The scene of sexual transgression is withheld, so that the high stakes of this story do not involve Ruby's male lover, but her love of newsprint; the object of affection that comes between husband and wife is not the coffee salesman or his aromatic present, but the piece of paper in which his coffee is wrapped.

This graphic betrayal begins casually. "She set the coffee on the table, just in the center." This emphasis on "centering" gives way to a scene in which the heroine's body decenters the careful layout of the newsprint, takes it over entirely; the paper's

well-regulated pages are subordinated to her fleshy whim as she
drags the paper in front of the fire and stretches out on top of it.
"Then she dragged the newspaper by one corner in a dreamy walk
across the floor, spread it all out, and lay down full length on top
of it in front of the fire." What kind of relation to language is
depicted here? "Her little song about the rain, her cries of surprise,
had been only a preliminary, only playful pouting with which she
amused herself when she was alone" (p. 22). In the slow-moving
heat of Welty's story another set of words begins to take shape
beneath the heroine's body: the newsprint seems to change character. "Presently she stirred and reached under her back for the
newspaper. Then she squatted there, touching the printed page as
if it were fragile" (p. 22). The heroine of "A Piece of News" has
begun to recover an "otherness" of language, to find, in her perusal
of words, something tender and elemental. "She did not merely
look at it—she watched it, as if it were unpredictable, like a young
girl watching a baby. The paper was still wet in places where her
body had lain" (pp. 22–23). As the animal print of her body displaces
the newsprint, the words on the page grow gravid; the newspaper
catches her own form of speech; it comes to life like a damp form
of writing. "Crouching tensely and patting the creases away with
small cracked red fingers, she frowned now and then at the blotched
drawing of something and big letters that spelled a word underneath."
The reference to this newspaper's freight as a "small bundle" is
achingly clear. As she crouches down like a woman about to deliver
a child, Ruby Fisher first smoothes out the creases of the paper
which by now have taken her imprimatur. She watches and assists
as something "blotched" and unformed begins to emerge "underneath" her body. Although the movement resembles birth, these
motions do not give rise to something biological, but instead to the
spelling of a set of letters, and then a word:

Her lips trembled, as if looking and spelling so slowly had
stirred her heart.
          All at once she laughed.
          "Ruby Fisher!" she whispered.   (p. 23)

In imposing her body on this text Ruby Fisher has given birth to herself and this birthing—for her—is wonderful. She discovers half a dozen, then a dozen new words and labors tenderly to spell them all. This tenderness does not prepare her for the shock of what she reads. "The little item said: 'Mrs. Ruby Fisher had the misfortune to be shot in the leg by her husband this week.' " Deciphering this text is a challenge for Ruby Fisher. The dissemination of its meaning is slowed down since she has to leave the longest word—"misfortune"—until last. Once this is deciphered she must repeat the whole sentence out loud—"like conversation," Welty says. " 'That's me,' she said softly, with deference, very formally" (p. 23).

What is Welty up to? Her story of Ruby Fisher's encounter with this "little" newspaper item is too contrived to allow us to read the passage naively. Perhaps this narrative within a narrative is meant to function as a kind of excess—a form of textual violation that exceeds the sociolect, that overgoes social norms by doubling them, by making them visible. Wittgenstein suggests that in the sentence reality is compared with itself,[4] and Welty gives us a set of sentences that enact this doubling, that allow the violence women experience at the hands of patriarchal culture to be read in a context in which Ruby Fisher's life story can be compared with itself. To read Welty's story in this way, however, reduces "A Piece of News" to mere social commentary. To take our reading further we must develop the terms we have borrowed from Hannah Arendt and ask ourselves other questions about the newspaper's "unpredictability." What about the "animality" of its letters? And what about Ruby Fisher's *pleasure* in this text?

While the print Ruby Fisher's body has left on the page is erotic, it is also quite violent; while it is potentially conversational, Ruby's efforts to speak are stillborn. Her voice is met with this gothic roar: "The fire slipped and suddenly roared in the house already deafening with the rain which beat upon the roof and hung full of lightning and thunder outside" (p. 23). Frightened, she jumps up and runs to the door. " 'You Clyde!' screamed Ruby Fisher at last, jumping to her feet. 'Where are you, Clyde Fisher?' " These outer noises which threaten her pleasure seem to come from her husband; she recognizes the voice of male culture. "A shudder of cold brushed over her in the heat, and she seemed striped with anger and bewilderment" (p. 23). Giving birth to her own word, Ruby Fisher is "striped" by something else, marked by "a flash of lightening, and she stood waiting, as if she half thought that would bring him in, a gun leveled in his hand. And then, almost in amazement, she began to comprehend her predicament: it was unlike Clyde to take up a gun and shoot her" (p. 24).

Welty's story seems to be examining the woman speaker's predicament within masculine languge; the word's violence is given an objective correlative in Clyde and his gun. And yet there is something touching and uncanny in Ruby's certainty that the story she reads is delightfully her own. When she discovers that these words are not real predictions, that Clyde has not, in fact, appeared in a bolt of lightening, language starts to pour out of Ruby in a flood of intensity: "She bowed her head toward the heat, onto her rosy arms, and began to talk and talk to herself. She grew voluble." Ruby begins her narrative by reminding herself that even if Clyde should hear about her fling with the traveling salesman he would not care to shoot her. Clearly "the account in the paper was wrong. Clyde had never shot her, even once. There had been a mistake made." But as she contemplates her hypothetical safety "a spark flew out and nearly caught the paper on fire. Almost in fright she beat it out with her fingers. Then she murmured and lay back more firmly upon the pages" (p.25). This passionate relation of body to text is wonderful; Ruby is maintaining her possession of language as long as she can, and this relation, for her, is erotic. Lying back on the newspaper she begins to imagine another story about her death in which, wearing a brand-new nightgown and lying in a corpselike pose, she overhears Clyde murmuring, "Ruby, I done this to you." Immersed in her fantasy, Ruby replies: "That is the truth, Clyde—you done this to me," and proceeds, fantastically, to die—"composing her face into a look which would be beautiful, desirable, and dead" (p. 26).

Welty's story seems to affirm Adrienne Rich's assertion in "Sibling Mysteries" that women can only live as themselves if

they escape from their father's or husband's language. According
to this view of speech, language, controlled as it is by masculine
culture, cannot have a "feminine" meaning. But this is not Welty's
emphasis. Instead, she points to an openness in the newsprint
through which Ruby's imagination can slip; Welty points to the
potential these words have to be possessed "differently," to act
unpredictably.

        As the fantasied story continues and Ruby maintains
her position *on top* of the newspaper, her revery is interrupted.
Clyde does appear; he stands over her body letting cascades of
water stream over her body and onto the floor. The newspaper
narrative and Ruby's own story are suddenly unbearably close as
Clyde pokes Ruby "with the butt of his gun," and asks "What's
keepin' supper?" He sits down to the table, "making a little tumult
of his rightful wetness and hunger. Small streams began to flow
from him everywhere." Clyde's power comes into the room in a
deluge, threatening to drown Ruby's passion, threatening to soak
the paper "still wet in places where her body had lain." As she
brings his dinner Clyde teases her, half gruffly, half violently: "Don't
you talk back to me. You been hitch-hikin' again, ain't you?" and
starts to laugh, but by this time Ruby is so absorbed in her own
world "she had not even heard him. She was filled with happiness.
Her hand trembled when she poured the coffee. Some of it splashed
on his wrist" (p. 28). When her "rightful wetness" competes mildly
with his own, his response is immediate anger. "Some day I'm
goin' to smack the living devil out of you" (p. 29).

        Once Clyde has finished eating, she brings him the
newspaper, her face bright with delight. "It excited her even to
touch the paper with her hand, to hear its quiet secret noise when
she carried it, the rustle of surprise." Clyde's response is quick and
naive: "It's a lie," he insists. " 'That's what's in the newspaper
about me,' said Ruby, standing up straight. She took up his plate
and gave him that look of joy. . . . 'Well, I'd just like to see the
place I shot you!' he cried explosively" (p. 29). If Clyde is associated
with the fatality of words and of weapons, he also shares Ruby's
vulnerability to the word's unpredictability in a peculiar way. "Slowly
they both flushed, as though with a double shame and a double

pleasure." It is, the narrator says, "as though Clyde might really have killed Ruby, and as though Ruby might really have been dead at his hand." The possibility stands between them, "rare and wavering"—like a stranger—until Clyde snatches the paper from her and tosses it into the fire, where it floats for a moment and bursts into flame. Now he glances at the paper's masthead and sees that Ruby has been reading not a Mississippi, but a Tennessee paper. " 'That wasn't none of you it wrote about.' He laughed, to show that he had been right all the time." Ruby refuses this realism: "It was Ruby Fisher! . . . My name is Ruby Fisher!" she cries, until Clyde begins to joke with her, to smack her cheerfully "across her backside" (p. 35). Ruby answers with silence:

> Ruby folded her still trembling hands into her skirt. She stood stooping by the window until everything, outside and in, was quieted before she went to her supper.
> It was dark and vague outside. The storm had rolled away to faintness like a wagon crossing a bridge. (pp. 30–31)

The storm is originally associated with the masculine power of interrupting, of marking things with a deluge grander than a woman's text. But by the end of "A Piece of News" this storm is a feminine force that has already gone away. Its passing mocks us with the recognition that, for Ruby Fisher, "everything, outside and in, was quieted." Does Welty's story, then, confirm even more than it challenges the notion that women are alienated from the sociolect, that, when we are not silent, we speak an oppressor's language?

As I have argued, this theory has its own oppressive power—it helps to elide Ruby's happiness in seizing the word as her own. Since Welty's text offers this happiness as a communal moment, in order to understand Welty's text we need to seize upon two things at once: both the meaning of those utopian moments when Ruby Fisher discovers the word's power to act—its potential forms of natality—and also those distopian moments when Ruby's speech mirrors her culture's misogyny.

Given these contradictory voices within Welty's story, how do we define its "theory" of language, how define the "poetic" that informs "A Piece of News"? To understand these operations it will be useful to appropriate Roland Barthes' theory of writing from *Writing Degree Zero*—not because this theory is "correct," but because it gives us a schema which helps illuminate Welty's text.

In *Writing Degree Zero* Barthes distinguishes between language, style, and writing, or *écriture:* three elements that must, he says, be included in any theory of writing. The first two terms, "language" and "style," are oppositional. Language represents, for Barthes, the familiar spaces of everyday life; insofar as "language" reflects culture's norms it is dictatorial—words are spoken as reflex; they involve little choice. Style, in contrast, sings out from deep within an author's "secret and personal mythology, the subnature of expression."[5] Style comes from the body and preserves a life "outside the pact which binds the artist to society." Exotically, "style" is part of the speaking voice that insists on cohabiting with what is forbidden. "It is the decorative voice of hidden, secret flesh."

In Welty's text "style" and "language," in Barthes' sense of these words, come awkwardly together in the opening scene. The newspaper is made up of words that are dictatorial; these words meet the opposition, the imposition, of Ruby's body, her "hidden, secret flesh." Throughout the story the overt message of the newspaper remains very much the same—the structure of words and the world they reflect are stolid and powerful. But these words act as if they have been altered by Ruby's bodily presence, and Ruby herself experiences them in a new way. "In her very stillness and pleasure she seemed to be hiding there, all alone. And at moments when the fire stirred and tumbled in the grate, she would tremble, and her hand would start out as if in impatience or despair" (p. 22). Ruby's hand darts out toward the newspaper; it begins to spell out the words of a name which both is and is not her secret signature. According to Barthes, this is the way that style itself functions:

Under the name of style a self-sufficient language is evolved which has its roots only in the depths of the author's personal and secret mythology, that subnature of expression where the first coition of words and things takes place, where once and for all the great verbal themes of his existence come to be installed. Whatever its sophistication, style has always something crude about it: it is a form with no clear destination, the product of a thrust, not an intention. . . . Its frame of reference is biological or biographical, not historical: it is the writer's . . . glory and his prison. (p. 11)

Language keeps the writer in line; style plunges her toward pleasure and myth, but neither alone can produce what Barthes calls "writing." Language and style remain "blind forces" which bind the writer to culture and to biological identity, but their risky amalgam—writing itself—is an act that "remains full of the recollection of previous usage, for language is never innocent," but also transcends previous usage to form an "anti-communication" which challenges the closure of language, which borrows the "animality" of style and is intimidating (p. 16).[6]

If the word, with its masochistic potency, remains full of negative power in Ruby's text, then something extra happens to this negativity, for by adding to proscriptive language the subversive increment of Ruby's own "style"—her own excitement and pleasure in this printed speech—even her husband can feel new possibilities in the combination of newspaper and body. He feels that he must intervene, must disrupt Ruby's capacity to reread and rewrite a social scene that he alone should have power to enunciate.

But if it is the possibility for "écriture" that Clyde Fisher destroys, if it is the threat of writing itself that has entered and threatened their marriage, then we must also reiterate that Ruby's transgressive sexuality is not the point of Welty's story. Instead, it is Welty's alignment of this sexuality with a repressive order of words that Ruby might learn to reorder in terms of her evolving libidinal pleasure. Welty does point to Ruby's inability to write her own story, but she emphasizes the missing terms of Ruby's text not just to hold the absence of this writing open for us, but to get us to see its presence, to see Ruby's enormous pleasure in inscriptive possibility. Welty does not point to some contaminating influence inherent in language itself; for her the issue is not just the deadliness of the father's word but the birth of woman's writing from the very sources that oppose it: "Again she looked at him in delight. It excited her even to touch the paper with her hand, to hear its quiet secret noise when she carried it, the rustle of surprise."

In "A Piece of News" we find an unexpected relation dramatized between woman and language. Welty focuses on the natal power of the word—its capacity to be unpredictable. The word's potential to call, to hold open, to gather new meanings is foregrounded in Welty's text as she explores her heroine's pleasure in slowing the word down, in liquidating former meanings so slowly, so erotically, that we can almost hear words change tone. In "A Piece of News" we discover the heroine's need for an alternative alphabet, but it is Welty's suggestion that this alphabet is already held within her primary language, that it is already held in the male text—but in chrysalis.

Having established in Welty's text and in *Villette* two different ways in which we can begin to redefine the tendency in feminist criticism to name women as mere objects of masculine discourse, I want to take up another question, to suggest that we examine a more fundamental assumption of gynocriticism, namely, the assumption that each woman shares with other women an intrinsic relation to language as such. To this end we will look at three texts by Welty's American contemporaries: Adrienne Rich's "Sibling Mysteries," Mary Oliver's "Mussels," and Elizabeth Bishop's "In the Village." In each instance we will see that the *images of language* each woman writer uses to describe her speaker's or heroine's relation to "masculine" words differ from those images of language employed by her female contemporaries. Each of these texts could be said to offer a different theory of the woman writer's practice and a different way of theorizing woman's ability to unlimit her language.

In looking at these four texts together my purpose is not simply to challenge de Lauretis' insistence in *Alice Doesn't* that woman "has no access to the codes of the invisible city which represents and absents her" (p. 35), but to challenge the notion that women writers have a single, and easily definable relation to language—an idea we also see reflected in Elaine Showalter's "Feminist Criticism in the Wilderness":

The appropriate task for feminist criticism . . . is to concentrate on women's access to language, on the available lexical range from which words can be selected, on the ideological and cultural determinants of expression. The problem is not that language is insufficient to express women's consciousness but that women have been denied the full resources of language and have been forced into silence, euphemism, or circumlocution. (p. 193)

Are these the best terms we have for describing women's powers of inscription? In putting four different texts up for analysis simultaneously I hope to avoid the tendency in feminist criticism to try to find coherence or unity where there is none—to impose a reductive theory of women's writing upon writers whose practices are diverse and heterogeneous. The problem with theories that unify is that by imposing commensurability where there is difference, they can blind us to the diversity of work that goes on in women's texts.[7]

Adrienne Rich's "Sibling Mysteries" will offer what is the most radical, but also, by now, the most conventional of feminist speech-worlds. The poem begins in a mythic, incantatory fashion as Rich spins a fantasy of the emotions women shared aeons ago when a sense of connectedness and primordial closeness allowed them to work easily together—their lives interrupted, but not stunted by the rhythms of childbirth. These women neither feel alienated from one another nor from the children who cling to their mothers' backs like tiny animals. Able to smell "the rains before they came," to feel "the fulness of the moon / before moonrise," these primitive women possess a rudimentary but powerful writing: "Remind me . . . how we traced our signs by torchlight / in the deep chambers of the caves."[8]

These happy times are over, Rich's poem tells us. Mythic sisterhood—with its festive carnality, its access to feminine language—has been destroyed by "progress" that has led women into the isolation of the nuclear family. Contemporary mothers are unable to scent, much less to articulate the needs of their children. Even the consolations of birth (and its aftermath when the mother "floated great and tender in our dark / or stood guard over us") are gone; the mother now sends her daughters "weeping" into the father's "law"; she is imagined as someone monstrous, regal, "erect, enthroned, above / a spiral stair . . . her woman's flesh was made taboo to us" (pp. 48–49).

   "Sibling Mysteries" is about a journey from silence to speech, a journey shared by two sisters who desire the same body: "Remind me how we loved our mother's body," Rich intones, "our mouths drawing the first / thin sweetness from her nipples / our faces dreaming hour on hour / in the salt smell of her lap" (p. 48). This euphoric world of salt and sweetness is inherently ruptured, the companionate tenderness of the mother's body evanescent, for she seems to love "'the strange male body first / that took, that took, whose taking seemed a law." The project of Rich's poem is to disrupt this paternal law, to describe a return to the arms of the mother, the source not only of comfort, but of poetic speech itself. Within Rich's schema, however, this speech requires a sacrifice; it requires no less than the death of the father.

   Is this death necessary? For Rich the unrest, the social alienation that leads to women's silence is an historical artifact and has an historical cure. The death of the father and the symbolic burning of words written in support of his laws frees these daughters to speak their own desires. Before his death, "there were years you and I / hardly spoke to each other." But when these sisters are called home to tend to their dying father, this silence hurries away: "then one whole night / our father dying upstairs / we burned our childhood, reams of paper, / talking till the birds sang" (p. 51).

   In the *Metamorphosis* the sister who wants to speak her mind loses her tongue and finally her body: Philomela and her sister Procne are turned into birds. But in Rich's poems birds are chosen as metaphors of a new kind of metamorphosis, of a woman's ritualized awakening from silence to speech, and as the sisters talk until morning their voices blend into another traditional masculine form, the *aubade,* or dawn song. In Ovid's poem Philomela and Procne are punished for their murder of Tereus; they are transformed into birds who retain the power of song. But in Rich's poem the birds and the women remain separate; the sisters keep Philomela's lyricism, Procne's violence, and Tereus' power of speech. Unlike the primordial women of the poem's opening fantasy these sisters keep their separateness from each other as well: "words flash from you I never thought of / we are translations into different dialects / of a text still being written" (p. 51). But now at least these barriers are down:

> I call you from another planet
>
> to tell a dream
> Light-years away, you weep with me
>
> The daughters never were
> true brides of the father
>
> the daughters were to begin with
> brides of the mother
>
> then brides of each other
> under a different law
>
> Let me hold and tell you   (p. 52)

This ending is breathtaking. Mysteriously, these women have earned access to other women's bodies and to their own powers of myth making. The word "bride" has been loosened from its patriarchal context and freed to spin in a feminine orbit.

The question for the feminist critic—in the light of what Rich's poem describes—is whether there can be a women's literature that does not demand the death of the father? In the *Pleasure of the Text* Roland Barthes insists that "Death of the Father would deprive literature of many of its pleasures. If there is no longer a Father, why tell stories? Doesn't every narrative lead back to Oedipus? Isn't storytelling always a way of searching for one's origins?"[9] For Barthes, if we dismiss the father's presence—or, to put this another way, if we do away with his tantalizing absence, his orphic teasing of the orphan son—speech, poetry, writing become impossible. But for Rich the death of the father and the destruction of his language is the only enabling act. It provides a space of emancipation in which the feminine voice may discover itself, in which each woman finds, in the speech of her feminine other, new sonorousness.

Rich's poem begins to define, then, a poetics of women's emancipation which involves the obliteration of the father's body and the father's tongue and its joyous replacement with the speech of sister or mother.[10] As such "Sibling Mysteries" also implies a poetics of women's writing consonant with recent feminist theories about the relation of women's discourse to masculine speech. According to Elaine Showalter:

The feminist obsession with correcting, modifying, supplementing, revising, humanizing, or even attacking male critical theory keeps us dependent upon it and retards our progress in solving our own theoretical problems. What I mean here by "male critical theory" is a concept of creativity, literary history, or literary interpretation based entirely on male experience and put forward as universal. So long as we look to androcentric models for our most basic principles—even if we revise them by adding the feminist frame of reference—we are learning nothing new. (p. 183)

Rich's text attempts to explode these androcentric models; she opens new space for her own writing by depicting the father's ritual death. Reading her poetry we return to the spirit of Irigaray's insistence in "When Our Lips Speak Together" that women must "get out" of men's language.[11]

How useful are these principles as arbiters of women's texts? My position is that we need to invent more inclusive metaphors to define woman's powers of speech, and that this invention will take us in a variety of directions. I am in disagreement with the voice in Rich's poem saying that the death of the father and the woman writer's repudiation of paternal speeh is the best route to writerly freedom (especially since Rich uses Ovid to such fine effect), just as I am in disagreement with Showalter's position that it is unhealthy for feminist critics to dabble in the father's texts:

Some feminist critics have taken upon themselves a revisionism which becomes a kind of homage; they have made Lacan the ladies' man of *Diacritics* and have forced Pierre Macherey into those dark alleys of the psyche where Engels feared to tread. According to Christiane Makward, the problem is even more serious in France than in the United States: "If neofeminist thought in France seems to have ground to a halt," she writes, "it is because it has continued to feed on the discourse of the masters." (pp. 183–84)

I have been arguing that this feeding on the discourse of the masters can be salubrious. In this midst of making this argument, however, I do want to recognize the political value of Showalter's point of view. As Hélène Cixous says so passionately in her interview with Verena Conley:

To touch upon feminine writing frees, liberates language, word usage. Of course, one cannot imagine a political liberation without a linguistic liberation; that is all very banal. . . . It is not by chance that all the regional movements grab on to their language. It is in order to escape, if you would like, the language of the father. It is in order to take something from a language which would be less authoritarian. It is a lot of work.[12]

My suggestion has been that there are many different kinds of "work" that women writers have done and can do in their texts, and that while Rich prescribes one kind of relation to orality there are other ways this work can be done. In this spirit, I want to look at a poem that uses "feeding" as its central metaphor: "Mussels," by Mary Oliver. In this reading of "Mussels" I will suggest that the relation of male to female texts is depicted here in another key. The dominant culture can become a site for female creativity, a site where a commodious, empowering relationship to the poetic tradition can be worked out.

In "Mussels" we do not enter the separatist universe filled with the pleasures of the mother-child dyad that we encountered in "Sibling Mysteries." The speaker of Oliver's poem is neither so privileged that she can recover the visionary speech Rich shares with her sister, nor so hungry that she looks for the epic speech with which Rich's poem begins. While Rich's speaker asks her sister to recall a legendary past, to "remind me how we walked / trying the planetary rock / for foothold / testing the rims of canyons /

fields of sheer / ice in the midnight sun" (p. 47), Oliver's poem abandons the sublime mode; it is set in a rip, a tear, in a cave by the seashore. The rocks of this cave—its floor and walls—are encrusted with the bodies of mussels.

The cave offers Oliver's speaker an intriguingly liminal point for beginning her poem. It is in such a cave in Book 5 of *The Prelude* that Wordsworth has visions, in such a cave that Don Juan meets Haidee. In Oliver's poem a similar meeting occurs. The poet enters a boundary world where mussels sing—like so many surrealists—and the female poet can go down to gather their song:

> In the riprap,
>   in the cool caves,
>   in the dim and salt-refreshed
>   recesses, they cling
> in dark clusters,
>   in barnacled fistfuls,
>   in the dampness that never
>   leaves, in the deeps
> of high tide, in the slow
>   washing away of the water
>   in which they feed,
>   in which the blue shells
> open a little, and the orange bodies
>   make a sound,
>   not loud,
>   not unmusical, as they take
> nourishment, as the ocean
>   enters their bodies.[13]

These little animals, with their orange bodies and blue shells, make grotesque, but not unbeautiful sounds, suggesting that the poet is not just collecting mussels, but music, poetry—sounds already clumped together in units of meaning.

"Mussels" begins by depicting a new female domain. Typically, caves are feminine spaces, and Oliver's speaker takes special pains to emphasize the sexual nature of her explorations:

> At low tide
> I am on the riprap, clattering

                  with boots and a pail,
         rock over rock; I choose
            the crevice, I reach
            forward into the dampness,
               my hands feeling everywhere
         for the best, the biggest.   (p. 44)

The female poet's relation to this space is erotic, but it is also antithetical, for the mussels do not want to be gathered by this female speaker. Like the rosebuds of Herrick and Lovelace, they resist the poet's gathering. Is this because their presence in Oliver's poem has a consonance with male language that is not only titillating, but disturbing? These are mussels that cluster about the sides of the cave, creating its meaning and music; they mediate the aura of this "female" space and, initially, resist this female gatherer's cooption.

In *The Madwoman in the Attic* Gilbert and Gubar discuss the ways in which caves function as female spaces. The cave, as "womb-shaped enclosure" is also "a house of earth, secret and often sacred."[14] Like the caves they explore, the cave in Oliver's poem is in the "deeps"—it is dangerously out of bounds, but also "salt-refreshed." But the site of Oliver's poem differs in a number of ways from the caves Gilbert and Gubar describe. They analyze a story of Simone de Beauvoir's in which four women squat in a cave weaving cloth and taking care of their children. Three of the women are decrepit, bereft of light, in contrast to their polygamous husband who has just returned from the sunny marketplace where he has been discussing "world affairs with other men."[15] This man can come to the cave for refreshment and still go back to the "vast universe," but "the women of this underground harem are obviously buried in (and by) patriarchal definitions of their sexuality." As patriarchy's tragic victims they experience "immanence with no hope of transcendence, nature seduced and betrayed by culture, enclosure without any possibility of escape."[16] In Oliver's poem the mussels are feeding, like this husband, on the materials around them, but the poet wants, in turn, to feed upon them. The space of the cave has not lost its secret, sacred aura because of their presence. Instead, the poet enters and claims the cave as her own;

she is not afraid of her relation to these musseltexts; it is they who are afraid of being read, afraid of being gathered by her.

Gilbert and Gubar emphasize the tragic relation of women to their own interior space:

Individual women are imprisoned in, not empowered by, such caves, like Blake's symbolic worms, "Weaving to Dreams the Sexual strife / And weeping over the Web of life." How, therefore, does any woman— but especially a literary woman, who thinks in images—reconcile the cave's negative metaphoric potential with its positive mythic possibilities? Immobilized and half-blinded in Plato's cave, how does such a woman distinguish what she is from what she sees, her real creative essence from the unreal cutpaper shadows the cavern-master claims as reality? (p. 95)

In Oliver's poem we get one kind of answer. Oliver makes the point—if allegorically—that male images of women, here represented in the singing mussel shells, are themselves blind to the beauties of a female bard:

> they, who have no eyes to see with
>   see me, like a shadow,
>   bending forward. Together
>   they make a sound
>   not loud,
>   not unmusical, as they lean
>   into the rocks, away
>   from my grasping fingers.   (p. 5)

For Oliver's speaker the cave's "negative metaphoric potential" is gathered—condensed and consumed in such a way that the "positive mythic possibilities" of this space can be reimagined. Oliver's narrator is someone who both *is* the cave and is *in* it, who can move freely about exploring its chthonic powers before returning to the surface to berate and rename this space's negative meaning. This revision does not take the form of discovering a new female tradition, but expropriating a male one. The narrator looks vehemently for mussels "to twist from the wet rocks . . . to devour."

To characterize as woman centered the poetic Oliver's poem discovers, we must question Gilbert and Gubar's assertion that the best way to chart a female literary tradition is to reconstruct a writer's female lineage:

Where the traditional male hero makes his "night sea journey" to the center of the earth, the bottom of the mere, the belly of the whale, to slay or be slain by the dragons of darkness, the female artist makes her journey into what Adrienne Rich has called "the cratered night of female memory" to revitalize the darkness, to retrieve what has been lost, to regenerate, reconceive, and give birth.

What she gives birth to is in a sense her own mother goddess and her own mother land. (p. 99)

This journey back to the cave to recover lost Sibyl's leaves is a journey of empowerment, an emancipatory quest for Gilbert and Gubar as well as for the authors they analyze. But this journey is always imperfect, the questers ambivalent. Gilbert and Gubar describe Mary Shelley's introduction to *The Last Man.* "But it is possible . . . for the woman poet to reconstruct the shattered tradition that is her matrilineal heritage. Her trip into the cavern of her own mind, despite (or perhaps because of) its falls in darkness, its stumblings, its anxious wandering, begins the process of remembering. . . . Going 'down to the woman' of Fate . . . the woman writer recovers herself as a woman of art" (pp. 98–99). Oliver's poem captures this ambivalent quality. The cave is feminine, but the problems that encrust its walls—the mussels of her poem—are male signatures which have owned and preinterpreted the cave's meaning.

Oliver's poem also suggests, however, that we should be confident about the woman writer's use of male signatures. Shelley talks about a time when she discovered a cave with a male companion, who names the cave, and Gilbert and Gubar comment that "the woman may *be* the cave, but—so Mary Shelley's hesitant response suggests—it is the man who knows the cave, who analyzes its meaning, who (like Plato) authors its primary parables." They add that "the cave is a female space and it belonged to a female hierophant" (p. 96). But we have seen that for Oliver the woman writer's journey is neither a journey toward the male signature nor a journey in which—as for Adrienne Rich—the writer looks only to her feminine past for meaning. Oliver's poetry does not counsel rejecting, but feeding on, incorporating the strange music of men whose words must be seized, seasoned, redescribed, redefined. Thus her verse asks us to emend Gilbert and Gubar's description of women writers' necessary relation to their foremother's sybilline script. Although the cave has been named by male writers, woman's journey can be one of seizing, of changing this naming and reinventing the scene of woman's empowerment. Unlike Ulysses, Oliver's speaker does not fall apart when she hears the siren call of those male voices who have defined her. Instead, she gathers and transforms them; she feeds on them and writes a new song.

In comparing Rich's "Sibling Mysteries" and Oliver's "Mussels" I have established two different relations the woman writer may have with the language she speaks. For Rich, creativity happens in two stages. After killing the father and burning his language, the sisters can discover a separatist world in which the mother's body, her writing may be remembered. But for Oliver the female poet requires the construction of a scene of trespass and expropriation. For her the central danger we inherit from male speech is the danger that we will continue to regard this speech as the oppressor's language instead of using it for our own hungry ends.

My point is that we can construct several valid accounts of the woman writer's relation to language, and that we must recognize that a number of strategies may be effective in overturning the violence of a dominant discourse. Feminist critics have been searching, over the past decade, for a feminist "poetics," for a gendered theory of language and writing that will help us to name and to account for the general structures of women's texts. One of the places we have sought such a theory is in describing and analyzing the woman writer's relation to a "patriarchal" discourse. As Myra Jehlen suggests in "Archimedes and the Paradox of Feminist Criticism":

The autonomous individuality of a woman's story or poem is framed by engagement, the engagement of its denial of dependence. We might think of the form this necessary denial takes . . . as analogous to genre, in being an issue, not of content, but of the structural formulation of the work's relationship to the inherently formally patriarchal language which is the only language we have.[17]

But I want to say that we cannot generalize about women's writing this easily, any more than we can make abstract principles from the contradictory "laws" I seem to have derived from Rich's, and then from Oliver's poems. If one of the language games commonly played by feminist critics is killing the father's text to allow the mother or daughter to speak, there are other equally valid games. Let us look at Elizabeth Bishop's "In the Village."

       "In the Village" seems to support our most negative theories about women's writing, especially Cixous' insistence in "The Laugh of the Medusa" that women speak a father tongue that obscures, even crushes a hypothetical mother tongue that might provide the writer with a vital relation to speech. "In the Village" tells the story of a pensive child who, to preserve herself and become a writer, turns from the uncontrolled, frightening, animal sounds made by her mother's body to the controllable articulations of a symbolic father. The heroine—who is Bishop herself as a little girl—finds solace in the craft of the paternal blacksmith whose laborious music resonates through the village of Bishop's childhood. "In the Village" begins eerily, like a Schoenberg tone poem. Bishop evokes "a scream, the echo of a scream," hanging over "that Nova Scotian village. No one hears it; it hangs there forever, a slight stain in those pure blue skies, skies that travelers compare to those of Switzerland, too dark, too blue, so that they seem to keep on darkening a little more around the horizon—or is it around the rims of the eyes?"[18] This "stain" has the tenacity of the ghost under the stairs: "it just came there to live, forever—not loud, just alive forever. Its pitch would be the pitch of my village. Flick the lightning rod on top of the church steeple with your fingernail and you will hear it." The scream resonates like the unpleasant sound of a fingernail rasping across metal, but remains indecipherable.

       Although Bishop's story opens with a surreal evocation of the scream hovering over the village, her prose zeros in on the village itself, inside the house where a child's mother is having a fitting. A dressmaker is pinning a purple dress to the mother's body; for years the mother has worn nothing but black. The child associates the mother's new dress with the vulgarity of badly bound books: "Drummers sometimes came around selling gilded red or green books, unlovely books, filled with bright new illustrations of the Bible stories. The people in the pictures wore clothes like the purple dress, or like the way it looked then" (p. 252). Feeling uncomfortable with the mother's charged presence, the child calls up one of these biblical references to help steady her mind: "The dressmaker was crawling around and around on her knees eating pins as Nebuchadnezzar had crawled eating grass. The wallpaper glinted and the elm trees outside hung heavy and green, and the straw matting smelled like the ghost of hay."

The young Elizabeth uses symbols self-protectively— here to displace her anxiety from the mother to the dressmaker. Elizabeth associates the dressmaker with the mad Nebuchadnezzar, a characterization that both expresses and refuses her mother's madness. This displacement does not work properly, however, and the child's mind turns to more durable displacements: she listens for the sound of the blacksmith's hammer—its heavy "clang":

Oh, beautiful sounds, from the blacksmiths' shop at the end of the garden! Its gray roof, with patches of moss, could be seen above the lilac bushes. Nate was there—Nate, wearing a long black leather apron over his trousers and bare chest, sweating hard, a black leather cap on top of dry, thick, black-and-gray curls, a black sooty face; iron filings, whiskers, and gold teeth, all together, and a smell of red-hot metal and horses' hoofs. (pp. 252–53)

Unlike her mother's cry the blacksmith's note is deliberately constructed; it is a form of work that helps the blacksmith to elaborate the human environment, and a communicative act, a gesture in which one human being draws another human being toward himself in order to constitute a community. This "clang" protects the child from what she has feared all along:

Clang.
The pure note: pure and angelic.

The dress was all wrong. She screamed.
The child vanishes. (p. 253)

Where has she gone? The incestuous closeness of the mother's body and her inchoate sounds have made the child "vanish." But she reappears somewhere else, in a site where the scream is ciphered and contained, where it is made safe by the paternal metaphor that rises up to enclose it. Two kinds of vanishing, then, are possible: the child can vanish into oneness with the mother, can disappear into that space where there are no seams or boundaries holding them apart, or she can vanish out of maternal discourse altogether and move into the zone of paternal saying, and this is where the young Elizabeth wants to go. "The child vanishes. . . . The child is visiting the blacksmith" (p. 253).

The scream inhabits a realm separate from the blacksmith's "language." As in Rich's poem we have a split between maternal and paternal discourse, but this time it is the mother's "word" that is dangerous. The father's shaping sounds give the child a sense of orientation and direction, of nonliminality; they give her a degree of autonomy from her own lived experience. Thus Bishop's story seems to focus on the alienating necessity—for the woman writer—of escaping from the mother's scream into the father's speech—here symbolized in the rhythmic makings of the blacksmith's hammer. What is liberating in Oliver's poem becomes an obsessive necessity.

If this interpretation of Bishop's story feels familiar, it is because feminist critics who write in the Lacanian mode have constructed theoretical coordinates to map these parental pleasures and dangers. According to Anika Lemaire, paternal language is the only discourse that allows the order of the world to be endlessly constituted; it "allows acts of reflexion and of consciousness upon the world and upon sense impressions to be carried out."[19] The father's language, his *nom* or "no," keeps us safe from reality; it "provides the mind with an autonomy from lived experience, allowing it to maintain a distance between itself and the lived experience." Since language works by conjuring up a "presence against a ground of absence," we can make theoretical distinctions between "the real" and the language which stands in for it, but in speaking or writing we are forced to ignore these distinctions. As Lemaire says, "this act of substituting a sign for a reality is also an operation of mediation whereby the subject places himself at a distance from the lived experience and is thus able to locate himself as a subject distinct from his surroundings."[20]

If "In the Village" can support the view that paternal discourse offers refuge from the throb of maternal immediacy that the mother's scream represents, the feminist critique of paternal discourse is that it distances women from themselves; such discourse demands a terrible autonomy from our lived experience as women. But I have suggested that there are other ways feminist critics can read the woman writer's relations to "patriarchal speech." "In the Village" is also a story about the hope of the paternal name. While Bishop seems to take refuge in the patronym, she actually uses the "name of the father" to hold open the "name of the mother" in a new way.

Robert Giroux describes "In the Village" as a tale that shelters the sheltering word of the father. He admires its oppositions between mother and father tongue:

The story with which this book ends, "In the Village," a prose-poem about an idyllic yet fearful childhood, records her terror at her mother's scream and the solace and refuge she sought, and found, in the "beautiful pure" sound—clang—that Nate the blacksmith made on his anvil. There seems to be general agreement that this story is a masterpiece.[21]

Howard Moss also analyzes Bishop's story in terms of this antimony:

The mother's scream hangs over the landscape, and yet the story is marvellous in bringing the curative into play at almost the same time the reader is faced with pain. The clang of the blacksmith's hammer rises to drown out the mother's scream. Innocence confronts the nightmarish and the pastoral with the same steady look. The nature world— the child leading the cow to pasture—and the smithy's magic are set against the horrors of the disrupted house, where adults weep and tell lies, and the child is forbidden to know what she already half guesses.[22]

I have suggested that the paternal order the blacksmith's hammer represents is more complicated, its relation to the mother's scream more ambivalent, than either critic realizes. First, the blacksmith's shop is filled with vestiges of a female body:

In the blacksmith's shop things hang up in the shadows and shadows hang up in the things, and there are black and glistening piles of dust in each corner. A tub of night-black water stands by the forge. The horseshoes sail through the dark like bloody little moons and follow each other like bloody little moons to drown in the black water, hissing, protesting. (p. 253)

The cloacal darkness of the blacksmith's shop is also the site of death for what is most feminine in his world—those "bloody little moons" which "drown in the black water." Here the male function predominates in a peculiarly antagonistic relation to the feminine which sails through the air "hissing, protesting." Bishop emphasizes the blacksmith's capacity to quiet these sounds. "Inside, the bellows creak. Nate does wonders with both hands; with one hand." The relation between his making and the silencing of the scream is metonymically explicit:

Outside in the grass lie scattered big, pale granite discs, like millstones, for making wheel rims on. This afternoon they are too hot to touch.
    Now it is settling down, the scream. (pp. 253–54)

Once more Bishop is setting up a dichotomy between scream and "word," between the frightening closeness of the mother's body and the resolution of the father's making. But her story also points to an irresolution in this dichotomy. Language, the word of the father, does not keep its part of the bargain; it continually slips out of place:

"There's that mourning coat she got the first winter," says my aunt.
    But always I think they are saying "morning." Why, in the morning, did one put on black? How early in the morning did one begin? Before the sun came up? (p. 254)

This "otherness" of language breaks into Bishop's story again and again in a way that invites us to question the easy resolutions Giroux and Moss find here. Shortly after the child's arrival, when her grandmother is going through memorabilia, the child breaks the "curdled elastic" holding together a packet of postcards. The postcards cascade to the floor; they reveal crystalline buildings which are overshadowed, surrounded, like the village itself, by precipitous syllables.

Some cards, instead of lines around the buildings, have words written in their skies with the same stuff, crumbling, dazzling and crumbling, raining down a little on little people who sometimes stand about below: pictures of Pentecost? What are the messages? I cannot tell, but they are falling on those specks of hands, on the hats, on the toes of their shoes, in their paths—wherever it is they are. (p. 255)

Words in Bishop's story have oddly spectral properties; they rain down from the sky—shimmer from the place where the scream itself hovers. Those words and objects associated with the mother and grandmother have a special penumbra. "See the grains of rice?" the grandmother says, when the child looks at the mother's delicate teacups "with little pale-blue windows" in them. The rice grains have disappeared. "They were put there just for a while and then they left something or other behind." What the mother is, what she leaves, both is and is not there. Even her handiwork has an odd, fragile quality:

And the smell, the wonderful smell of the dark-brown stains. Is it roses?
A tablecloth.
"She did beautiful work," says my grandmother.
"But look—it isn't finished."
Two pale, smooth wooden hoops are pressed together in the linen. There is a case of little ivory embroidery tools.
I abscond with a little ivory stick with a sharp point. To keep it forever I bury it under the bleeding heart by the crab-apple tree, but it is never found again. (p. 257)

The child steals the embroidery stick—her metaphorical pen—but when it vanishes, the child possesses nothing from the mother she can use to create or communicate. Only the blacksmith's work has an aura of permanence.

Nate sings and pumps the bellows with one hand. I try to help, but he really does it all, from behind me, and laughs when the coals blow red and wild.

"Make me a ring! Make me a ring, Nate!"
Instantly it is made; it is mine. (p. 257)

Bishop's story repeats, in a dozen different scenes, this
dichotomy between the evanescent, treacherous signs of the feminine
and the perdurable masculine. And yet, when women's words or
objects vanish, they vanish *into* the child as the father's symbols
do not. Thus the seamstress whose bosom is "full of needles with
threads ready to pull out and make nests" and whose house is a
minefield of "scraps of cloth and tissue-paper patterns, yellow,
pinked, with holes in the shapes of A, B, C, and D in them" is
an emblem of the mother's dangerous capaciousness; she possesses
vestigial letters but not the words these letters must form to be
safely legible. Things disappear in the seamstress' house: "A gray
kitten once lay on the treadle of her sewing machine, where she
rocked it as she sewed, like a baby in a cradle, but it got hanged
on the belt. Or did she make that up? But another . . . lies now
by the arm of the machine, in imminent danger of being sewn into
a turban" (p. 258). Finally, when the seamstress gives the child a
nickel, dropping it "in the pocket of the red-and-white dress that
she has made herself" (p. 259), the child puts it in her mouth "for
greater safety on the way home" and swallows it. Its metallic
blessings persist: "Months later, as far as I know, it is still in me,
transmuting all its precious metal into my growing teeth and hair"
(p. 259). The father's ring may feel permanent and satisfying, but
it remains external, superfluous, a mere possession. The dressmaker's
ciphers are dangerous, contaminating, but they give the child an
intermittent power; they flash upon her inward mind with the blissful
persistence of those crytalline words that fall in the picture postcards
onto Pentecostal people.

In a final scene, the child plays with the grandmother's
body, adorning her hair. The grandmother uses combs to keep her
hair tidy, and the child seizes one of them, with "longer teeth than
the others." "I pretend to play a tune on it; then I pretend to play
a tune on each of the others before we stick them in." What
women make may be lost, but it is also full of meaning: "my
grandmother's hair is full of music. She laughs" (p. 260). This

making has an alternate power to protect the child from what she fears. After making her grandmother's head full of music, Bishop recalls that

I am so pleased with myself that I do not feel obliged to mention the five-cent piece. I drink a rusty, icy drink out of the biggest dipper; still, nothing much happens.

We are waiting for a scream. But it is not screamed again, and the red sun sets in silence. (p. 260)

In the end the mother is unable to come into the father's or grandfather's world, into their language. She is sent to a sanatorium; every week the grandmother sends a package of chocolates or cake or a jar of preserves. The package is addressed

in my grandmother's handwriting, in purple indelible pencil, on smoothed-out wrapping paper. It will never come off.

I take the package to the post office. Going by Nate's I walk far out in the road and hold the package on the side away from him.

He calls to me. "Come here! I want to show you something."

But I pretend I don't hear him. But at any other time I still go there just the same. (p. 272)

The words made for or by the mother must be kept separate from the father's making. "Every Monday afternoon I go past the blacksmith's shop with the package under my arm," Bishop says, "hiding the address of the sanatorium with my arm and my other hand."

Why must the child keep these two alphabets separate? Is she simply ashamed of these words associated with the mother, or does she want to keep them safe from the blacksmith's hammering? In *Post-Partum Document* Mary Kelly explores a similar split between her child's unformed "writing" and the "symbolic" itself. Kelly explains that "the repression, condensation and displacement of graphemic signifiers in the child's text, suggest a writing anterior to speech, an insistence of the letter in the discourse of the unconscious which is resistant to signification as such."[23] This messy, pre-oedipal "writing" is blotted out by the writing that culture inscribes in the child:

The graphic rhetoric of children's books . . . such as A is for apple, B is for balloon, C is for cake, etc., implies a certain coagulation of the signified, underlining the logocentric bias of the system of language to which the letter ultimately subscribes; a system that privileges naming and the proper name and that pronounces the beginning of writing with the child's inscription of his father's name. (p. 167)

In thinking about language we tend to follow the second arc of Kelly's analysis—the line about language's propriety, its inscriptions of the proper name, and to ignore the remainder, the excess, the "writing anterior to speech"—which speaks "otherwise," which slips from the page. But my point about the images of language Bishop creates in "In the Village" is that Bishop delineates the child's fear and affection for both of these scripts. She outlines the child writer's discovery of "paternal" language's propriety, of the inscriptive power of the proper name, but she also shows us that one of the values of the *"propre"* is its capacity to hold onto the remainder, the excess, the mother's "writing anterior to speech" that makes speaking pleasurable.

For the mother, the child's text is a fetish object; it desires her. The polymorphous perversity of the letter explores the body beyond the limit of the look. The breast (e), the hook (r), the lack (c), the eye (i), the snake (s); forbidden anatomies, incestuous morphologies; the child's alphabet is an anagram of the maternal body. (p. 188)

My suggestion is that Bishop discovers, in "In the Village," a way to make us aware that both alphabets, both languages do and do not coincide. She writes her story as a palimpsest in which the slate can never come clean, and though the blacksmith's hammer civilizes "the bloody little moons" of feminine discourse, Bishop's story is *not* written in his mode—but in a language that gives us both alphabets simultaneously.

For Kelly these alphabets are also simultaneous. As the child writes, what emerges are "faeces, mark, imprint, utterance; a residue of corporality subtends the letter and overflows the text" (p. 188). But the letter enacts the child's separation from this corporality. "With the inscription of his proper name, the child is instituted as the author of his text. Each purposeful stroke disfigures the anagram, dismembers the body" (p. 188). In Bishop's story the blacksmith's hammer mimics this disfiguring stroke. Here, as Kelly says, "with the child's insistent repetition of the Name, he appropriates the status of the Father, the dead Father, the absent Father, the pre-conditon of the 'word.' The incestuous meaning of the letter is ciphered by the paternal metaphor" (p. 189). Thus the child and the mother are separated from their incestuous bond "through their mutual inscription in an order of extra-familial discourse and social practice."

The usual reading of "In the Village" stresses the ways in which Bishop focuses on this moment of entering paternal language and separating from the mother's anguished script. But the ending of "In the Village" is more complex than any simple notion of paternal metaphor intimates. As the child describes her journey over the bridge to the post office (the journey in which the grandmother's inscription is hidden from the blacksmith), Bishop describes a world that has escaped all this ciphering; she tells about the small trout in the nearby stream who refuse to be caught, who hover, like the scream, in the transparent elements outside the village:

From above, the trout look as transparent as the water, but if one did catch one, it would be opaque enough, with a little slick moon-white belly with a pair of tiny, pleated, rose-pink fins on it. The leaning willows soak their narrow yellowed leaves.
Clang.
Clang.
Nate is shaping a horseshoe. (pp. 273–74)

The river represents a force impervious to the blacksmith's sound, as if the persistence of the rhythms of the body, the "little bloody moons" which Nate drowns, still hover in these social margins, still mobile, still visible. Juxtaposed with this stream-world, the scream is also transformed. Having found its symbolic double the scream grows more beautiful and more transparent:

Oh, beautiful pure sound!
It turns everything else to silence.
But still, once in a while, the river gives an unexpected gurgle. *"Slip,"* it says, out of glassy-ridged brown knots sliding along the surface.
Clang.

And everything except the river holds its breath.

Now there is no scream. Once there was one and it settled slowly down to earth one hot summer afternoon; or did it float up, into that dark, too dark, blue sky? But surely it has gone away, forever.

It sounds like a bell buoy out at sea.

It is the elements speaking: earth, air, fire, water.

All those other things—clothes, crumbling postcards, broken china; things damaged and lost, sickened or destroyed; even the frail almost-lost scream—are they too frail for us to hear their voices long, too mortal?

Nate!

Oh, beautiful sound, strike again! (p. 274)

The promise that opens in the phrase "It sounds like a bell buoy out at sea," seems at first to refer to the blacksmith's "clang" alone—to the pure, merry note of his hammer. But the three prepositions before the phrase "It sounds" refer directly to the scream, making the story's resolution, its depiction of this the final, beautiful sound, more than a representation of the clang, of Nate's saving creativity; Bishop's text depicts another sort of natal moment: "are they too frail for us to hear their voices long? . . . Oh, beautiful sound, strike again!" Bishop's story ends with an impassioned apostrophe to the mother's voice which is gathered and cherished by language itself.

The tension between two supposedly inimical sounds breaks open the tidy structure usually imposed on Bishop's text; it gives us access to another reading of the woman writer's possible relation to speech. Rather than recording an escape from mother to father, Bishop's story is the record of woman's writing as a profoundly flexible activity. At first this flexibility seems to involve a refusal of the lingering cry of the mother and an embracing of the cool, staccato sound of the blacksmith's hammer. But while the child tries to keep the two alphabets separate, the adult poet looks for the point of their juncture. Bishop's text keeps returning to and lingering over the scream to let us know that the blacksmith's noise is valuable—but only insofar as it helps the writer not simply to escape from, but to call toward, to hold open the mother's voice in a new way. The story moves toward that emancipatory moment where the adult writer can call the mother's speech into such nearness that it reveals just how much "maternal" content the father's word contains.

To understand how this works we must consider another function of naming. For Lemaire, language bestows distance, allows its speakers to experience the order of the world, to hold onto a useful alienation from what really is. But language is also, as Heidegger has taught us, a site of gathering, of assembling, of "letting stay." The word can call things into a distant and magical nearness. As Heidegger writes in "The Origin of the Work of Art": "the temple-work, in setting up a world, does not cause the material to disappear, but rather causes it to come forth for the very first time and to come into the Open of the work's world. . . . The work moves the earth itself into the Open of a world and keeps it there. *The work lets the earth be an earth.*"[24] In a sense, Bishop's text lets the scream be a scream, but she also countenances her own desire for proximity to that scream, her own desire for maternal nearness by mapping the blacksmith's "clang" and the mother's scream onto one another. Heidegger comments on our need for such mapping: "in order to hear a bare sound we have to listen away from things, divert our ear from them, i.e., listen abstractly. In the thing-concept . . . there is not so much an assault upon the thing as rather an inordinate attempt to bring it into the greatest possible proximity to us."[25] The paternal word may operate as the place of gathering those meanings we want to bring into nearness, and the gathering word ceases, in this moment of nearness, to be paternal. Bishop's text makes this work of gathering visible.

Can Bishop's text offer another theory of practice, another way of looking at women's transformation and defiance of a paternal discourse? Yes. The argument goes something like this. If Bishop's text gives us a split between a mother and father tongue, she also reveals their dependence on one another when she shows us the slipping of the mother's signifier into and "under" the "name" of the father. Because Bishop reveals this slippage in the final paragraphs of her story, the paternal word which her story seems to celebrate changes its tone, for Bishop shows that it has contained the hissing, protesting sound of the mother's voice all along, that

it represses, but can also be made to yield, the little bloody moons
which fascinate and frighten the child—as well as something else
that is beautiful: the child's desire to draw the mother's word into
safety, into beauty, into proximity with her own desires.

If we are to describe the woman writer's relation to
language with any accuracy we must recognize that the word qua
word is not reproduced in women's texts; we never peruse there
a simple version of the "paternal" letter. Instead, the woman writer
works with *an image of language*—with words whose meaning is
mitigated and refracted by a multivocal clamoring. This is to say
that alien words not only do the work of representing, but are
themselves represented. To focus on the woman writer's silence or
circumlocution misses the ways in which writing offers this alternate
space, this space that not only "represents" words, but intimidates
them.

Let me return to my assertion that "Alice Can." What
I have established in my analysis of these four texts is that there
are a variety of language games the woman writer can play, and
that if we must construct a "poetic" or theory of women's writing,
it must take this variety into account. Is our only alternative a
theory of relativistic practice within women's writing? No. As Richard
Bernstein points out in *Beyond Objectivism and Relativism,* rival
paradigm theories can be "logically incompatible" and thus in conflict
with one another, unable to be measured against each other point
by point, but still comparable—that is, capable of being compared
against each other in numerous ways.[26] This is the direction my
analysis has taken. In looking at four different works and the differing
poetics that they imply, we have not been confronted with a "babble"
of "incommensurable languages," but with a powerful orientation
toward language "that has direction." Any incommensurability among
these works should not frighten us into a relativistic reading of
women's writing, since I would define these texts as part of a
dialogic community involved in inventing an emancipatory relation
to the dominant discourse. I want to suggest that these texts share
three traits. The first is a pleasure in language, a celebration of the

word's engagement of the senses, of the otherness of speech. Second, these texts share a preoccupation with *images of language*.[27] Literary women not only use speech and find themselves used by speech; they also create images of speech that aid in the collapse of hegemony. "Thanks to the ability of a language to represent another language while still retaining the capacity to sound simultaneously both outside and within it, to talk about it and at the same time to talk in and with it," Bakhtin explains in "Discourse in the Novel," "and thanks to the ability of the language being represented simultaneously to serve as an object of representation while continuing to be able to speak to itself—thanks to all this, the creation of specific novelistic images of languages becomes possible."[28]

Finally, each of these writers creates images of language that portray a second level of linguisticality, that allow the woman writer to enter into dialogue with a given word's limitations. What we see in the woman writer's reinvention of what had seemed monovocal is a multivoiced dialogue: a *struggle* going on within discourse itself. In these "images of language" we encounter both a dominant discourse that resists other points of view and an impetus to consume this discourse, to subvert it or replace it or reveal its subtext.

Thus each of these texts involves the invention of a pleasurable and emancipatory relation to language. Both Bishop and Rich attempt to collect within the word a new feminine residue: Rich by rejecting the language of the father and Bishop by using it to call toward the missing speech of the mother which has been repressed or lost. As we have seen in Bishop's story, the blacksmith's hammer begins to evoke this maternal speech not only by the power of association, but because Bishop allows the sliding of one signifier under the other to be reenacted in her writing and then reversed.

Oliver is not interested—as Rich and Bishop are—in recollecting what has been lost. For her, woman's relation to the dominant register of language may be transgressive, but it is also empowering. The problem for her speakers is not whether one can wrest language from men and give it new meaning, but how to go about satisfying the enormity of one's own verbal hunger. Finally, in Eudora Welty's "A Piece of News" the heroine has the power of joining language and style, but not the power of combining them in a writing that has self-conscious or critical dimensions. But while Welty's story comments on one woman's verbal repressions, she reveals the subtext of pleasure which might allow these repressions to be renegotiated.

In analyzing these texts I have been working toward a theory more complex than the idea that women are oppressed by language, or that women's lexical or syntactical coordinates are limited. As we have examined these four different texts, each one has given us a different reading of the woman writer's relation to speech. Oliver affirms woman's power to seize male language. Rich describes the woman writer's need to destroy the father's language; Bishop wants to conserve the father's speech in order to reveal the way it has served as a reservoir for the mother's voice, and Welty discovers for her heroine a site of pleasure in the word that reveals conventional language as the site of women's liberatory practice, a potential Welty seizes and acts out for herself.

Thus each of these texts offers a different theory of practice, but within these differences each text finds this common ground. First, these works reveal an erotic relation to language—imaged as mother's milk, as the blacksmith's note in which the child escapes from and rediscovers the mother, as a sensual relation with a newspaper, and as the consumption of singing shellfish which, consumed, describe the possibility of writing another story. Second, these works formulate emancipatory strategies in relation to a dominant discourse, by including an image of that dominant discourse itself. It is this recurrent combination of pleasure in speech and an emancipatory interest in the most oppressive tenets of masculine culture that reminds us that "Alice Can." What I have begun to argue for is the variety with which women writers are able to construct for themselves a dialectical, empowered relation to speech, and having established this in some of its richness and variety, my question in the chapters that follow will be: how is it that women writers have participated in praxis-oriented and trans-formative modes of writing—in dialogue, in social revision, in communicative interaction with one another and with masculine culture?

FIVE

Writing as Action:
A Vindication
of the Rights of Women

Conley: Do you think that your mode of writing is able to transform, to change the situation of women? Is there a strategic value?

Cixous: I do not know whether I can effectuate transformations. But one always arrives at something when something that has been silenced is expressed, when something that has been inhibited expresses itself. It is true that it liberates something.

Conley: Do you consider your writing to be an action?

Cixous: Yes, I think so. I think that there is also a test of reading. Texts with a strong "femininity," like some—not all—the texts of Lispector, put to test a certain *jouissance*. There are people who resist, who feel it as threat, while others are relieved by this very kind of rhythm.

Conley, "An Exchange with Hélène Cixous"

A *Vindication of the Rights of Women* is a difficult book for the modern reader, a book even feminist readers may have trouble applauding. First, the originalities of Wollstonecraft's work have become so commonplace that we must place it among those invisible works Woolf describes as "books so true that they seem now to contain nothing new in them." A *Vindication* contains a remarkable range of insights, ranging from Wollstonecraft's anger at Chinese footbinding (reminiscent of Mary Daly's *Gyn-Ecology*), to her concern that women be taught about their anatomies (reminiscent of *Our Bodies, Ourselves*). Since Wollstonecraft expounds ideas taken up in dozens of recent feminist texts, little of what she says strikes us as new—most of it has been spelled out at greater length and in more modern detail. By itself this familiarity might appease us if Wollstonecraft's prose held other felicities. But as a child of the Enlightenment Wollstonecraft practices her rational arts upon us without ceasing. Clear thinking is more important than feeling, reason than sensibility; passion is a trap for women, since constant use of "lower" modes of perception deprives women of reason and dignity.

In a series of essays dedicated to "honey-mad women," to devising a theory of the emancipatory value of play, where does Wollstonecraft fit in? Her text does not lend itself to a celebration of the "animality" of the letter. As Josephine Donovan notes in *Feminist Theory: The Intellectual Traditions of American Feminism,*

> Wollstonecraft . . . reflects the Stoic bias of the age. It is by subduing one's "animal nature," through the imposition of disciplined reason that one achieves dignity and virtue. "When we are gathering the flowers of the day, and revelling in pleasure, the solid fruit of toil and wisdom should not be caught at the same time." "He who will pass life away in bounding from one pleasure to another [will] . . . acquire neither wisdom nor respectability of character."[1]

The second problem the modern reader encounters in Wollstonecraft is her lack of mischief and high-spiritedness; we miss a certain pleasure in her text. *A Vindication* focuses on three consecutive ideas. Women have been reduced to the status of slaves—they are trained to please men. However, as creatures made in God's image, women are also created as rational beings. It follows that women should be educated not for man's glory, but for their own. Wollstonecraft sifts through these arguments page after page; her prose is dogged and elegant in pursuit of its logic, but in our post-theological age the arguments lack suasive power.

Although these arguments were timely for Wollstonecraft's contemporaries, and although they inspired other feminists to write passionate texts well into the nineteenth century (Margaret Fuller's *Woman in the Nineteenth Century* is the most stirring example), Wollstonecraft's excessive praise of rationality makes her well-reasoned, "unbodily" text seem monologic and single-voiced, closed in on itself, a quintessential theoretical text.[2] Wollstonecraft's *Vindication* is difficult to read because of its high degree of abstraction, its obsession with theory. Does Wollstonecraft belong, then, among those women writers accused by French feminists of capitulating to "phallogocentrism"?

"Men . . . begin from a theoretical platform that is already in place, already elaborated," says Marguerite Duras. "The writing of women is really translated from the unknown, like a new way of communicating rather than an already formed language."[3] Wollstonecraft's writing is not "translated from the unknown"; she glories in the "already formed language" that Duras condemns. As Mary Poovey explains:

Wollstonecraft seems very aware of two dangers: the danger of indulged feelings and the danger of inviting the charge of "feminine hysteria," which might subvert her debut in the form of masculine logic. She wants to express and harness emotion, for she knows the very real power of her own experience and longings. Yet, unsure of how to credit personal feeling, uncomfortable with the physical forms in which her imagination projects its gratifications, she retreats into the masculine literary conventions whose artifice she claims to despise. Reliance on rhetoric is for her a form of indirection that distances her from her own unreliable emotion without sacrificing its force. At the same time, it permits her to project the appearance of masculine assertiveness without having to take personal responsibility for it.[4]

Such willing ventriloquism is tantamount to silence. "Throughout the course of history, [women] have been mute, and it is doubtless by virtue of this mutism that men have been able to speak and write." Xavière Gauthier condemns women's aphasia, but she sees the same symptom mirrored in women who talk like men. For Gauthier the aphasic woman and the woman who mimics male speech are equally maimed. "As long as women remain silent, they will be outside the historical process. But if they begin to speak and write *as men do,* they will enter history subdued and alienated; it is a history that, logically speaking, their speech should disrupt."[5]

In accusing Wollstonecraft of employing this "appearance of masculine assertiveness," I also want to insist that her text's theoretical base is open (amidst its logic and abstraction) to emotions, bodily rhythms, pulses of vision that we miss if we see her "stoic bias" only. If modern readers do not experience the emancipatory vigor of Wollstonecraft's text, it may be because the focus on the woman writer's victimization by her culture's "logocentrism" has allowed us to overlook her strategies of resistance to victimization; feminist theory has not focused specifically on the woman writer's capacity for dialogue, for inventing abnormal discourses, for play. If one of the recurring capacities of the woman writer is her desire to invent emancipatory strategies that disrupt and reformulate the terms of the dominant culture, we must rescue the emancipatory potential of older texts by exploring these language games and making them visible.

My project in the next four chapters will be to describe a set of emancipatory practices in women's writing. We have seen that it is useful to examine the ways in which women's texts are engaged in praxis, in active social "work." In this chapter I want to focus on dialogue as an emancipatory strategy and to describe the ways in which Mary Wollstonecraft enters into conversation with male texts, specifically, with Rousseau's *Émile,* as a way of renegotiating its derisive energy. To make Wollstonecraft's bravado clearer, I will outline three additional areas in feminist theory that need reevaluating: 1) the use of "silence" as metaphor to describe women's relation to speech, and the assumption that women's speech can only be represented by an "absence"; 2) the assumption that women have primarily been represented as objects who circulate through culture and through men's texts, and that, as circulating "objects," women are outside culture—they give social texts the marks of coherence at the price of their own alienation; 3) the assumption that dialogue with the dominant tradition is useless to the woman writer as an emancipatory strategy because it always involves representations of a complicitous or oppressive discourse, and such representation inevitably reenacts this oppression.

In "Gynesis" Alice Jardine suggests that conventional genres such as narrative are ineffective as emancipatory forms because their elements "are recognized as existing only at the level of the fantasies which have entrapped us. To endlessly analyze those fantasies is to ask for repetition."[6] My own tendency is to be less skeptical.[7] I want to suggest that representations of suspect or complicitous modes of speech can give rise to "abnormal discourse," and to focus on just such a language game at the end of Wollstonecraft's dialogue with Rousseau—namely, a collective fantasy that takes the form of an address to the women of England. This address rises unexpectedly out of those "fantasies which have entrapped us." It is an "abnormal discourse" that comes into play not in spite of, but because of Wollstonecraft's dialogue with the dominant tradition.

SILENCES

"Literary history and the present are dark with silences," says Tillie Olsen, "some silences hidden; some the ceasing to publish after one work appears; some the never coming to book form at all."[8] In Silences Tillie Olsen has created an eloquent typology of literary quietness. She asks us not only to think about texts lost from our lexicons, but to consider, among women especially, the volume of texts never written. Olsen distinguishes between the "natural silences" most writers experience (moments of renewal or gestation for the sake of the work—what Olsen calls "the natural cycle of creation"), and spaces empty, even, of this latent work. According to Olsen it is women who have known these silences most intimately. Despite the exceptions—women unmarried or childless, women whose work has survived because they were freed from domestic duties by the death of a father or brother—Olsen explains that the majority of women who wanted to write were unable to protect their creativity. Even within this century (the date of her essay is 1972), she estimates that one woman writer has been reviewed, canonized, or anthologized for every twelve men. By drawing our attention to the tragic lacunae in writers' lives, Olsen reminds us of writing whose loss is invisible either because it has been obscured by work that did manage to come to fruition— or worse, invisible because a potential woman writer lacked time, money, or confidence, and failed altogether to produce.

Although Olsen's Silences provides a moving testimonial to writing that did not happen and to the fragility of the writing that did, we must be careful about misusing her evidence. Since

Olsen, since Wittig, since our rediscovery of *A Room of One's Own*, we have grown accustomed to noticing how socially imposed silences are figured in women's texts, and we have begun to read these "unnatural silences" as an essential part of women's plots, to emphasize the vulnerabilities, fragilities, interruptions, the absences in women's writing, and to valorize these absences as the most characteristic aspect of women's scripts. Translated into feminist theory, Olsen's poignant discoveries have achieved the status of feminist myth, and this myth has begun to legislate what we see when we read women's texts.[9]

Let me hasten to add that Olsen's discoveries have been indispensable both politically (in instigating self-consciousness and giving rise not only to feminist criticism as a collective enterprise but to anthologies of women's writing like *The Norton Anthology of Literature by Women*), and pragmatically (as an essential tool to help us think about textual lacunae). Using Olsen's terms we can, for example, discover in Carson McCullers' "The Ballad of the Sad Cafe" an extended meditation on the woman writer's silence. McCullers' story ends with an image of "Twelve Mortal Men" who work on a chain gang and lack every freedom but the freedom of voice:

All day there is the sound of picks striking into the clay earth, hard sunlight, the smell of sweat. And every day there is music. One dark voice will start a phrase, half-sung, and like a question. And after a moment another voice will join in, soon the whole gang will be singing. The voices are dark in the golden glare, the music intricately blended, both somber and joyful. . . . It is music that causes the heart to broaden and the listener to grow cold with ecstasy and fright.[10]

The situation of these enslaved men offers a stark contrast to the lonely fate of the story's heroine. Miss Amelia, who peers occasionally from behind a shutter in her boarded-up house, possesses "a face like the terrible dim faces known in dreams—sexless and white, with two gray crossed eyes which are turned inward so sharply that they seem to be exchanging with each other one long and secret gaze of grief" (pp. 3–4). Miss Amelia's excessive interiority is matched by her broken voice. "Her voice has lost its old vigor;

there was none of the ring of vengeance it used to have when she would mention 'that loom-fixer I was married to,' or some other enemy. Her voice was broken, soft and sad as the wheezy whine of the church pump-organ" (p. 70). In the space between Amelia's voicelessness and the chain gang's song, an entire history of the gendered nature of discourse might be written. Both genders have been mutilated by social circumstance, but unlike the chain gang, Miss Amelia's incarceration is permanent; she never hears a dialogic response.

Olsen's metaphors offer enormous analytic power, but they also have the power to divert our attention from other voices in women's texts. While Olsen's work has helped us see that the missing producer of missing texts is most often a woman, and while her descriptions of her own and of Rebecca Harding Davis' restricted productivity have helped us examine women's writing in new ways, *Silences* has also contributed to a myth about feminine silence that does not always reflect women writers' real strengths. For example, in reading a work like *A Vindication,* critics have focused on the ways in which Wollstonecraft has either been silenced by her culture or else been complicitous in its values. But what does Wollstonecraft say about silence? She quotes Rousseau's commandment that women be mute and then attacks his words vehemently. For Rousseau, women should not speak out of turn:

We ought not, therefore, to restrain the prattle of girls, in the same manner as we should that of boys, with that severe question, *To what purpose are you talking?* but by another, which is no less difficult to answer, *How will your discourse be received?* In infancy, while they are as yet incapable to discern good from evil, they ought to observe it, as a law, never to say any thing disagreeable to those whom they are speaking to: what will render the practice of this rule also the more difficult, is, that it must ever be subordinate to the former, of never speaking falsely or telling an untruth.[11]

Wollstonecraft replies, "To govern the tongue in this manner must require great address indeed; and it is too much practised both by men and women.—Out of the abundance of the heart how few speak!"[12] She meets Rousseau on his own turf and outdoes him in the business of coining maxims.

Instead of looking at women's silence, I want to examine women's noise and articulateness in inventing emancipatory strategies to empower themselves in relation to a tradition that restricts their right to speak. To this end we will examine Mary Wollstonecraft's A Vindication from two different perspectives. We will look at the dramatization of Wollstonecraft's persona, first, in the poetry of William Blake, and second, from the perspective of Wollstonecraft's written dialogue with Rousseau in A Vindication. The discovery of emancipatory moments in A Vindication may seem perverse to those in sympathy with Olsen's ideas, but I want to suggest that for women, writing is not just an act that permits the overcoming of personal silence, but of men's silence as well, since writing, as physical act, gives women an unprecedented power of dialogue with the dominant tradition, a power, above all, of interrupting that tradition and revealing its violence.

This vision of women's writing asks that we controvert Derrida's thesis that writing and speech are coequal. Although both written and oral speech are dangerous practices in which we are always at risk (either vulnerable to "logocentrism" or else at a loss for words), writing also permits the quotation and revision of alien languages.[13] In a world where women are not allowed public speech, writing gives the literary woman a physical power the spoken word often lacks: namely, the power to cite someone else's words at length in order to interrupt the citation and change its intent. Let us consider what the possibility for carrying on these scriptive conversations means.

Legend has it that the heroine of Blake's "Visions of the Daughters of Albion" is modeled on Mary Wollstonecraft, a writer whose friendship Blake valued and whose work he read and admired. At the poem's beginning the heroine, Oothoon, is trapped in a sweet and insipid persona; a persona she is not able to cast off, even after she has been raped by the villainous Bromion and rejected by her lover Theotormon. Like the children of the Songs of Innocence, Oothoon's imagination is active and vulnerable. She speaks in simple verse, addressing the radiant "Marygold of Leutha's vale" in language generous, naive, and unabashedly sexual:

Art thou a flower! art thou a nymph! I see thee now a flower;
Now a nymph! I dare not pluck thee from thy dewy bed?
The Golden nymph replied; pluck thou my flower Oothoon the
    mild
Another flower shall spring, because the soul of sweet delight
Can never pass away. She ceas'd & clos'd her golden shrine.[14]

Oothoon plucks the flower and is suddenly rent by Bromion's thunders; her happy sensuality has made her vulnerable to sexual attack. Raped by Bromion, she is also defined by him:

Bromion spoke. Behold this harlot here on Bromions bed,
And let the jealous dolphins sport around the lovely maid;
Thy soft American plains are mine, and mine thy north & south:
Stampt with my signet are the swarthy children of the sun:
They are obedient, they resist not, they obey the scourge:
Their daughters worship terrors and obey the violent.
                                              (plate 1, ll.18–23)

Protesting her innocence, Oothoon refuses to become part of Bromion's story. But she is already implicated. Her openness becomes a frightening masochism, a desire to disempower herself by reflecting the laws of her jealous lover Theotormon. "Silent I hover all the night, and all day could be silent / If Theotormon once would turn his loved eyes upon me; / How can I be defild when I reflect thy image pure?" (plate 3, ll. 14–16)

Can we generalize from Oothoon's story about woman's relation to silence? Oothoon's willingness to be silent and to reflect Theotormon's angry ideology seems all too familiar. But Blake also insists on defamiliarizing this story. He describes an Oothoon who overcomes Theotormon's commands, and he dramatizes the ways in which both Bromion and Theotormon are afraid of her. At first, these men express their fear by talking too much; they ask fanatical questions: "And is there not one law for both the lion and the ox? / And is there not eternal fire, and eternal chains? / To bind the phantoms of existence from eternal life?" Bromion shakes the caverns of existence with his lamentations, and Oothoon waits "silent all the day . . . and all the night" hoping for a more sympathetic response (plate 4, ll. 23–25). After Bromion's and Theotormon's hysterical negations, she hears nothing. Finally, she breaks their silence and her own:

> O Urizen! Creator of men! mistaken Demon of heaven:
> Thy joys are tears! thy labour vain, to form men to thine image.
> How can one joy absorb another? are not different joys
> Holy, eternal, infinite! and each joy is a Love.
>
> (plate 5, ll. 3–6)

Blake's poem presents us with a dazzling birth, with the emergence of Oothoon as a heroine who charts her own complex mythology, who formulates her own set of beliefs and declares them passionately to the world. Initially demure and self-effacing, Oothoon is a woman who casts herself willfully into some wild, fiery furnace of mind and emerges—demonic *and* rational—a liberated feminist goddess. Or does she? By the end of the poem Oothoon seems to have resolved all internal conflicts; she has challenged Theotormon's oppression and rejected Bromion's heckling. Her only dilemma is that, in her freedom, she has lost her community; she finds herself separated not only from Theotormon, but from the "Daughters of Albion," those Englishwomen who have witnessed her journey:

> Arise you little glancing wings, and sing your infant joy!
> Arise and drink your bliss, for every thing that lives is holy!
>
> Thus every morning wails Oothoon. but Theotormon sits
> Upon the margind ocean conversing with shadows dire.
>
> The Daughters of Albion hear her woes, & eccho back her sighs.
>
> (plate 8, ll. 9–13)

Oothoon cannot converse with this female chorus, whose blank echoes simply mimic her cries. Her victory is empty, and in the final illumination Blake shows her sad-faced and disembodied—soaring above the earth in an aphonic universe where she has lost contact with every voice but her own.

Oothoon achieves insight into her plight as a woman and into the conditionality of her world, but no one will recreate this world with her; her buoyancy is limited by the silence of others.[15] Blake's poem bears witness to Oothoon's dialogic being, to her fundamental need as a being in conversation with others. Blake also insists on Oothoon's dialectical power to mediate the social contradictions she encounters through her own public discourse. But since the rhythms of speech are intrinsically dialogic, since speech cries out for others who respond, her speech comes to an end. Oothoon cannot carry this conversation further by herself.[16]

Thus the dilemma Blake's poem projects is not woman's speechlessness, but man's; not that Oothoon needs this dominant discourse to define herself, but that she must be able to interrupt and transform men's words if she is to alter her world. By lapsing into silence Oothoon's male interlocutors refuse to recognize Oothoon's powers of self-definition, but equally crucially, they refuse to submit their words to her interjections.

To make this point another way, we can ask: what makes Theotormon and Bromion silent, what are they afraid of? The conventional answer is that Oothoon's world view frightens them. But Bromion and Theotormon are equally frightened of having a conversation with her, of making their ideas vulnerable to dialogue with a woman's world view. As Gadamer explains:

A conversation is a process of two people understanding each other. Thus it is characteristic of every true conversation that each opens himself to the other person, truly accepts his point of view as worthy of consideration and gets inside the other to such an extent that he understands not a particular individual, but what he says.[17]

Following Gadamer's metaphor, to converse with another is to "get inside the other," to return to the womb: in Theotormon's and Bromion's fantasy, to enter the "feminine" body of Oothoon's speech. To be controlled by a woman's body of speech is frightening; it portends the loss of masculine boundaries.[18]

DIALOGUE

My goal in this reading of Blake's "Visions" has been to problematize our readings of dialogue and silence in relation to "patriarchal" discourse. Although feminist critics have recognized that women are dialogic beings—beings who thrive on conversation, beings in whom language is a reality—they have also argued that women are silenced by masculine culture and trapped by masculine language. This language is said to disrupt the unrestricted play of women's writing. I have begun to stress another aspect of women's life within speech, to say that women are also dialogic beings for whom the unexpected does happen: that in writing women can subvert past silences and refashion the terms of a repressive discourse. Even though the fact and theme of women's silence is recurrent and may seldom, even in the best of circumstances, reach the stage of "text" to recur as theme, this does not mean that we should ignore emergent structures in women's writing that speak out against this silence. To return to Hannah Arendt: "the life span of man running toward death would inevitably carry everything human to ruin and destruction if it were not for the faculty of interrupting it and beginning something new, a faculty which is inherent in action."[19] I have been arguing that we need to understand more about the systematic recurrence of this interruption in the writing of women. Arendt reminds us that when "beginning" is viewed from the viewpoint of ordinary processes, any extraordinary action "looks like a miracle": a new action always appears as unexpected; it is the "infinite improbability which occurs regularly" (p. 246). I am optimistic that we can begin to characterize this regularity in women's texts, to see, with Arendt, the action women and men are capable of "by virtue of being born. Only the full experience of this capacity can bestow upon human affairs faith and hope" (p. 247).

My thesis is not that emancipatory dialogue is easy for either gender. If philosophers still cherish the fiction, as Habermas says, "that Socratic dialogue is possible everywhere and at any time," it is because they are blind to the systematic distortions of our life within speech:

From the beginning philosophy has presumed that the autonomy and responsibility posited with the structure of language are not only anticipated but real. . . . Only when philosophy discovers in the dialectical course of history the traces of violence that deform repeated attempts at dialogue and recurrently close off the path to unconstrained communication does it further the process whose suspension it otherwise legitimates: mankind's evolution toward autonomy and responsibility.[20]

Feminist critics have suggested that the woman writer is immutably trapped by this violence. But writers like Mary Wollstonecraft have discovered these "traces of violence" and begun to talk back. Wollstonecraft's dialogue with Rousseau in A *Vindication of the Rights of Women* is a reconstruction of the violence his text imposes on women. In drawing Rousseau out, drawing him into a conversation, Wollstonecraft succeeds in changing the tenor of this violence and awakening voices that have been repressed.

Like Oothoon, Wollstonecraft achieves a prose style that assaults the reader with dizzying spirals of prose. But unlike Oothoon, Wollstonecraft can create the conversations she needs because the act of writing can give her uncanny power over her conversational partners. Writing, as physical act, gives the woman writer a space in which she can expropriate men's texts and treat these texts as bodies. These embodied texts are mortal, penetrable, excitable; they become imperfect sites of that sometime thing we call "patriarchal discourse." Thus male bodies and texts can be made to circulate through women's texts—breaking that circuit of meaning in which women have been the objects of circulation. Wollstonecraft's dialogue with Rousseau in the *Vindications* serves double ends. First, she quotes his texts liberally—in order to decontextualize his misogyny, to place it in a context she can control. Then she draws Rousseau into a conversation that, like Theotormon and Bromion, he would prefer to resist. But since Wollstonecraft is controlling his words, she can change their import by revealing their violence. Finally, Wollstonecraft corrects this violence with her own ideas.

If Wollstonecraft's prose can be characterized by the abruptness and energy with which she seizes the role of speaking subject and constructs fictive dialogues with silent male interlocutors, why isn't this perception at the center of Wollstonecraft criticism? If Wollstonecraft's prose has this dialogic capacity, why haven't feminist critics invented a theory that accounts for its partial wisdom, its emancipatory glee?

In order to understand the power of Wollstonecraft's writing, we need to re-evaluate the woman writer's relation to dialogue. We will consider three theories that will let us recover a framework for seeing dialogue as an emancipatory mode.

Philosophers have recently begun to renew their faith in the power of dialogue, in the transformative energy of conversation. In *Philosophy and the Mirror of Nature* Richard Rorty insists that philosophy itself is a form of conversation, an exchange of questions and ideas, rather than a deliberate, "accurate" inquiry into the "glassy essence" of things. Rorty explains that there is no single epistemology offering us the knowledge we need to describe the world as it is. As we think and talk and move through the world, we begin to change things, and our descriptions inevitably alter. These descriptions alter the world as well; we can never come closer to the "truth" because, as we talk, truth itself changes. Given this fluctuating state of things, it is our business to pay more attention to thinkers who are, in Rorty's terms, "edifying" rather than "systematic": philosophers like Dewey, Wittgenstein, or Heidegger whose goal is not to deepen our knowledge of the fundament, but to disrupt our limiting notions of what truth should be. Edifying philosophers, Rorty explains,

refuse to present themselves as having found out any objective truth (about, say, what philosophy is). They present themselves as doing something different from, and more important than, offering accurate representations of how things are. . . . One reason they manage as well as they do is that they do not think that when we say something we must necessarily be expressing a view about a subject. We might just be *saying something*—participating in a conversation rather than contributing to an inquiry.[21]

To describe philosophers as women or men who neither mirror reality nor look for foundational structures of truth, but who participate in flux, who are creative conversationalists, does not mean their labor lacks validity. In carrying on such conversations we can, Rorty says, "perform the social function which Dewey called 'breaking the crust of convention,' preventing man from deluding himself with the notion that he knows himself, or anything else, except under optional descriptions" (p. 379). To interrupt the status quo so that new beliefs and ideas emerge in the world and give us new things to think and language games to play: this, for Rorty, is the "hero's" task. Conversation is the ultimate emancipatory act:

Given leisure and libraries, the conversation which Plato began will not end in self-objectivation—not because aspects of the world, or of human beings, escape being objects of scientific inquiry, but simply because free and leisured conversation generates abnormal discourse as the sparks fly upward. (p. 389)

For Rorty, abnormal discourse is something that happens when someone enters into the conversation who does not know its convictions, or who sets them aside (p. 320); it is any discourse that interrupts "agreed-upon criteria for reaching agreement" and refuses to carry on with the normative course of an argument (p. 11).

Rorty's ideas are, to say the least, problematic, but his descriptions of "abnormal discourse" can be useful for the feminist critic. We will see that in Wollstonecraft's *Vindication* something unusual does happen in her conversation with the tradition, that "the sparks" of a new kind of conversation do indeed fly upward as Wollstonecraft speaks. This is to suggest that, despite feminist conventions insisting upon the limits of any communicative system invented and controlled by men, we should not overlook the momentum provided by the peculiar intersection of body and word in women's written (and, to a different degree, in spoken) conversation, nor should we ignore the ways in which women writers have used the act of writing as a site for appropriating and beginning to reformulate male discourse by turning this discourse in the direction of women, by making men speak.[22] We cannot adapt Rorty's view of dialogue for our own ends, however, before challenging his view of language.

Rorty's description of language as such, his theory of how speakers relate to the words that they speak, is surprisingly naive.[23] Confident of our capacity to use words to direct a change of fate, Rorty insists that language changes according to need. "It is the commonplace fact that people may develop doubts about what they are doing, and thereupon begin to discourse in ways incommensurable with those they used previously" (p. 386). It is not simply that linguistic change happens, but that it comes at no cost:

Meditation on the possibility of such changes, like reading science fiction, does help us overcome the self-confidence of "philosophical realism." But such meditation does not need to be supplemented by a transcendental account of the nature of reflection. All that is necessary is the edifying invocation of the fact or possibility of abnormal discourses, undermining our reliance upon the knowledge we have gained through normal discourses. (p. 386)

Rorty does admit that "normal discourse" tends to block the flow of conversation by presenting itself as canonical. But this tendency is not something Rorty finds dangerous. He insists that "abnormal discourse" is capable of emerging from "normal discourse" to change things, even in the worst of circumstances. The emergence of philosophers like Wittgenstein and Dewey proves that these simple emancipatory moments are possible, even recurrent. If this sounds like my argument about women's writing, the similarity is deceptive. At the heart of Rorty's project we find the positivist belief that men and women can change themselves by changing their self-descriptions: "man is a self-defining animal. With changes in his self-definition go changes in what man is, such that he has to be understood in different terms" (p. 350). We have seen that women's relation to language is more complex. For example, when Oothoon changes her self-definition, she still is not understood by the men who inscribe and inhabit her world. Instead, she is obliterated, excised from their discourse.

Rorty dismisses this possibility: "The sense in which human beings alter themselves by redescribing themselves is no more metaphysically exciting or mysterious than the sense in which they alter themselves by changing their diet, their sexual partners, or their habitation" (p. 351). Metaphysics aside, the political implications of any of these changes could be impressive. To put the case against Rorty succintly, his view is that the structure of language is commensurable with human needs. The unexpressed is always the will-be-expressible.

Rorty is not alone in his beliefs. Philosophers like Gadamer celebrate the liberatory powers of dialogue; language for them is singularly unproblematic. Gadamer explains the dynamics of conversation in the following way:

Language, then, is not the finally found anonymous subject of all social-historical processes and action, which presents the whole of its activities as objectivations to our observing gaze; rather, it is by itself the game of interpretation that we all are engaged in every day. In this game nobody is above and before all the others; everybody is at the center, is "it" in this game. Thus it is always his turn to be interpreting.[24]

Gadamer's belief that "everybody is at the center" brings us to a second view of dialogue, to its gender and class-based critique. Adrienne Rich has already spoken for this point of view; her ideas are reiterated by H. J. Giegel:

The oppressed class not only doubts the ability of the ruling class to conduct the dialogue, but also has good reasons for assuming that each attempt on its part to enter into a dialogue with the ruling class will only serve as an opportunity for the latter to strengthen the security of its domination.[25]

Giegel's view matches Jameson's discussion of dialogue in *The Political Unconscious*. Jameson says that dialogue is absolutely nonrevolutionary because it is only possible through the "unity of a shared code." Those who argue with an oppressor can only argue in the oppressor's language.

For Mikhail Bakhtin "normal" discourse offers the writer something less than the easy purchase on transformation of Rorty and Gadamer, but something more than the "abstract imperative" of Giegel and Jameson. For Bakhtin linguistic norms are "the generative forces of linguistic life," which, even as they "struggle to overcome the heteroglossia of language" or to "unite and centralize verbal-ideological thought," also give rise to a "growing heteroglossia."[26] In contrast to the hermeneutic and Marxian readings of dialogue, Bakhtin argues that language is always "alive and developing" along its own fault lines, that the life of every language system is marked by struggle "among socio-linguistic points of view." "Abnormal" discourse cannot establish itself easily.

> The word in language is half someone else's. It becomes "one's own" only when the speaker populates it with his own intention, his own accent, when he appropriates the word, adapting it to his own semantic and expressive intention. Prior to this moment of appropriation, the word does not exist in a neutral and impersonal language (it is not, after all, out of a dictionary that the speaker gets his words!), but rather it exists in other people's mouths, in other people's contexts, serving other people's intentions: it is from there that one must take the word, and make it one's own. (pp. 293–94)

For Rorty "edifying" philosophers live at the changing edge of social discourse as its dialogic elite, while for Jameson dialogue is communal but inert; it implies commitment to a shared diacritic. But for Bakhtin, dialogic language is "alive and developing"—a development that is not "abnormal," but is continually transformative (a transformation carefully monitored, but not always overcome by conservative resistance). "Language is not a neutral medium that passes freely and easily into the private property of the speaker's intentions; it is populated—overpopulated—with the intentions of others. Expropriating it, forcing it to submit to one's own intentions and accents, is a difficult and complicated process" (p. 294). It is this appropriative mode of dialogue that gives *A Vindication* its energy and allows Wollstonecraft to fight against Rousseau's words, which are "overpopulated" with misogynous meaning. To see how this expropriation works (and why both Rorty's and Jameson's models of dialogue are finally inadequate), we need to examine Wollstonecraft's expropriation of a cultural code that she supposedly lacks the scriptive power to change: namely, the circulation of women.

THE TRAFFIC IN WOMEN

According to Lévi-Strauss, the traffic in women holds social structures together. As Teresa de Lauretis explains, in his theory, "women are not simply goods or objects exchanged by and among men," but also "signs or messages which circulate among 'individuals' and groups, ensuring social communication."[27] In this model women's two social functions are reproduction and the maintenance of social cohesion. Possessed by men, women pass among them in order to keep the social order intact. This division of labor extends to the use of language as well, since women are not simply objects in the form of circulating goods, but objects in the form of speech, and thus offer society duplicate modes of cohesion.

Although Teresa de Lauretis and Gayle Rubin have beautifully deconstructed this myth system, the traffic in women is still a social force to be reckoned with, and a number of philosophers and critics write as if this system is permanently in place. In Terry Eagleton's *The Rape of Clarissa,* for example, Eagleton criticizes Clarissa's status as an item of exchange, but treats this status as if it were normative:

The patriarchal structure of all known societies is perhaps nowhere more evident than in the fact that the fundamental unit of exchange, the founding gift, is women. In this sense, the letter of *Clarissa* can be seen not only as sign of female sexuality but as nothing less than *the woman herself,* that circulating property which cements the system of male dominance. What "circulates" in the novel, what unifies its great circuits of textual exchange, is simply Clarissa herself, whether as daughter or lover, rival or confidante, protégée or property-owner. It is on the trading, withholding, surrendering or protecting of Clarissa that the currency of all that letter-writing is founded.[28]

Why is this reading problematic? Eagleton resists Lévi-Strauss' syllogisms even as he gives in to them. Clarissa becomes the super-glue of society; her body can multiply the sites of desire because of her "object" status in patriarchal discourse:

Clarissa's body is itself the discourse of the text. It is the signifier which distributes others to their positions of power or desire, fixing them in some fraught relation to her own mysteriously inviolable being.
    To claim as much is to argue that Clarissa acts in the novel as the "transcendental signifier." (pp. 56–57)

Just as Clarissa's body is empty of personal meaning, so her acts of writing are empty of power. For Clarissa, to act or not to act comes to the same thing.

If letter-writing is in one sense free subjectivity, it is also the function of an ineluctable power system. Certainly no activity could be more minutely regulated. To "correspond" is to implicate a set of political questions: Who may write to whom, under what conditions? Which parts may be cited to another, and which must be suppressed? Who has the authority to edit, censor, commentate? (p. 50)

Who indeed? According to Eagleton, writing (for Clarissa, not Lovelace), becomes a "private, always violable space, a secret enterprise fraught with deadly risk. In an oppressive society, writing is the sole free self-disclosure available to women, but it is precisely this which threatens to surrender them into that society's power" (p. 49).

Eagleton aims at historical accuracy, and he notes correctly that women's writing was even more circumscribed in the eighteenth century than it is today. But his generalizations lack the dialectical capacity to discover scriptive operations outside the realm of this particular notation; he ignores the woman writer's capacities to turn the malleability and iterability of male script against itself. When Eagleton insists that Clarissa's letter writing is fixed in relation to "an ineluctable power system" we should ask whether his argument bears this out, or whether, in so arguing, Eagleton perpetuates his own version of gender asymmetry.

For writing, as Lovelace goes on to imply, does indeed possess a body, a thick and violent material being: it is a matter of record and contract, seal and bond, tangible documentation which may be turned against its author, cited out of context, deployed as threat, testimony, blackmail. It is the "iterability" of script—the fact that its materiality allows it to be reproduced in changed conditions—which makes it such an efficient instrument of oppression. (p. 48)

Eagleton does not ask why Clarissa is unable to seize this "thick and violent material being" and cite it out of context, or turn the scripts she receives against their masculine author. "The free utterances of the heart, once taken down in writing, may always be used later in evidence against the speaker" (p. 48), Eagleton says, but it is Lovelace's capacity, and his alone, to pervert the text against its author, to shackle her "with her own signs." "The utterance of the moment, once paralysed to print, is then secured for the most devious interpretative uses" (p. 49).

Despite his best efforts to make *The Rape of Clarissa* a profeminist text, Eagleton still writes Clarissa's story as if subjectivity is masculine, and the dreadful things that happen to Clarissa— and to her writing—happen because women's scripts are inevitably powerless. But this same thickness and violence of script can be appropriated by the female writing subject as well.

In noting that Eagleton's enthusiasm for Clarissa's helplessness is born of his sympathy for women's oppression, we should also note that Lévi-Strauss shares some of Eagleton's sympathy; Lévi-Strauss does not exclude women from the race of "mankind." As de Lauretis notes in *Alice Doesn't,* Lévi-Strauss

compromises by saying that women are also human beings, although in the symbolic order of culture they do not speak, desire, or produce meaning *for themselves,* as men do, by means of the exchange of women. One can only conclude that, insofar as women are human beings, they are (like) men. In short, be he naked or clothed by culture and history, the human subject is male.[29]

One of de Lauretis' projects is to show the inadequacy of this point of view—not in terms of its inadequacy as an ethic, as Rubin does—but by critiquing its power as theory:

The universalizing project of Lévi-Strauss—to collapse the economic and the semiotic orders into a unified theory of culture—depends on his positing woman as the functional opposite of subject (man), which logically, excludes the possibility—the theoretical possibility—of women ever being subjects and producers of culture.[30]

In *Alice Doesn't* de Lauretis limits the achievement of this female subjectivity to the feminist projects of consciousness raising and self consciousness. I want to frame women's roles as "subjects and producers of culture" differently—in terms of women's power of writing, a power, peculiarly, that allows women to exchange the meanings of men's words, to circulate men's names through their texts in a manner that begins to shake up, though not, alas, to completely eradicate, the old traffic in women.

How does this happen in *A Vindication?* In "Animadversion on Some of the Writers Who Have Rendered Women Objects of Pity, Bordering on Contempt," Wollstonecraft quotes lavishly from Rousseau's *Émile,* explaining that she needs to reproduce Rousseau's own words exactly "lest my readers should suspect that I warped the author's reasoning to support my own arguments" (p. 78). In quoting so freely, does Wollstonecraft warp her own reason instead? No, for Wollstonecraft's representation of Rousseau's words recontextualizes his ideas. She takes his authoritative text and constructs a conversation with it; in quoting she begins to rescind Rousseau's sayings, to make them dialogic and vulnerable. While the traffic in women is a "game" designed by men for the serious purpose of forging homoerotic boundaries, Wollstonecraft attempts to reverse the direction of this bonding; she makes Rousseau's name circulate through her text as a new object of exchange and bond between women.

Wollstonecraft's attack on Rousseau is organized around a structure of statement and reply. "I shall begin with Rousseau, and give a sketch of his character of woman, in his own words, interspersing comments and reflections" (p. 77). Wollstonecraft's initial quotations from Rousseau are lengthy—some a whole page— while Wollstonecraft's early replies remain brief and ironic. At the same time, Rousseau's words are shifted into Wollstonecraft's diction:

He then proceeds to prove that woman ought to be weak and passive, because she has less bodily strength than man, and hence infers, that she was formed to please and to be subject to him, and that it is her duty to render herself *agreeable* to her master—this being the grand end of her existence. (p. 78)

If Wollstonecraft's early arguments against this position are brief and thus moderately "passive," by the end of her argument Rousseau has grown silent; the quotations and paraphrases disappear, and Wollstonecraft's own words take over.

Wollstonecraft's seizure of Rousseau's power is no easy matter. As Bakhtin reminds us,

not all words for just anyone submit equally easily to this appropriation, to this seizure and transformation into private property: many words stubbornly resist, others remain alien, sound foreign in the mouth of the one who appropriated them and who now speaks them; they cannot be assimilated into his context and fall out of it; it is as if they put themselves in quotation marks against the will of the speaker.[31]

Wollstonecraft's early conversations with Rousseau confront this resistance. Carefully vehement, she does not argue with him directly, but reminds her reader that she has "already asserted that in educating women these fundamental principles lead to a system of cunning and lasciviousness" (p. 78). This angry glance in Rousseau's direction launches a more forceful attack. Women have not been created for the glory of man:

Supposing woman to have been formed only to please, and be subject to man, the conclusion is just, she ought to sacrifice every other consideration to render herself agreeable to him. . . . But . . . I may be allowed to doubt whether woman was created for man: and though the cry of irreligion, or even atheism, be raised against me, I will simply declare, that were an angel from heaven to tell me that Moses's beautiful, poetical cosmogony, and the account of the fall of man, were literally true, I could not believe what my reason told me was derogatory to the character of the Supreme Being. (pp. 78–79)

Like Oothoon, Wollstonecraft challenges religious authority with passion and reason. Oothoon builds spiraling stories which emphasize her society's repressiveness.

With what sense does the parson claim the labour of the farmer?
What are his nets & gins & traps. & how does he surround him
With cold floods of abstraction, and with forests of solitude,
To build him castles and high spires. where kings & priests may
        dwell.
Till she who burns with youth. and knows no fixed lot; is bound
In spells of law to one she loaths: and must she drag the chain
Of life, in weary lust! must chilling murderous thoughts, obscure
The clear heaven of her eternal spring?   (plate 5, ll. 17–24)

In "Visions of the Daughters of Albion" "she who burns with youth" does not have courage equal to her mental clarity, but as the narrator of A Vindication, Wollstonecraft does; she lashes out at Rousseau: "and, having no fear of the devil before mine eyes, I venture to call this a suggestion of reason, instead of resting my weakness on the broad shoulders of the first seducer of my frail sex" (p. 79).

Although Wollstonecraft challenges Rousseau's assumptions, she has not yet challenged his words directly. Instead, she focuses on Moses' "poetical" (hence irrational) version of history, and only then, in seeming to attack Satan, does she set a new tone for quoting Rousseau's text. By implication, Rousseau becomes complicitous with Satan as "first seducer": like Satan he lures women away from the sweet light of reason. And once Wollstonecraft has challenged his logic, Rousseau's words also become susceptible to dispersion. She interrupts his sentences with a particularizing "says Rousseau," or "Rousseau adds." With this "interspersing" of comments Rousseau's sentences seem more fallible; they are now capable of being parodied and stylized. For what Wollstonecraft is creating is not only a summary of Rousseau's politics, but also an image of Rousseau's style and of the typographic permeability of that style.

While in the novel a parody of someone else's style may seem invisible or intrinsic as it is seamlessly incorporated into the narrative (think, for example of Austen's portrayal of Emma), in Wollstonecraft's essay this stylization becomes extrinsic and occurs when she replies to Rousseau as if the two of them were engaged in real conversation. In order to achieve this effect, Wollstonecraft first has to locate his prose within reach, "in a zone of potential conversation with the author" (Bakhtin, p. 46). This zone of "dialogical contact" is partly achieved by interrupting the linear flow of Rousseau's prose. The first quotation is interrupted by a startling footnote ("what nonsense!") while elsewhere Wollstonecraft challenges the authority and distance of Rousseau's prose simply by interrupting his speech with his own name. " 'It being once demonstrated,' continues Rousseau, 'that man and woman are not, nor ought to be, constituted alike in temperament and character, it follows of course that they should not be educated in the same manner.' "[32] In addition to being Satanic, Rousseau is now someone who "continues" instead of commands, whose prose can be interrupted at the whim of the person quoting him. Wollstonecraft's message is that these are the words of a particular and particularly vulnerable person: words that not only can be challenged, but can be deleted and replaced by ellipses. Each of these gestures takes Rousseau's "authoritative word" and makes it dialogic.

Wollstonecraft removes Rousseau's language from the distanced, nondialogic zone where she finds it and makes it available for alteration. As his hieratical stance is challenged, his prose grows open to change, disagreement, conflict: it acquires a relative, particular status. My point is not, of course, that Wollstonecraft solves the woman writer's problems by becoming a feminist hierat, by taking on Rousseau's authority. Many of her descriptions of how to right the wrongs of women still seem inadequate, and her best ideas no longer describe a fully feminist project. However, we can learn something about women writers' emancipatory strategies when we examine Wollstonecraft's disabling of Rousseau's authority. She achieves a great deal simply by making his prose conversational.

If Wollstonecraft refutes Rousseau's text mildly at first, at the same time she continues interrupting it for several pages with footnotes, ellipses, and counterarguments that work by analogy. Then, after her third lengthy citation of his text, Wollstonecraft's prose begins to heat up; her attacks grow wilder and more vehement. At this point Rousseau is exclaiming about the need for feminine self-restraint in order to keep women free from self-injury:

To prevent this abuse, we should teach them, above all things, to lay a due restraint on themselves. The life of a modest woman is reduced, by our absurd institutions, to a perpetual conflict with herself: not but it is just that this sex should partake of the sufferings which arise from those evils it hath caused us.[33]

While Wollstonecraft has treated Rousseau's statements with a modicum of detachment and diffidence, by now a textual intimacy has been established between Rousseau's voice and her own, and suddenly she begins to treat their interaction as a conversation of

equals in which she has as much power to direct and to shape
Rousseau's words as he has to shape them himself. Her rebuttal
presents itself as a continuation of Rousseau's thought:

And why is the life of a modest woman a perpetual conflict? I should
answer, that this very system of education makes it so. Modesty,
temperance, and self-denial, are the sober offspring of reason; but when
sensibility is nurtured at the expence of the understanding, such weak
beings must be restrained by arbitrary means, and be subjected to
continual conflicts; but give their activity of mind a wider range, and
nobler passions and motives will govern their appetites and sentiments.
(p. 82)

With this direct commitment to dialogue, the tempo of Wollstonecraft's prose picks up and is followed by a rapid succession of
"his" and "hers" paragraphs in which Rousseau is allowed to speak
for only a few lines before Wollstonecraft intervenes. His authoritative
word is thoroughly removed from its "distanced zone" and made
more tentative, quizzical, and unreliable, until finally she interrupts
in mid-paragraph and challenges directly: "I shall not boggle about
words, when their direct signification is insincerity and falsehood.
. . . How could Rousseau dare to assert. . . ." (p. 85). Wollstonecraft's logic is convincing, but her manner is more impressive still.
At last she is attacking Rousseau's language directly, and distinguishing the moral order of his words from her own. It is now the
male who trespasses when he speaks, and ought to be silent, while
woman's voice speaks with authority.

Only after establishing this contrast between her fierce-
ness and his folderol does Wollstonecraft cite Rousseau's dictums
about women's silence. The middle sequence of Wollstonecraft's
"conversation" has consisted of a rhythmic sequence of "his"
paragraphs followed by "her" replies. Now Wollstonecraft mounts
a heated debate in which quotations from Rousseau are inserted in
paragraphs which begin and end with Wollstonecraft's own statements, and quotations from Rousseau are assaulted by a series of
angry rhetorical questions reminiscent of Oothoon's questions to
Urizen. As Rousseau's statements grow shorter, they seem to drown
in Wollstonecraft's prose; she accuses him of nonsense and inco-

herence, of dealing in "unintelligible paradoxes." In analyzing Rousseau's motives in coining such a poor philosophy of education, she also claims the colleague's right to censure and praise him:

But peace to his manes! I war not with his ashes, but his opinions. I war only with the sensibility that led him to degrade woman by making her the slave of love. . . . The pernicious tendency of those books, in which the writers insidiously degrade the sex whilst they are prostrate before their personal charms, cannot be too often or too severely exposed. (p. 91)

In "The Visions of the Daughters of Albion" when Oothoon cannot speak with Theotormon, she is unable to converse with the Daughters of Albion. But in A Vindication, when Wollstonecraft makes Rousseau her unwilling dialogic partner, she suddenly finds herself addressing the "objects" of her own discourse, the women of England.[34] The belatedness of this address is, perhaps, reprehensible. Wollstonecraft has not constructed a model of feminine solidarity or feminist community; A Vindication is not the ideal feminist text. But Wollstonecraft's appropriations of Rousseau's speech make possible the discovery of a new subject of address by the end of this conversation. She addresses her countrywomen directly, speaks toward a collective, feminine consciousness that has not appeared in her text before. Wollstonecraft does not continue speaking in or toward this collective, but in her passionate recovery of sisterhood we can recognize one of the emergent practices Raymond Williams praises in Marxism and Literature:

What matters, finally, in understanding emergent culture, as distinct from both the dominant and the residual, is that it is never only a matter of immediate practice; indeed it depends crucially on finding new forms or adaptations of form. Again and again what we have to observe is in effect a pre-emergence, active and pressing but not yet fully articulated, rather than the evident emergence which could be more confidently named.[35]

It is Wollstonecraft's reinvention of her place in the conversation of culture that makes this pre-emergence possible, for when Wollstonecraft reverses a norm and makes Rousseau into a new kind of circulating social message, she makes him into both a speaking partner and a sign. Rousseau—formerly the generator and arbiter of signs—is turned into someone who circulates: a sign whose meaning and value is designated by a woman.

I have suggested that Wollstonecraft's power over the circulation of Rousseau's name places Wollstonecraft in the role of producer of culture—and not just its sign or commodity. I have added that feminist anger at Wollstonecraft is just; she is willing to put women's names in circulation as well, and she accepts too heartily the economic, sexual, and philosophic terms of her culture. But after her debate with Rousseau, she is suddenly enabled to inscribe women in the very place both Rousseau and Lévi-Strauss refuse to inscribe them:

> Let us, my dear contemporaries, arise above such narrow prejudices! If wisdom be desirable on its own account, if virtue, to deserve the name, must be founded on knowledge; let us endeavour to strengthen our minds by reflection, till our heads become a balance for our hearts; let us not confine all our thoughts to the petty occurrences of the day, or our knowledge to an acquaintance with our lovers' or husbands' hearts; but let the practice of every duty be subordinate to the grand one of improving our minds, and preparing our affections for a more exalted state! (p. 92)

Wollstonecraft has not only put Rousseau's name in new circulation, she has established that desire itself is not the sole property of men, but the volatile possession of women—a message Margaret Fuller picks up when she "echoes" Wollstonecraft's text in tones so unlike the blank echolalias of Blake's "Daughters of Albion" that I must echo them here:

> Women of my country!—Exaltadas! if such there be,—women of English, old English nobleness, who understand the courage of Boadicea, the sacrifice of Godiva, the power of Queen Emma to tread the red-hot iron unharmed,—women who share the nature of Mrs. Hutchinson, Lady Russell, and the mothers of our own revolution,—have you nothing do to with this?[36]

SIX

The Novel and Laughter:
Wuthering Heights

We hear pleasurable echoes of Fuller's and Wollstonecraft's calls to action in the writings of Hélène Cixous.

Write! and your self-seeking text will know itself better than flesh and blood, rising, insurrectionary dough kneading itself, with sonorous, perfumed ingredients, a lively combination of flying colors, leaves, and rivers plunging into the sea we feed.[1]

All three writers ask women to rise up, to renew their sense of collective empowerment. But Cixous' brave sensuality seems a far cry from Wollstonecraft's or Fuller's. Is this sensual surplus Cixous' reason for emphasizing the hiatus between her own work and that of her feminist foremothers? In "The Laugh of the Medusa" Cixous defines older writing as the site of systematic repression, "where woman never has *her* turn to speak." The history of writing "has been one with the phallocentric tradition," a tradition that lacks a maternal lineage:

There have been failures—and if it weren't for them, I wouldn't be writing (I–woman, escapee)—in that enormous machine that has been operating and turning out its "truth" for centuries. There have been poets who would go to any lengths to slip something by at odds with tradition—men capable of loving love and hence capable of loving others and of wanting them, of imagining the woman who would hold out against oppression and constitute herself as a superb equal, hence "impossible" subject, untenable in a real social framework. (p. 249)

I have three quarrels with Cixous' point of view. First, women *have* been "at odds" with the tradition. Second, this pivotal work did not happen because of some "lapse" in patriarchal attentiveness, but because a particular woman writer was capable of acting, because women have participated in the invention of a countertradition of emancipatory strategies. Third, Cixous' ideas shackle our sense of what is radical in women's writing, make us miss the liberatory potential of older texts: both the work these texts continue to do in the present, and the political work these texts did in their own time. And Cixous' is not the only repressive voice. We need to overcome both the limited vision of history that Cixous presents, and the limited belief in the crisis potential of narrative she shares with other postmodern theorists.[2] "Only the poets—not the novelists, allies of representationalism" have been able to challenge the status quo, Cixous says, "because poetry involves gaining strength through the unconscious and because the unconscious, that other limitless country, is the place where the repressed manage to survive" (p. 250). Kristeva shares this skepticism: "Narrative is one of the forms of binding, sublimation, and repression of the drive charge against the curbs imposed by community structures."[3]

In this chapter I want to describe the nineteenth-century novel as a form with an emancipatory force: a force based on the novel's interrogatory relation to social codes and its explosive use of laughter. Cixous, like Kristeva, does find subversive potential in laughter: "You have only to look at the Medusa straight on to see her. And she's not deadly. She's beautiful and she's laughing" (p. 255). The Medusa's laugh sweeps away every impediment:

To write. An act which will not only "realize" the decensored relation of woman to her sexuality, to her womanly being, giving her access to her native strength; it will give her back her goods, her pleasures, her organs, her immense bodily territories which have been kept under seal. . . . An act that will also be marked by woman's *seizing* the occasion to *speak,* hence her shattering entry into history, which has always been based *on her suppression.* (p. 250)

The Medusa's laugh is intoxicating, but Cixous' insistence on an opposition between this modern Medusa and historical women's repressions must be called into question. The seizure of the body's wicked music has animated women's texts for some time. In fact, I want to begin this chapter with a conundrum, to set up a puzzle we will solve by the chapter's end. Why, in its opening pages, is *Wuthering Heights* such a funny book? What is the relation of comedy to the woman writer's productivity? Why has Emily Brontë's humor in *Wuthering Heights* been ignored by feminist and non-feminist critics alike?

Anyone returning to *Wuthering Heights* after long absence will be startled at the laughter bubbling up through its early pages. Recalling the elegiac tone of Lockwood's benediction or his irritating class biases and hypochondria, even seasoned readers of Brontë's novel forget that Lockwood begins the novel as an amusing character. Although Lockwood is neither as graceful as Chaplin nor as sympathetic as Keaton, like them he gets himself into a number of amusing scrapes. Dogs attack him, cold water is thrown on him, and both events are told in the manner of slapstick; Brontë has as much fun as the inhabitants of the Heights poking fun at him. The humor does not just consist of things done to Lockwood; he is author—in a space of twenty pages—of an amazing number of bloopers. He mistakes a cushion of dead rabbits for Catherine Heathcliff's household pets; he imagines Catherine to be the wife of each of the men of the Heights in turn; he calls her a "beneficent fairy."[4] But the best bit of comedy prefigures a gathering in another Victorian text: the tea party in *Alice in Wonderland*. In the scene where Alice has joined the Mad Hatter, the March Hare, and the Dormouse for tea, and the Dormouse starts to tell the story of the three little sisters who live in the bottom of a well, Dodgson's technique matches Brontë's, for both use nonsequitur; they employ an illogical "logic" to disturb the referential potential of their own texts.

The Dormouse had closed its eyes by this time, and was going off into a doze, but, on being pinched by the Hatter, it woke up again with a little shriek, and went on: "—that begins with an M, such as mouse traps, and the moon, and memory, and muchness—you know you say things are 'much of a muchness'—did you ever see such a thing as a drawing of a muchness?"

"Really, now you ask me," said Alice, very much confused, "I don't think—"

"Then you shouldn't talk," said the Hatter.[5]

We find a similar use of nonsequitur in Lockwood's tea-time conversation with the second Catherine. In this scene Lockwood tries politely, like Alice, to make sense of the inhabitants of the Heights. He also wants to obtain some simple information, but Catherine is no more helpful to him (and no less obstreperous) than the March Hare:

"Mrs Heathcliff," I said, earnestly, "you must excuse me for troubling you—I presume, because with that face, I'm sure you cannot help being good-hearted. Do point out some landmarks by which I may know my way home—I have no more idea how to get there than you would have how to get to London!"

"Take the road you came," she answered, ensconcing herself in a chair with a candle, and the long book open before her. "It is brief advice; but as sound as I can give." (pp. 57–58)

Lockwood's polite, highbrow speech is disturbed by the sour tones of Catherine's laughter. What is this broadly sketched humor doing in a passionate tragedy like Wuthering Heights?

Mikhail Bakhtin describes laughter as one of the unofficial "languages" that works—with gaiety and abandon—to disrupt the official language of the status quo. He is particularly interested in the ways in which laughter operates within moments of parody. While mimicry is not simply repetition, but an act that "rips the word away from its object, disunifies the two, shows that a given straightforward generic word—epic or tragic—is one-sided, bounded, incapable of exhausting the object," parody is more precocious:

parodying forces us to experience those sides of the object that are not otherwise included in a given genre or a given style. Parodic-travestying literature introduces the permanent corrective of laughter, of a critique on the one-sided seriousness of the lofty direct word, the corrective of reality that is always richer, more fundamental and most importantly too contradictory and heteroglot to be fit into a high and straightforward genre.[6]

For Julia Kristeva laughter also has this polyvocal intensity. Laughter, for her, is the bodily eruption that "lifts inhibitions by breaking through prohibition . . . to introduce the aggressive, violent, liberating drive. . . . When practice is not laughter, there is nothing new; where there is nothing new, practice cannot be provoking: it is at best a repeated, empty act."[7] What inhibitions are lifted at the beginning of Wuthering Heights? And what is the role of parody in lifting these inhibitions?

To answer this question we need to consider not only the comic beginning of Wuthering Heights, but the present status of the novel as a nineteenth-century women's genre. Virginia Woolf has already set the terms for this discussion in A Room of One's Own. In this courageous book Woolf revises our view of an entire era of history. She celebrates an epic change in women's status which, she says, deserves greater attention on the part of historians than either the Crusades or the Wars of Roses. "Towards the end of the eighteenth century," Woolf says, "the middle-class woman began to write." For Woolf, this writing is world-historical: "For if Pride and Prejudice matters, and Middlemarch and Villette and Wuthering Heights matter, then it matters far more than I can prove in an hour's discourse that women generally, and not merely the lonely aristocrat shut up in her country house among her folios and her flatterers, took to writing."[8] In a context where writing becomes a permanent arena of conversation among women, the individual woman writer can begin to introduce subversive practices into a masculine literary climate. Habermas puts this function of writing more technically:

It is only late in history that discourses have lost their sporadic character. Only when certain domains of discourse are institutionalized to such an extent that under specifiable conditions a general expectation exists, that discursive conversations will be initiated, can they become a systematically relevant mechanism of learning for a given society.[9]

Virginia Woolf's tone is more elegiac than Habermas', but her point is the same; she wants to praise the anonymous and not so anonymous women writers of the eighteenth century for the discursive ambience they provided the writers who came after them.

But why, Woolf asks, did nineteenth-century women choose a form so mundane and unwieldy? Since the muse was female, it would have made sense for women to turn to verse: "The 'supreme head of song' was a poetess. Both in France and in England the women poets precede the women novelists" (p. 69). And yet when Woolf looks at the "early nineteenth century" sitting on library shelves, "here, for the first time, I found several shelves given up entirely to the words of women. But why, I could not help asking, as I ran my eyes over them, were they, with very few exceptions, all novels?" And why were their styles and subject matters so very different? "Save for the possibly relevant fact that not one of them had a child, four more incongruous characters could not have met together in a room—so much so that it is tempting to invent a meeting and a dialogue between them" (p. 69).

Woolf is astonished at the mysterious common detail, but her answer to the question—Why did women write novels?—is largely negative. First, since "the original impulse was to poetry," Woolf concludes that nineteenth-century women wrote fiction because it was easier to write; women's "domestic" sensibilities were in tune with the communal sensitivity that novel writing demands. The woman writer "had been educated for centuries by the influences of the common sitting room. People's feelings were impressed on her; personal relations were always before her eyes" (p. 70). Most women were not allowed to study philosophy or Latin rhetoric, but since they were required to be thorough students of human manners, the novel became their most "natural" outlet: a springboard for feminine observation.

Second, the novel became the genre of choice for women writers because of its formal formlessness. A mode well-suited for those who lived and wrote in a common sitting room, the novel offered the woman writer a genre that could be interrupted. The novel's rambunctiousness means that in its composition, "less concentration is required" (p. 70). As proof, Woolf cites the famous case of Jane Austen, who wrote all her novels in public, "with no study to repair to," and Austen's plight becomes an argument for

Woolf's stirring appeal—her insistence that women must have rooms of their own.

While I applaud Woolf's politics, I want to question her insistence that the novel is the genre women choose because it is the form of least resistance. Although Austen was subjected "to all kinds of casual interruptions," the novel is not the form she (and Eliot and Gaskell and the Brontës) selected because it permitted these interruptions. Rather, Austen, Eliot, Gaskell, and the Brontës chose the novel because it allowed them both to disrupt a dominant literary tradition and to interrogate their surroundings. As a multi-voiced, multilanguaged form—a form inviting the novelist to parody other discourses and portray a dialogic "struggle among socio-linguistic points of view"—the novel is a genre that encourages its writers to assault the language systems of others and to admit into these language systems the disruptive ebulliance of other speech and of laughter.

Discussions of women's novels in the decades after *A Room of One's Own* have not fared much better. The novel has been represented as a form of constraint rather than as a force of praxis and change. Instead of celebrating the novel's capaciousness as a form—its penchant for containing and refracting older genres, and for putting these genres into question or crisis—the novel has earned a reputation as a compromised form that gives in too easily to the marriage plot and to romance. For example, in *Becoming a Heroine,* a delightfully confessional study of the ways novels affect their audiences, Rachel Brownstein argues that novels offer entrancing, dangerous educations for unsuspecting girl readers. In particular, Brownstein focuses on the restrictions imposed on women's imaginative lives by acts of novel reading: "Girls, enjoined from thinking about becoming generals and emperors, tend to live more in novels than boys do, and to live longer in them." What the novel offers its feminine audience is not only longevity, but the compensation of self-containment. "The marriage plot most novels depend on is about finding validation of one's uniqueness and importance by being singled out among all other women by a man."[10] Readers of novels live in melodramatic worlds that blind them to the economic dangers of heroineship:

The man's love is proof of the girl's value, and payment for it. Her search for perfect love through an incoherent, hostile wilderness of days is the plot that endows the aimless (life) with aim. Her quest is to be recognized in *all* her significance, to have her worth made real by being approved. When, at the end, this is done, she is transformed: her outward shape reflects her inner self, she is a bride, the very image of a heroine. For a heroine is just that, an image; novel heroines, like novel readers, are often women who want to become heroines. (p. xv)

Even though Brownstein's book makes delectable reading, and even though her critique of heterosexual ideology is partially right, she seems to read novels as if we find nothing in them but models for our own plots or characters. From this point of view, the novel is dangerous since "women who read have been inclined since the eighteenth century to understand one another, and men, and themselves, as characters in novels" (p. vviii).

For Myra Jehlen in "Archimedes and the Paradox of Feminist Criticism," the novel also means danger. Complicitous in middle-class norms, the novel reduces the collective and political dimensions of everyday life into individual psychomachias: "what is peculiar to this genre is that it locates the internal problems of its society still deeper inside, inside the self . . . this approach tends to vitiate the distinction between the private self and the world out there that is the powerful crux of middle-class identity."[11] Jehlen's argument is powerful: the novel is irresponsible because it refuses to see social problems in communal terms. Instead, political events are internalized; they become the responsibility of the individual soul. Like Brownstein, Jehlen wants to reduce the effects of the novel to the effects of its plot and to its reading of character: "it is women's ability to act in the public domain that novels suppress" (p. 90). Form is especially complicitous in this suppression: "I am suggesting that George Eliot was compelled by the form of her story to tell it as she did, that the novel as a genre precludes androgynously heroic women while and indeed *because* it demands androgynous heroes" (p. 92).

We should question the notion that the novel does one thing, that there is a single and heroine-centered way to read novels.[12] Of course, the insistence that we explain the novel in terms of its "unitary" structure has a long-lived tradition. For Dorothy Van Ghent in *The English Novel;*

a novel itself is one complex pattern, or Gestalt, made up of component ones. In it inhere such a vast number of traits, all organized in subordinate systems that function under the governance of a single meaningful structure, that the nearest similitude for a novel is a "world."[13]

Reading Brownstein and Jehlen we recognize that Van Ghent's assumptions about novelistic unity still have practical power. What has changed are her moral assumptions. For Van Ghent the novel must be an orderly unit: a "good novel is one that can be analyzed." In her literary universe, "the sound novel, like a sound world, has to hang together as one thing. It has to have integral structure" because "our only adequate preparation for judging a novel evaluatively is through the analytical testing of its unity . . . its ability to make us more aware of the meaning of our lives."[14] For Brownstein or Jehlen, it is the novel's resemblance to the "sound world"—especially its tendencies to mimic and reinforce the conservative impetus of this world—that is most suspect. The novel is dangerous precisely because it reinforces the conventional meanings of women's lives.

I have argued that the novel's form is more heterogeneous and dazzling in its subversiveness than Woolf, Brownstein, Jehlen, or Van Ghent admit. We could profit from a catastrophe theory of the novel—one that accounts for its appearance of linearity, but notices that novels are marked with caesuras, holes, pauses, shifts onto different ground. The novel is less about character or subordination or unity than it is a "field of force," an arena for the display of warring social formations.[15]

Although the language is Jameson's, the source for this argument is Mikhail Bakhtin, who argues that the novel is both heteroglossic (or many-voiced) and dialogic (that is, it permits and promotes a dialectical interaction between words, between styles, between points of view). The results can be radical:

The prose art presumes a deliberate feeling for the historical and social concreteness of living discourse, as well as its relativity, a feeling for its participation in historical becoming and in social struggle; it deals with discourse that is still warm from that struggle and hostility, as yet unresolved and still fraught with hostile intentions and accents; prose art finds discourse in this state and subjects it to the dynamic-unity of its own style.[16]

We see this dynamic in Lockwood's conversation with Cathy—his politeness is immediately evaluated and immersed in conflict. "Fraught with hostile intentions and accents," the novel is a genre that invites the novelist to conjoin disparate languages, to incorporate disruptive points of view. It offers a site of struggle and refuses to incorporate (without heteroglossia, without bombarding with dialogue) the structures of myth, religion, and other forms of patriarchal ideology. "The novel begins," Bakhtin says, "by presuming a verbal and semantic decentering of the ideological world, a certain linguistic homelessness of literary consciousness, which no longer possesses a sacrosanct and unitary linguistic medium for containing ideological thought" (p. 367). Lukacs shares this insistence on the novel's "linguistic" or "transcendental homelessness" in The Theory of the Novel, although to different ends.[17] We need to set this image of the novel's "transcendental homelessness"—its lack of mythic center and loss of a coherent world view—in dialogue with Woolf's image of the woman novelist's domestic spirit—her status as an interrupted artist who produces novels when she should be writing poems.

In emphasizing the scripture virtues of interruption and "homelessness" I do not wish to challenge Woolf's valiant theme: her argument that the woman writer requires an education, tradition, and room of her own. Nor do I wish to question Woolf's insistence that the middle-class writer's limited role—her socially inscribed need to provide continuity for her family—has been costly. What I wish to suggest is that while the novel may be produced within the materially continuous space of the sitting room, it is also a form that refuses contiguity with this space, that disrupts and permits women to violate socially prescribed roles by inviting their depiction of a range of responses to conventional problems. This is to reverse Woolf's thesis about the novel's interruptibility and to argue that the novel is an emancipatory form which permits the woman novelist to refuse and revise other literary genres.

The fact that the novelist conceives of her work in an atmosphere of disruption is, according to this thesis, entirely promising. It suggests a covert perception of writing as trespass, of writing as a force of interruption in which the ideas of "unity" or "the tradition" or even "the novel" are continually challenged by the alien rhythms of everyday life and the interrogative rhythms of the writer's own body.[18] The interruptions that Woolf describes as the source of the novel's benignity acquire the status of transgressions which the novelist must weave into the uneven textures of her work until what is challenged by this unevenness is the very idea of logocentrism, of any singular, patrilocal claim to truth. The rhythms of the interrupted woman writer preclude a naive participation or belief in novelistic unity, confirming Derrida's notion that

the idea of the book, which always refers to a natural totality, is profoundly alien to the sense of writing. It is the encyclopedic protection of theology and of logocentrism against the disruption of writing, against its aphoristic energy, and . . . against difference in general. If I distinguish the text from the book, I shall say that the destruction of the book, as it is now under way in all domains, denudes the surface of the text. That necessary violence responds to a violence that was no less necessary.[19]

Catherine Earnshaw's behavior in *Wuthering Heights* already calls the normative status of "the book" into question. Her marginal writing is the prototype of the novel as the site where violence surfaces, where the "aphoristic energy" of women's writing begins to usurp the encyclopedic grasp of the tradition itself.

To make this point more forcefully I want to compare three different genres by Emily Brontë in order to argue that the novel's formal properties place the nineteenth-century woman novelist at the locus of maximum struggle. We will examine a sampler Emily Brontë embroidered at the age of eleven, a poem written a year or two before *Wuthering Heights,* and then *Wuthering Heights* itself. Not surprisingly, the sampler (a variation on verses from the *Old Testament* and *The Book of Common Prayer)* provides no space for the proliferation of alien and contending points of view. It presents a form of single-voiced, authoritative discourse not refracted by other discourses. The poem, in contrast, *does* provide a space for this struggle, but while it is polyvocal, it is not dialogic; the multiple voices that come together in "The Philosopher's Conclusion" are not in conversation but are made to speak as one voice under enormous lyric pressure. In *Wuthering Heights,* however, Brontë seizes a form with an emancipatory dimension—the voices struggling to enter into productive dialogue in the poem come together but do not merge; they provide the reader with an opportunity to examine their own genesis. In *Wuthering Heights* Brontë uses shifting narrative patterns and shifting narrators to examine some of the material conditions that have given rise to the class and gender conflicts that the sampler and poem repress.

Brontë's sampler is a shocking piece of material culture. The sampler contains short quotations from the *Psalms, The Book of Common Prayer,* and *Proverbs.* The words of the proverb provide standard dicta; they are meant to emphasize the speaker's humility, and, in a voice like that of the whirlwind replying to Job, to remind us of God's greater power. But if we remember that these words have been copied painstakingly onto her sampler by an eleven-year-old-girl with a passion for writing, the words acquire another dimension. "The words of Agur, the son of Jakeh . . . Surely I am more brutish than any man." Not only does the sampler begin by invoking a male lineage, but the "brutishness" of the girl child who makes this sampler becomes a prohibition: "I neither learned wisdom nor have the knowledge of the holy . . . who hath gathered the wind in his fist? . . . Every word of God is pure . . . he is a shield unto them that / put their trust in him. Add thou not unto his words, / lest he reprove thee, and thou be found a liar."[20] This injunction against feminine speaking is not one Brontë followed, for she wrote copiously throughout most of her life. And yet the prohibition haunts Bronte's writing.

Brontë's sampler gives the moment when Lockwood attacks Cathy in *Wuthering Heights* a new resonance. While the neat, even stitches of the young seamstress's sampler counsel verbal humility, Emily Brontë imagines Catherine Earnshaw at a similar age devouring blank, open spaces. "Catherine's library was select,"

Lockwood observes. "Its state of dilapidation proved it to have been well used, though not altogether for a legitimate purpose; scarcely one chapter had escaped pen and ink commentary . . . covering every morsel of blank that the printer had left" (p. 62). But in the opening chapters of *Wuthering Heights,* Catherine pays for this marginalia with her blood. After reading Catherine Earnshaw's diaries, Lockwood dreams again. Terrified at the noise of a fir bough tapping against his window, Lockwood breaks the glass, but instead of the fir bough his "fingers closed on the fingers of a little, ice-cold hand!"

> The intense horror of nightmare came over me; I tried to draw back my arm, but the hand clung to it, and a most melancholy voice sobbed, "Let me in—let me in!"
> "Who are you?" I asked, struggling, meanwhile, to disengage myself.
> "Catherine Linton," it replied shiveringly. "I'm come home, I'd lost my way on the moor!"
> . . . . .
> As it spoke, I discerned, obscurely, a child's face looking through the window—terror made me cruel; and, finding it useless to attempt shaking the creature off, I pulled its wrist on to the broken pane, and rubbed it to and fro till the blood ran down and soaked the bedclothes: still it wailed, "Let me in!" and maintained its tenacious gripe, almost maddening me with fear. (p. 67)

This is a scene that male critics have found inexplicable in its violence. The usual explanation for this scene is that it *is* inexplicable, that we all hoard within us a primordial violence. But examining Bronte's transition from sampler to poem to novel will suggest another reading of this scene, one requiring us to rethink the relation of women's writing and violence.

If the novel offers a preliminary context in which we can criticize Lockwood, the sampler represents a context devoid of critique; it employs the abstracting power of an authoritative word— a word that claims to be hierarchically higher than its readers—a word permitting no play. This word demands unconditional allegiance. "Authoritative discourse permits no play with the context framing it, no play with its borders, no gradual and flexible transitions, no spontaneously creative stylizing variants on it," as Bakhtin says. "One must either totally affirm it or reject it."[21]

While needlepoint, quilting, and embroidery have been celebrated as part of a rediscovered female aesthetic, Brontë's sampler moves outside this aesthetic; its plain style leaves no room for female inscription. Already we can see a flexibility the novel allows that the "frame" of the sampler does not. Novels have margins for writing in, and they can provide images of such marginal writing. But the sampler ends with a *Gloria Patri:* "Ye saints on earth, ascribe, with heaven's high host, / Glory and honor to the One in Three; / To God the Father Son and Holy Ghost, / As was and is and evermore shall be." Not only is paternity the sampler's main theme, but the structuring of Brontë's script into neat rows of stitches prevents the intrusion of the disruptive female body. There is nothing in the making of this sampler, at least in its material workmanship, that tells us this seamstress is a "writing subject" at war with her culture's discourse. But if the frame of the sampler is limiting, Brontë goes beyond these limitations in a lyric poem that takes up the sampler's themes. "The Philosopher's Conclusion" plays with male voices; it trespasses in patriarchal territory and describes the crisis and contradiction that the sampler leaves out.

"The Philosopher's Conclusion" is a poem enormously at odds with itself, full of fragments and voices that collide as they speak. The poem opens with a death wish:

"Enough of Thought, Philosopher;
Too long hast thou been dreaming
Unlightened, in this chamber drear
While summer's sun is beaming—
Space-sweeping soul, what sad refrain
Concludes thy musings once again?"[22]

The poem begins with an echo of "Expostulation and Reply," but the poem soon veers from the sunlit dialogues of Wordsworth's conversation poems toward a demonic landscape whose speaker is homeless and alienated. The voices expressing this alienation seem out of control. Stanza two echoes the helpless prettiness of Wordsworth's Lucy poems *("O for the time when I shall sleep / Without identity, / And never care how rain may steep / Or snow may cover me!"*), while stanza three echoes the booming tones of Milton's Satan:

> "No promised Heaven, these wild Desires
> Could all or half fulfil;
> No threatened Hell, with quenchless fires,
> Subdue this quenchless will!"   (ll. 7–14)

Whereas the sampler restricted the range and multivocality of woman's speech, in the poem this same speech goes berserk. The speaker imagines herself as an incongruous amalgam of Wordsworth's male speaker, of Lucy, and of Milton's rebellious archangel. The combination is especially unsettling because these contrasting voices never turn toward one another. Instead, the speaker's frenetic energy spills into another persona:

> —So said I, and still say the same;
> —Still to my Death will say—
> Three Gods within this little frame
> Are warring night and day.   (ll. 15–18)

The poem glosses its own predicament. These gods are the Romantic trinity: Milton, Wordsworth, and Coleridge. But they are also the Holy Trinity of the sampler. The "One in Three" reappear as warring gods trapped within the speaker's body, and in the "little frame" of her poem as well. While there is no description of this "war" in the sampler itself, within the frame of the poem this struggle is both named and located; the poem sets up the conditions for its own critique. But this epic battle collapses into lyric defeat:

> Heaven could not hold them all, and yet
> They all are held in me
> And must be mine till I forget
> My present entity.
>
> O for the time when in my breast
> Their struggles will be o'er;
> O for the day when I shall rest,
> And never suffer more!   (ll. 19–26)

This loss and suffering is compounded; the poet does not give authority over these three warring gods to her speaker, but to a

masculine spirit. Under his authorship, the body language repressed
in the sampler begins to flow freely.

"I saw a spirit standing, Man
Where thou dost stand—an hour ago;
And round his feet, three rivers ran
Of equal depth and equal flow—

"A Golden stream, and one like blood
And one like Sapphire, seemed to be,
But where they joined their triple flood
It tumbled in an inky sea."

Once again, the poem heaves toward a subversive description of
the female poet's trauma as the three gods are transformed into
fecund rivers that speak, subliminally, of female blood and excre-
ment. But these rivers are controlled by a spirit who bleaches their
potential for healthy defilement of the tradition. As the spirit assim-
ilates the "inky sea" into dazzling light, the only space left for the
poem's speaker is in the blank margins.

"The Spirit bent his dazzling gaze
Down on that Ocean's gloomy night,
Then—kindling all with sudden blaze,
The glad deep sparkled wide and bright—
White as the sun; far, far more fair
Than the divided sources were! "   (ll.
27–40)

The precursor poem for these stanzas is Coleridge's
"Kubla Khan." In Brontë's poem the "inky sea" replaces Coleridge's
"sunless sea" and "Alph" is replaced by rivers that begin to be
heard, like the shimmering voices of "Kubla Khan," "prophecying
war." But in "The Philosopher's Conclusion" this "war" is dis-
couraged by the unifying obsession of the Coleridgean "Spirit." The
speaker turns her attention to the panacea of a masculine muse.

—And even for that Spirit, Seer,
I've watched and sought my lifetime long;
Sought him in Heaven, Hell, Earth and Air,
An endless search—and always wrong!

Had I but seen his glorious eye
Once light the clouds that 'wilder me,
I ne'er had raised this coward cry
To cease to think and cease to be—

I ne'er had called oblivion blest,
Nor stretching eager hands to Death
Implored to change for lifeless rest
This sentient soul, this living breath.

O let me die, that power and will
Their cruel strife may close,
And vanquished Good, victorious Ill
Be lost in one repose.   (ll. 41–56)

If, in the first half of "The Philosopher's Conclusion" we witness an incipient war between the personae of Lucy, Satan, Wordsworth's expostulatory speaker, and the poet of "Kubla Khan," in the last half of the poem we witness a discrepancy between what Brontë and Coleridge feel they are entitled to say as poets; between what the male poet of the nineteenth century can do *with* his muse and what his female counterpart must do *for* hers. For male poets the muse is enabling, a liminal figure who presides over the poem's birth, but in Brontë's poem the speaker feels powerless in relation to her muse.[23]

As we have seen, this presiding spirit stands above three rivers—of gold, of sapphire, and one "like blood"—and as they tumble into the "inky sea" of the poem, he kindles this chaos into a light which whitens with his gaze. He has the power to unify this cacophonous mixture of voices, to hear and aestheticize Brontë's bickering gods. But this unification is precisely what repulses the combat that might give Brontë's poem political clout. Under the gaze of this male spirit, the speaker alienates herself from the sources of creative power; she controls neither the seminal nor menstrual fluids of poetry which flood toward him in rivers of gold, sapphire, and blood: stunning sources of erotic and cosmic energy. Because the gender boundaries of Coleridge's poem remain unchanged in Brontë's verse, this masculine spirit will not function as Brontë's muse; her speaker's "coward cry" emerges as a pallid version of Coleridge's grandiose wishfulness. Deprived of the "divided sources" she needs to fuel her combat with a misogynous tradition, her voice finally collapses. Why does Brontë capitulate to the worst of Coleridge's terms?

With its sweet ironic voices, its exquisite seriousness, its binary frame of reference, its insistence on unity, the frame of the traditional lyric poem can be restricting for the woman writer. Coleridge depends on the cooption of the Abyssinian maid and of the woman wailing for her demon lover for his poem's eroticism: "Could I revive within me / Her symphony and song . . . I would build that dome in air." In the lyric's miniature space epic moments are built upon women's bodies, while the opportunity for a woman writer to enter into great debate with oppressive social and literary forces is paradoxically miniaturized.[24] Since the voices she inherits from the tradition are already written upon, already "mastered," the woman writer requires a scriptive context inviting the explosion of this mastery. Within the lyric's small compass, these inherited voices may remain unitary, intact, closed off to further debate. As we saw in the analysis of the bilingual heroine in chapter 2, the refraction of voices that women inherit from the tradition is often a dialectical process requiring multiple voices and multiple situations of rupture or dialogue for its success. Thus in "The Philosopher's Conclusion" Brontë acknowledges that the "laws" of these voices are in conflict with the desires of her female speaker, but she does not discover a context for prolonging this conflict; in reevoking the gender boundaries that deflect subversive desires, the speaker also gives into them. She barely begins to challenge the Romantic order she has inherited when the lyric's demand for self-identity intervenes; the poem can go no further than acknowledging this speaker's misery within this tradition, its complicity with her own death wish.[25]

The problem with working in the lyric mode (the mode as it was still conceived by Emily Brontë), is that Brontë feels an overpowering need to break this framework in some epic way, but has no form for such pyrotechnics; epic rupture is not yet encoded in the lyric form. But this rupture is precisely what the female poet needs to have her vision; she needs to break the sampler—shatter its frame, to splinter the coherence of the masculine tradition.

Now we can turn again to Woolf's question—why did these nineteenth-century women write novels?—and speculate that within the English tradition the lyric poem, for all its gorgeous attentiveness to the painful desires and limits of a culturally constructed "I," also denies its female speaker (until, let us say, the poetry of Emily Dickinson) formal access to the shifting voices, the plural perspectives, the openness to dialogue among diverse points of view that are necessarily in debate with one another in the invention of a female tradition. But the novel offers, in simple spatial terms, a place where the novelist can work with these voices over time and from a variety of angles—not to solve them, but to problematize them, to put them into process; the novel (by virtue of its multivoicedness, its strategies of interruption, and its long-windedness) multiplies its own spaces of volatility and transformation.[26]

Thus in *Wuthering Heights,* Brontë's conversation with her culture is not conveyed in isolated fragments, as it is in the frame of her poem—but projected into the voices of characters who are at war with one another—or with the frame of the novel itself. As a place of dialogism, parody, and laughter, the novel admits a new intersection of body and text, provides another way to rupture the authoritative, the normative, the social.

In coming back to Virginia Woolf's preoccupation with novelistic unity, we should also notice that Woolf undervalues the disruptive power of the novel form.[27] In analyzing *Jane Eyre,* she is critical of Charlotte Brontë's descriptions of Jane's visits to the airy rooftop—especially the passage where Jane expresses her longing "for a power of vision which might overpass that limit; which might reach the busy world, towns, regions full of life I had heard of but never seen." Jane's longing is followed by a change of tone, an insistence that "women feel just as men feel; they need exercise for their faculties and a field for their efforts as much as their brothers do." Woolf notes that this transition seems odd, even in the autobiographical context of Jane's narrative. It seems to come out of nowhere, as does Jane's abrupt reversion to storytelling: "When thus alone I not unfrequently heard Grace Poole's laugh."[28]

Woolf deplores this break in Brontë's style: "That is an awkward break, I thought. It is upsetting to come upon Grace Poole all of a sudden. The continuity is disturbed." While in Woolf's view Brontë has more genius than Austen, her indignation mars this genius—"one sees that she will never get her genius expressed whole and entire. Her books will be deformed and twisted. She will write in a rage where she should write calmly" (pp. 72–73).

I have suggested that the novel's advantage to the woman writer is precisely the fact that it promotes such deformity; Charlotte Brontë can say startling and audacious things about the relation of men and women, and then underscore their audacity with the madwoman's laughter, without losing the audience that needs to hear these ideas. While Woolf agrees that the central thing about the novel is its antagonism and complexity, she goes on to question whether Brontë's gender has interfered with her "integrity" as a novelist: "that integrity which I take to be the backbone of the writer" (p. 76). According to Woolf, this integrity is fundamental; in letting her private anger into this story, Brontë loses her audience: "Her imagination swerved from indignation and we feel its swerve" (p. 76). But the novel is precisely the form that allows the "swerve" to happen, the extraneous feeling to intrude. Far from marring, this openness to other voices gives the novel its special intensity and makes it one of those forms in which women can contend with the "systematically distorted" discourse of the tradition.

But how does the laughter with which *Wuthering Heights* opens count as one of these intrusions? Earlier I cited Kristeva's notion that "laughter is what lifts inhibitions by breaking through prohibition . . . to introduce the aggressive, violent, liberating drive."[29] In looking at Brontë's poem and sampler we have seen small space for this liberation. Both the sampler maker and the female lyric poet need a form that can better express drives directed against the authority of the dominant culture. But in *Wuthering Heights* Brontë starts with parody, with "an irruption of the drives against symbolic prohibition."[30] Once Lockwood is deauthorized, a second prohibition is lifted as the conflict between male authority and female script suddenly becomes visible in the scene in Catherine Earnshaw's bedroom where Lockwood grabs her hand and rubs it back and forth on the broken glass until her blood soaks the bedclothes. In the poem these female fluids are contained, bleached out. But the novel runs with a river of female blood—and gives us a vision of gender antipathy which is also a critique of the arbitrary power that even insipid male authority figures have to control, sadistically, the flow of this blood.

The multivoiced chambers of the novel reveal that this sadism comes, above all, from a fear of the intrusive, interrogatory power of female texts. For when we examine this scene from the perspective of Emily Brontë's childish sampler and the injunction it contains against female writing, Lockwood's attack on the hand that clasps his own is doubly macabre. "Some were detached sentences," Lockwood says of Catherine's writings, while "other parts took the form of a regular diary, scrawled in an unformed, childish hand" (p. 62). The phantom hand that Lockwood rubs back and forth in the broken window is also the "hand" that adds words to the blanks in other men's books. What Lockwood is afraid of is a "scratching" sound outside the window, a noise quite like writing, and a "hand" he has witnessed before.

Because we have laughed at Lockwood, his cruelty is not naturalized; the novel takes on the problems of poem and sampler as wound. And as this mad "scene of writing" continues, it is clear that Catherine's writing is feared because it is powerful; her words acquire a threatening life of their own. Snatching his hand through the hole he has made in the window, Lockwood panics:

I . . . hurriedly piled the books up in a pyramid against it and stopped my ears to exclude the lamentable prayer.
". . . Begone!" I shouted, "I'll never let you in, not if you beg for twenty years."
. . . . .
"It's twenty years," mourned the voice, "twenty years, I've been a waif for twenty years."
Thereat began a feeble scratching outside, and the pile of books moved as if thrust forward. (p. 67)

Catherine's weird scratching, her writing from the "wild zone" outside the window, has the power to move these books in a new direction, to thrust against the thrust of Lockwood's exclusion. And, I have argued, this thrust is the special gift of the novel. For if in Brontë's poem the "frame" or structure or gender limit that the sampler enacts is brought *into* the text and made problematic—still, the poem describes and enacts its own impotence to overthrow this limit. But in *Wuthering Heights* this same frame or limit is brought into the text and this "inside" is challenged and crossed; the novel marks, again and again, an "ideological tearing" in its own social fabric.

I have argued that *Wuthering Heights* begins with the voice of a male narrator who is both cruel and silly, whom we immediately discredit as an authoritative voice because the passage from poetry to novel, from high seriousness to incipient laughter, forces us to experience those sides of the object (in this case Lockwood's misogyny and Catherine's powerfulness) that are not ordinarily glossed in a "high" genre or style. But I will also grant that once the authoritative masculine voice is parodied, the patriarchal voices conspiring against the woman writer remain as cruel as they have been in Brontë's earlier texts. This misogynous gesture is nonetheless emancipatory. The social and literary frameworks supporting male authority have been shattered by a form of multivocality that puts into question the binary opposition Brontë's poem takes for granted. Brontë's text is now open to a new sort of movement, to a practice that splits the subject open and reveals the cultural formations through which this subject has been produced.

We must press this reading one step further, for the theory of novel production I am espousing stands at one remove from Bakhtin's theories of "dialogism." While in *The Political Unconscious* Jameson describes the novel as something that happens to its primary materials, as a process rather than a form,[31] I would add that the novel not only goes to work on its primary materials, but itself becomes a primary material that its own succeeding chapters respond to and revise. We need to supplement a dialogic theory of the novel with a reading of narrative that emphasizes other modes of struggle. Kristeva's *Revolution in Poetic Language* offers such emphasis.

According to Kristeva our usual ways of reading prevent us from seeing that what we read is continually moving toward the outer limits of social and textual practice:

Our philosophies of language, embodiments of the Idea, are nothing more than the thoughts of archivists, archaeologists, and necrophiliacs. Fascinated by the remains of a process which is partly discursive, they substitute this fetish for what actually produced it. (p. 13)

Most analyses of texts are narratives of "the sleeping body"—they look for meaning by examining this body "in repose, withdrawn from its socio-historical imbrication, removed from direct experience." Kristeva insists that this "sleeping body"

points toward a truth, namely, that the kind of activity encouraged and privileged by (capitalist) society represses the *process* pervading the body and the subject, and that we must therefore break out of our interpersonal and intersocial experience if we are to gain access to what is repressed in the social mechanism: the generating of signifiance. (p. 13)

The text, for her, is not "an archive of structures" but a practice "involving the sum of unconscious, subjective, and social relations in gestures of confrontation and appropriation, destruction and construction—productive violence" (p. 16).

If we follow this logic and examine the novel as process rather than form, we can no longer read the scene where Lockwood rubs Cathy's wrist on the broken glass as a simple expression of Brontë's anxieties about female authorship.[32] The scene is cathartic, but this catharsis can only occur because Brontë has parodied and deauthorized Lockwood, creating a new space for exploring the struggle between a masculine narrator whose authority has been challenged by laughter, and a demonic figure of female powerfulness who is trying to get back into the house of fiction to rewrite herself and the culture that excludes and confines her. When she reenters this house she does not come back as Lucy or as Catherine Earnshaw, but as Nelly Dean.

Why Nelly Dean? If Brontë's novel is as subversive as I am suggesting, why give its narration to a character, even to a female character, who is complicitous in the separation of Cathy and Heathcliff? Once again the text is operating on itself as primary material and putting into process what the earlier machinations of plot have uncovered. In order to preserve this process as process, to construct a text that remains involved in social struggle, the author must not only "introduce the violent, liberating drive," but also avoid the creation of a strong "focal point of transference" that would lock the text "into an identification that can do no more than adapt the subject to social and family structures." By keeping the text in Nelly's hands rather than Catherine's or Heathcliff's, Brontë changes the cathexis; as Kristeva's theory implies, she allows the particular ideologies (in this case those of class and gender) "that preoccupy the social group" reading the novel to be "put into play" by the very processes "of the subject they wanted to ignore" (p. 209).

For Kristeva "poetic language" is that discourse that captures, contains, and uses the alinguistic rhythms of the body to put the subject—and the social structure constructing that subject—into process. This process also works in the novel. While this process becomes the site where the text does its "work," at the same time the text needs a site of identification for its disruptiveness to be effective:

There is a strange problem in the way laughter works: the ego that laughs through the irruption of the drive charge tearing open the symbolic, is not the one that observes and knows. In order to make the irruptive charge pass into discourse . . . the instigator of laughter must bind or re-bind the charge. (p. 224)

After demonic laughter releases a charge—a forceful critique of Lockwood's highbrow paternalism—in Brontë's early chapters, Nelly Dean's role as narrator is to "re-bind" this charge, but in a particular way. Nelly is the only female character in *Wuthering Heights* who can continue speaking from Catherine's position outside the window. As Jane Gallop explains in *The Daughter's Seduction,* the "maid" is someone who exists both inside and outside the family. In Freud's

Dora "the nurse is desirable; her alterity is a stimulus, a tension.
. . . Her alterity is not just her femininity, not even just her not
belonging to the family, it is her not belonging to the same economic
class. It is not enough to seduce her. She must be expelled from
the family."[33] Nelly Dean is also expelled—but this expulsion has
a narrative as well as a social purpose. Brontë's novel makes use
of the nurse's ambivalent status. As Gallop explains: "For the analysis
to pass out of the imaginary, it must pass through a symbolic third
term—like 'des femmes' on the cover of Cixous's *Portrait de Dora,*
a term that represents a class" (p. 148).

To say that Nelly represents this third term is not to
idealize her character or her position in the novel as a member of
the "working class." Nelly is a rather charmless woman whose self-
effacement cannot hide the grudges she holds against all her "fam-
ilies." But these grudges are justified. Nelly is a sibling who is denied
siblinghood; a surrogate mother whose motherhood is denied, a
worker whose labor is undervalued. She is in the perfect position
to reintroduce disturbing drives into the narrative while holding these
drives in check. As Kristeva explains, "under the pleasing exterior
of a very socially acceptable differentiation, art reintroduces into
society fundamental rejection, which is matter in the process of
splitting" (p. 180).[34] Nelly combines this pleasing exterior with a
"fundamental rejection" of others and of her own "pleasing" role.

This ambivalent reading of Nelly is not the usual view.
For Van Ghent, Nelly provides a civil ground for the novel's inci-
vilities: "set over against the wilderness of inhuman reality is the
quietly secular, voluntarily limited, safely human reality that we find
in the gossipy concourse of Nelly Dean and Lockwood, the one an
old family servant with a strong grip on the necessary emotional
economies that make life endurable, the other a city visitor in the
country" who protects himself from "the insentient wild flux of
nature."[35] Juliet Mitchell stresses the continuity Nelly's presence
provides: "this second narrator is the nurse and this allows for a
continuity of insight which a description of the disruptions to their
growth experienced by the main characters would forbid."[36] My
suggestion is that Nelly offers a second ground for disruption; her
position within the novel as servant and female means that she

introduces a heterogeneity into the social structure that the reader at once registers and tries to repress.

In the opening scenes of *Wuthering Heights* Brontë has already admitted this "heterogeneous element" into her text. She challenges male authority by enacting a scene of crisis in which a pusillanimous male figure punishes a female figure for writing. "Textuality" repulses as ink turns to blood. But in this repulsion there is also relief; the dream-work of the text acknowledges the hierarchical violence of gender relations and one form of repression is lifted. As Kristeva writes in *Revolution in Poetic Language,*

in every kind of society and situation, the text's function is therefore to lift the repression that weighs heavily on this moment of struggle, one that particularly threatens or dissolves the bond between subject and society, but simultaneously creates the conditions for its renewal. (p. 27)

How is the text able to lift this moment of repression and permit the specular moment when the struggle between genders becomes visible?

Wuthering Heights' violence is usually ascribed to Cathy's and Heathcliff's passion. Their unworldly love is the source of the novel's amoral splendor: "the dramatic figures that Emily Brontë uses . . . are figures that arise on and enact their drama on some ground of the psychic life where ethical ideas are not at home."[37] But I am suggesting that we must also locate a "productive violence" in the novel's operations on its own materials, on those processes that allow Brontë to attack her anxieties about male authority and authorship and to refigure them.

If this sounds like Gilbert and Gubar's reading of *Wuthering Heights,* it should, for I am indebted to them. But I want to conclude this chapter by making a series of distinctions that will separate my reading of Brontë's novel from Gilbert and Gubar's in *The Madwoman in the Attic,* Jameson's in *The Political Unconscious,* and Eagleton's in *Myths of Power: A Marxist Study of the Brontës.*

In Gilbert and Gubar's provocative chapter on *Wuthering Heights* the authors operate under a certain constraint. In order to make their particular argument about the woman writer's "anxiety of authorship" fit Brontë's novel, Gilbert and Gubar feel the need to locate a symbol system in the book that will represent this anxiety. To produce this system they transform Heathcliff into another version of the madwoman and thus into an avatar of Emily Brontë's own psyche rather than locating this anxiety as an emotion in transit which changes as Brontë's text begins to work upon itself as a "primary material." "Despite his outward masculinity, Heathcliff is somehow female in his monstrosity . . . 'female'—on the level where younger sons and bastards and devils unite with women in rebelling against the tyranny of heaven."[38]

All of us, at one time or another, have identified with Heathcliff's victimization, with his gorgeous, sadistic rage, but Gilbert and Gubar must push this identification very far, indeed, to argue that women's writing in the nineteenth century is part of an effort to excavate a "real self buried beneath the copy selves" that Western society imposes on women.[39] Gilbert and Gubar deny the paradoxical reality of Heathcliff's character, namely, his emergence within the text as a predatory consumer of women who has, himself, been consumed.

In contrast, Jameson explores Heathcliff's ambiguous position as heroic protagonist and Byronic villain in Marxist terms.

Heathcliff is the locus of *history* in this romance; his mysterious fortune marks him as a protocapitalist, in some other place, absent from the narrative, which then recodes the new economic energies as sexual passion. The aging Heathcliff then constitutes the narrative mechanism whereby the alien dynamism of capitalism is reconciled with the im- memorial (and cyclical) time of the agricultural life of a country squire- dom.[40]

Both readings are brilliant, yet neither seems quite right, for just as Jameson's reading fails to account for the novel's dislocations, its switching of time frames and its eery, inexplicable opening, so Gilbert and Gubar's reading makes the book homogeneous with itself; the problems in chapter eight are a mirror image of the predicaments of chapter one. I would argue, instead, for a reading of *Wuthering Heights* that is heterogeneous and dialectical, a reading, like Jameson's, that makes the material contradictions of the novel problematic, and, like Gilbert and Gubar's, that makes Brontë's position as woman novelist one of the novel's chief contradictions. This reading would locate the trauma and reenactment of the woman writer's anxiety of authorship in the beginning of the book—explicitly in the scene I have glossed several times in which Lockwood cuts Cathy's hand. If we read this scene as gothic and parodic, as a tragic exegesis of masculine power which is, at the same time, a weirdly comic expulsion of this power, we have begun to account for several items most critics of the novel ignore: 1) the novel's opening humor, 2) the novel's preoccupation with class, and 3) the novel's shift from a masculine to a feminine narrator. We can also insist that the female narrator Brontë turns to is not simply an avatar of Brontë herself, but a troubled female voice riven by power asymmetries of both class and gender.

This brings me to the critique of Eagleton's analysis of *Wuthering Heights* in *Myths of Power*. Like Jameson, Eagleton focuses on what Emily Brontë's novel tells us about class politics, but his sympathy is so entirely with Heathcliff that Eagleton betrays his insistence that we must analyze the socially determined strata of the novel. He says that Catherine's choice between Heathcliff and Edgar Linton is "the pivotal event of the novel, the decisive catalyst of the tragedy. . . . In a crucial act of self-betrayal and bad faith, Catherine rejects Heathcliff as a suitor because he is socially inferior to Linton; and it is from this that the train of destruction follows."[41] But one of the odd characteristics of Brontë's novel, as Hillis Miller points out, is that it refuses to let us discover such a chain of causality.[42] Once Cathy is "captured" by the gender and class position of "young lady" that so bedazzles her, Heathcliff is equally "captured" by the dream of becoming a rapaciously self-made man, in order to "even" the class/gender asymmetries that separate them. Heathcliff leaves the Heights, and engages in a mysterious adventure of self-creation, since it is the prerogative of his gender to install itself in violent positions of owning people and property. He then returns to take up the story with Cathy again.

The fairy-tale ambience surrounding both Catherine's transformation into a lady and Heathcliff's into a rapacious protocapitalist points to the essentially "magical" status that class and gender asymmetry have acquired in Brontë's society. No one questions the validity of these transformations, for in the world of the novel there are no other rites of passage available to men or to women. Gender and class asymmetries are bound together with invisible ideological chains—a movement in one direction (discovering the idealized role of "lady") initiates an opposite movement in the same direction (discovering the lucrative role of capitalist landlord). Amidst this tumult of social formations and their discontents, Nelly Dean occupies a peculiar position that Eagleton's male-identified analysis ignores. Eagleton's sympathy with Heathcliff is too wholehearted:

Heathcliff's presence is radically gratuitous; the arbitrary, unmotivated event of his arrival at the Heights offers its inhabitants a chance to transcend the constrictions of their self-enclosed social structure and gather him in. . . . He is ushered into the Heights for no good reason other than to be arbitrarily loved. . . . Nelly hates him at first, unable to transcend her bigotry against the new and non-related."[43]

But Eagleton never asks why Nelly herself is not "ushered into the Heights . . . to be arbitrarily loved." Nelly hates Heathcliff because he is someone like herself—a person from outside the family, who is suddenly invited in, but on radically different terms from her own. The only way to make the inequalities of her status vis-á-vis Heathcliff's invisible again is to get rid of Heathcliff, which is exactly what Nelly tries to do.

Through the agency of Nelly Dean, Brontë expresses and exposes the absurdly tangled material or "objective" relations among economic classes and between men and women that have led not only to Cathy's marginal status and to Heathcliff's negative power, but to Nelly Dean's exclusion from economic and sexual scenes of power as well.[44] This is to say that Brontë's novel first sets up and then begins (especially in those scenes where Nelly describes Cathy's and Heathcliff's quick and fabulous initiations into the dynamics of class and gender) to explore the genesis of its own ideological limitations. This exploration is enabled by the novel's excitable form. Its writers may find themselves interrupted, but this interruption becomes the source of interrogation and laughter, the moment when broken form becomes force.

SEVEN

Toward a Theory of Play

The preceding chapters offer a reconstruction of textual moments in which women writers have met the forces of the dominant culture "with cunning and high spirits."[1] In this chapter I want to theorize these moments more explicitly by developing a theory of the woman writer at play. To theorize the woman writer's playfulness is to discover a language and set of practices that help us understand moments in women's texts we have overlooked because we lacked a framework or set of metaphors to encourage their description. It is my conviction that the feminist critic does not have enough linguistic practices—in the form of either metaphors or theories— to describe sites of mobility and freedom in women's texts. One way to gather these metaphors is to reevaluate the almost invisible uses to which ordinary practices like dialogue and novelization are put in women's writing. In theorizing "play" as an important activity of the woman writer at "work," I am looking for another descriptive category that will clarify the ways in which the woman writer introduces "free" energy into the "bound" energy of her culture's texts.

In search of such a theory, the preceding analysis of *Wuthering Heights* has brought us to the carnival beginnings of the novel, to laughter and the literary devices of parody and the carnivalesque: devices through which what is "high" and "superior" is made low and made laughable. En route to a theory of play should we also consider the woman writer's relation to carnival?

According to Mikhail Bakhtin the joyful relativity of the carnival world is engendered by laughter—a laughter that degrades, that materializes. As we saw in *Wuthering Heights,* this degradation through laughter has a healing capacity. But Bakhtin describes this degradation in terms of the low cultural status of the feminine body. "To degrade an object," as Bakhtin says, "does not imply merely hurling it into the void of nonexistence, into absolute destruction, but to hurl it down to the reproductive lower stratum, the zone in which conception and a new birth take place. Grotesque realism knows no other lower level; it is the fruitful earth and the womb. It is always conceiving."[2] These metaphors make sense to Bakhtin on the most primitive of biological levels—in describing the writing of men. But if to laugh—or write—is to hurl oneself and one's symbolic objects into the womb, to inseminate with laughter, then what about women's writing, how are we to describe with any pleasure our entry into the carnival of fiction?

Although a "feminist" answer to this question should begin by refusing Bakhtin's misogynist themes, in "The Laugh of the Medusa" Hélène Cixous does neither. She says that women should locate their writing, their laughter, where men have always located it: in the bodies of women. "Text my body—shot through with streams of song. . . . We will rethink womankind beginning with every form and every period of her body."[3] For Cixous, woman's body is already script or text, but rather than lamenting its overinscription Cixous asks women to write more, to rename and reimagine at its very source the relation of body to writing. The woman as writer "is never far from 'mother' (I mean outside her role functions: the 'mother' as nonname and as source of goods). There is always within her at least a little of that good mother's milk. She writes in white ink" (p. 251). And if the breast is to be imaged as verbal profusion, the genitals give even more:

Let the priests tremble, we're going to show them our sexts!
Too bad for them if they fall apart upon discovering that women aren't men, or that the mother doesn't have one. But isn't this fear convenient for them? Wouldn't the worst be, isn't the worst, in truth, that women aren't castrated, that they have only to stop listening to the Sirens (for the Sirens were men) for history to change its meaning? (p. 255)

Cixous' playful emphasis on woman as body and on writing as the exuberant expression of this body, on the laughter of women's genitals, on speech as milk, has seemed regressive—even dangerous—to those feminist theorists who argue that women need to separate speech and erogeny, since the woman writer has been immobilized by her culture's eroticization of the feminine body. But "The Laugh of the Medusa" risks this awkward terrain for good reason. Cixous' essay is deliberately written in the carnival mode; her writing encourages the loosening of old semiotic barriers; she insists that her reader be preoccupied simultaneously with language, with masculine myths about the bodily lower strata, and with laughter.

Men say that there are two unrepresentable things: death and the feminine sex. That's because they need femininity to be associated with death; it's the jitters that give them a hard-on! for themselves! They need to be afraid of us. Look at the trembling Perseuses moving backward toward us, clad in apotropes. What lovely backs! Not another minute to lose. Let's get out of here. (p. 255)

Derisive, abusive, offensive, Cixous brings her "conversation down to a strongly emphasized bodily level of food, drink, digestion, and sexual life," as do the clowns Bakhtin describes in *Rabelais* as typical of carnival and carnival writing: "One of the main attributes of the medieval clown was precisely the transfer of every high ceremonial gesture or ritual to the material sphere" (p. 20). Cixous shares with Emily Brontë an interest in the parodic and the grotesque. As Bakhtin reminds us: "not only parody in its narrow sense but all the other forms of grotesque realism degrade, bring down to earth, turn their subject into flesh" (p. 20).

If Cixous' bawdy, bodily language is designed to startle and amuse, to disrupt the status quo, to repolemicize our thinking about the relationship between philosophy, writing, and physicality, "The Laugh of the Medusa" is also, and seriously, an essay that has designs upon our reading of language as such. Cixous not only appropriates the carnival mode from men, but she invents new language games for women to play.[4] In Cixous' writing it is language itself (the "mad word," the "steed," or "barge") that is carnivalized—

language that is revealed in its sensuality and materiality, that must become carnal. It is not that language is returned to the body, but that the body is returned to language itself.[5]

Cixous plays fast and loose with the old dualities; in her texts we no longer see the world in terms of an opposition between a transcendent realm of language or culture and an immanent, degraded realm of the flesh. "And why don't you write? Write! Writing is for you, you are for you; your body is yours, take it. I know why you haven't written. (And why I didn't write before the age of twenty-seven.) Because writing is at once too high, too great for you, it's reserved for the great—that is for 'great men' " (p. 246). In puncturing these scribal myths, Cixous asks us to see that language has a material presence, that it is allied with our physical being. And in unmasking this alliance, Cixous challenges the central hierarchies or gender myths of our culture in which women are associated with nature while men "appear to have two natures as against women's single one." According to Mary O'Brien, woman's nature has always appeared to be different from "the Nature of Man" because her body is defined as *the* body while man's nature "transcends" the biological. The result, for women, is loss of prestige, power, self-esteem. "Idealist concepts of Man are concepts about this free-floating second nature, which, through the artificially created realms of civility, of politics, of philosophy, and, above all, of freedom, has transcended the contingencies of biological being."[6] While Bakhtin's ideas of carnival and carnivalesque writing insist on these divisions between culture and nature by describing a return from transcendence to immanence, from artifice to bios, from masculinity to femininity, Cixous collapses these categories. She refuses to acknowledge the myth of a "free-floating second nature," and she refuses the ideal of transcendence. Language is not a separate category, a region free from bios, nor is writing a practice to which women must "aspire." In fact, the reverse is true. For woman to produce a narrative that challenges present hierarchies and creates a space for their remaking, not only her body with its already vivid lower strata must be reimagined, not only the inseminated womb, or the female genitals, but "patriarchal" language itself must be given a new dimension, must be brought back to earth and made playful.

In this chapter I want to explore the implications of a "poetics" of play for women's writing. Cixous has said that the feminine writing of the future will be profuse, physical, utopian: "A woman's body, with its thousand and one thresholds of ardor—once, by smashing yokes and censors, she lets it articulate the profusion of meanings that run through it in every direction—will make the old single-grooved mother tongue reverberate with more than one language" (p. 256). But in describing the ways in which this multivocal writing occurs as an emergent or preemergent structure in eighteenth- and nineteenth-century women's writing, I have both celebrated Cixous' multivocality and challenged her vision of history. Now I want to suggest that one of the reasons we have not theorized this emergence is that we lack a feminist theory of play.[7]

There are good reasons to resist such a theory. First, play is regarded in our culture as a lesser impulse; defining a theory of women at play may look like a step backwards, an insistence that women rejoin the "weak." According to Arendt, labor is always regarded in our culture as superior to play:

All serious activities, irrespective of their fruits, are called labor, and every activity which is not necessary either for the life of the individual or for the life process of society is subsumed under playfulness. . . . The playfulness of the artist is felt to fulfil the same function in the laboring life process of society as the playing of tennis or the pursuit of a hobby fulfils in the life of the individual.[8]

Playfulness is associated with the apolitical, the acultural, with escape from the most productive of social constraints. "By relying on postures and possibilities already marked as feminine, women risk their own disempowerment," Linda Singer explains, "since those gestures are likely to be read as indications of the weakness with which women are already associated, and thus to be unthreatening to the strong."[8]

The second reason to resist a feminist theory of play is that most theorists have emphasized play's normative function.

They say that play helps the player adjust his or her subjectivity to social norms. In his famous essay on Balinese cockfighting Clifford Geertz explains that cockfighting is a game that

makes nothing happen. Men go on allegorically humiliating one another and being allegorically humiliated by one another, day after day. . . . *But no one's status really changes.* . . .

. . . Its function, if you want to call it that, is interpretive: it is a Balinese reading of Balinese experience, a story they tell themselves about themselves.[10]

Freud is even more explicit about the imitative nature of play:

It is clear that in their play children repeat everything that has made a great impression on them in real life, and that in doing so they abreact the strength of the impression and, as one might put it, make themselves master of the situation. But on the other hand it is obvious that all their play is influenced by a wish . . . to be grown-up and to be able to do what grown-up people do.[11]

In play children both anticipate their acquisition of adult powerfulness and relieve inner tensions by turning upon other children and exacting revenge for their powerlessness. In this view play allows children to rehearse the serious games of their parents and to negotiate symbolic transformations of unruly feeling states. In playing each child adjusts herself to social expectations and does not change those expectations to fit her own needs.

For Freud and Geertz play is a force that socializes and makes transgression safe; it sanctions the expression of hostilities in a context that reinstates repressions rather than questioning them. For example, in Lucille Clifton's "Admonitions" we see how, within the context of women's writing, Freud's and Geertz's theories might form the basis of a negative aesthetic of play. The speaker's tone is ludic, but her high spirits reinforce an undertone of pain:

> boys
> i don't promise you nothing
> but this
> what you pawn
> i will redeem

what you steal
i will conceal
my private silence to
your public guilt
is all i got

girls
first time a white man
opens his fly
like a good thing
we'll just laugh
laugh real loud my
black women

children
when they ask you
why is your mama so funny
say
she is a poet
she don't have no sense.[12]

If we feel dignity in "Admonitions," it is because Clifton's speaker inhabits a lifeworld so constrained by the desires of the dominant culture that she can only preserve her integrity by clowning. The point of her poem is to relay this constraint; thus her laughter does not resemble the subversive laughter Cixous and Kristeva celebrate. As Terry Eagleton notes, carnival is often "a *licensed* affair in every sense, a permissible rupture of hegemony, a contained popular blow-off as disturbing and relatively ineffectual as a revolutionary work of art. As Shakespeare's Olivia remarks, there is no slander in an allowed fool.[13]

The third reason we may want to resist a feminist aesthetic of play is that such an aesthetic involves a complicity with the very forms of the dominant culture Clifton's poem wants to critique. In *Les Guérillères* the games Wittig's women warriors inherit from an earlier, misogynous culture remain painful, even when the players laugh uproariously:

The game consists of posing a series of questions, for example, Who says, I wish it, I order it, my will must take the place of reason? Or,

Who must never act according to their will? Or else, Who is only an animal the colour of flowers? There are plenty of others such as, Who must observe the three obediences and whose destiny is written in their anatomy? The answer to all the questions is the same. Then they begin to laugh ferociously slapping each other on the shoulders. Some of the women, lips parted, spit blood.[14]

This association of play with violence, and with the helpless semiosis of women who spit blood, must be taken seriously.

For Gadamer, play undermines the solidity of the Cartesian subject; it involves a "to-and-fro motion" in which the player is absorbed, and "the burden of the initiative, which constitutes the actual strain of existence," removed. But Gadamer's optimistic description of play confirms the possible dangers of "gaming" for literary women and their readers. If the lightheartedness that comes from the relief of the "actual strain of existence" sounds contagious, it should also sound dangerous, for when Gadamer's terms are applied to women's participation in the games of patriarchy, this "relief" grows oppressive:

The attraction of a game, the fascination it exerts, consists precisely in the fact that the game tends to master the players. . . . The real subject of the game (this is shown in precisely those experiences in which there is only a single player) is not the player, but instead the game itself. The game is what holds the player in its spell, draws him into play, and keeps him there.[15]

If this is how play works, it is part of the nexus of power and constraint that Foucault describes as the "episteme," and it cannot offer useful emancipatory strategy for women who wish to change the dominant culture.

My counterresponse is to ask—if the play impulse implicates women in patriarchy—why have "phallocritics" repressed or appropriated or ignored the play impulse in women's texts? I want to suggest that there is a political dimension to play that Freud, Geertz, and Gadamer do not recognize. To explore this dimension, we will look at *The Land of Oz* by L. Frank Baum, a text that describes a boy's metamorphosis into a girl. Baum turns the hero of *The Land of Oz* (Tip—the playful, revolutionary boy who disorders and recombines) into Ozma, the well-mannered girl who mouths maxims of high insipidity. Tip is the perfect bricoleur, and he achieves maximum pleasure in the objects he plays with. But when Baum reveals that Tip has been a girl all along, that he is really Ozma—although with a boy's sensibility and in a boy's body—Baum sets about to replace this boy who says "no" to a world he dislikes with a girl who says "yes."

I want to use Baum's text to suggest that the repression of play within feminist theory mirrors the repression of women's play in the dominant discourse—and I want to begin to undo this repression—to recapture the concept of "play" for a feminist polemic. While Baum's story may seem an eccentric place to begin this analysis, children's stories have always offered a good place to comprehend the dominant myths of a culture, and L. Frank Baum's text is especially attentive to the unexpected connections between play and suffrage.

The central pleasure we experience in anticipating a recognition scene comes from our knowledge that the lost, long-sought person is not lost at all, but there, before our eyes, waiting for the moment of discovery to shine forth. In *The Land of Oz,* L. Frank Baum's sequel to *The Wizard of Oz,* this pleasure shines forth in the search for the lost Princess Ozma, daughter of the deceased "King Pastoria" and heir to his throne. The Wizard of Oz who botched Dorothy's flight back to Kansas is not such a bumbler in *The Land of Oz.* An adept in the white slave trade, he has sold Ozma to the wicked witch Mombi, who has enchanted the baby girl and given her a detective-proof identity. For years the citizens of Oz have searched for the lost princess, but *The Land of Oz* is not so much Ozma's story as the story of Tip, a young bricoleur who possesses an "elixir of life," a wonderful potion which allows him to bring his creations to life, and Jinjur, Baum's caricature of a suffragist, who leads a rebel army of women to conquer the Emerald City. While the stories of Tip and Jinjur seem disconnected, when the moment arrives for Glinda the Good to reveal Ozma's identity, we discover an oddity: Ozma, Jinjur, and Tip share the same gender.

"What did you do with the girl?" asked Glinda and at this question everyone bent forward and listened eagerly for the reply.

"I enchanted her," answered Mombi.

"In what way?"

"I transformed her into—into—"

"Into what?" demanded Glinda, as the Witch hesitated.

"Into a boy!" said Mombi, in a low tone.

"A boy!" echoed every voice; and then, because they knew that this old woman had reared Tip from childhood, all eyes were turned to where the boy stood.

"Yes," said the old Witch, nodding her head; "that is the Princess Ozma—the child brought to me by the Wizard who stole her father's throne. That is the rightful ruler of the Emerald City!" and she pointed her long bony finger straight at the boy."

"I!" cried Tip, in amazement. "Why, I'm no Princess Ozma—I'm not a girl!"

Glinda smiled, and going to Tip she took his small brown hand within her dainty white one.[16]

In Baum's text the border dividing "Ozma" from "Tip" is as emphatic and uncrossable as that boundary dividing Glinda's "dainty white" hand from Tip's boyish "brown" one. Tip resists this return to femininity by insisting on the sacredness of the male/female border; he does not want to give up his homoerotic companionship with the Scarecrow or Tin Woodsman or his birthright of frolic.

Why is this repression of girl's play in an old children's story important to the feminist critic? First, it can direct our attention to the fact that "playing," for all its associations with the nonactivity of the weak, tends to be represented in our culture as a masculine prerogative. If Gadamer can free the concept of play from its association with agency and individual creativity, he does not free play from its masculine gender: "The player himself knows that play is only play and exists in a world which is determined by the seriousness of purposes. But he does not know this in such a way that, as a player, he actually intends this relation to seriousness. Play fulfills its purpose only if the player loses himself in his play" (pp. 91–92). This masculinization of play has serious consequences. For Gadamer, play is an arena of freedom precisely because it undermines coercive boundaries between subject and object. In Gadamer's text, this privilege is reserved for male players.

It is obviously not correct to say that animals too play and that we can even say metaphorically that water and light play. Rather, on the contrary, we can say that man too plays. His playing is a natural process. The meaning of his play, precisely because—and insofar as—he is part of nature, is a pure self-presentation. . . .

. . . . Nature, inasmuch as it is without purpose or intention, as it is, without exertion, a constantly self-renewing play, can appear as a model for art. Thus Friedrich Schlegel writes, 'All the sacred games of art are only remote imitations of the infinite play of the world, the eternally self-creating work of art.' (p. 94)[17]

In making this distinction between "man" and "nature," Gadamer forgets that, at least in Western culture, the founding myth of "Nature" is also masculine. In Milton's *Paradise Lost* the invocation "Let there be play" is equal in force to God's "Let there be light":

> The Sixth, and of Creation last arose
> With Ev'ning Harps and Matin, when God said,
> Let th' Earth bring forth Soul living in her kind,
> Cattle and Creeping things, and Beast of the Earth,
> . . . . .
> The grassy Clods now Calv'd, now half appear'd
> The Tawny Lion, pawing to get free
> His hinder parts, then springs as broke from Bonds,
> And Rampant shakes his Brinded mane; the Ounce,
> The Libbard, and the Tiger, as the Mole
> Rising, the crumbl'd Earth above them threw
> In Hillocks. . . .[18]

This presumptive control from above, this direction of the playful activity of others by a booming male voice, is typical. In *Villette* when Lucy Snowe begins to feel light-hearted and mischievous, her mischief is controlled by M. Paul:

I stood a moment thinking, and absently twisting the handkerchief round my arm. For some reason—gladdened, I think, by a sudden return of the golden glimmer of childhood, roused by an unwonted renewal of its buoyancy, made merry by the liberty of the closing hour, and, above all, solaced at heart by the joyous consciousness of that treasure in the case, box, drawer upstairs,—I fell to playing with the handkerchief as if it were a ball, casting it into the air and catching it as it fell. . . . The game was stopped by another hand than mine—a hand emerging from a paletôt-sleeve and stretched over my shoulder; it caught the extemporised plaything and bore it away with these sullen words—

"Je vois bien que vous vous moquez de moi et de mes effets."

Really that little man was dreadful: a mere sprite of caprice and ubiquity: one never knew either his whim or his whereabout.[19]

To transform a handkerchief meant for grieving into a plaything, a bauble: this is the power that must be corrected; Lucy's error is to have created a game that does not include M. Paul.

At the beginning of *Northanger Abby* Catherine Morland shares Lucy's buoyancy:

What a strange, unaccountable character!—for with all these symptoms of profligacy at ten years old, she had neither a bad heart nor a bad temper . . . she was moreover noisy and wild, hated confinement and cleanliness, and loved nothing so well in the world as rolling down the green slope at the back of the house.[20]

Like the animals in Milton's creation, Catherine Morland feels close to earth and free from its gravity. But the repression of this childish play impulse is also the criterion for becoming a heroine.

Such was Catherine Morland at ten. At fifteen, appearances were mending; she began to curl her hair and long for balls; her complexion improved . . . her eyes gained more animation, and her figure more consequence. Her love of dirt gave way to an inclination for finery, and she grew as clean as she grew smart; she had now the pleasure of sometimes hearing her father and mother remark on her personal improvement. "Catherine grows quite a good-looking girl—she is almost pretty today," were words which caught her ears now and then; and how welcome were the sounds! (pp. 10–11)

Catherine's sensuous manner is given social form: "But from fifteen to seventeen she was in training for a heroine; she read all such words as heroines must read to supply their memories with those quotations which are so serviceable and so soothing in the vicissitudes of their eventful lives" (p 11).

We have seen that the difference between Tip and Ozma is that Tip is allowed to be creative, while Ozma, like Catherine Morland, must dabble in language games made by others. Tip's special gift in *The Land of Oz* is his capacity to act as bricoleur; he is a child creator who can recombine whatever he finds into forms that alter the direction of his story. But when Tip is changed back into Ozma, this power of invention is arrested. (Until then, Tip's inventions are wonderfully preposterous and include a flying "gump," a creature made out of an antelope head, two sofas, a broomstick, and a pair of palm-frond wings, as well as a contraption named Jack Pumpkinhead, made out of scraps of old lumber and a very ripe pumpkin.)

From the beginning Tip's preoccupations are stereotypically "boyish." Sent by Mombi to work in the fields or gather wood in the forest, "Tip often climbed trees for birds' eggs or amused himself chasing the fleet white rabbits or fishing in the brooks with bent pins." Only after he has satisfied his yen for adventure will he "hastily gather his armful of wood and carry it home" (p. 2). At other times, "when he was supposed to be working in the corn-fields, and the tall stalks hid him from Mombi's view, Tip would often dig in the gopher holes, or—if the mood seized him—lie upon his back between the rows of corn and take a nap." While Catherine Morland is "in training for a heroine," Tips slips "between the rows," digs up gophers instead of weeds and "by taking care not to exhaust his strength, he grew as strong and rugged as a boy may be" (pp. 2–3).

While Mombi is away, Tip makes something designed to scare her, a "terrorist text" with jointed hands and feet, and a huge pumpkin smile. Tip combines a deity's power of creating with Adam's of naming: " 'I must give him a name!' he cried. 'So good a man as this must surely have a name. I believe,' he added, after a moment's thought, 'I will name the fellow "Jack Pumpkinhead" ' " (p. 7). If Tip names Jack, only Mombi can bring the pumpkin figure to life; she sprinkles it with a magic elixir and Jack wakes up, creaky and awkward. Ignoring Mombi's part in his awakening, he addresses Tip as "Father," whereupon Mombi decides that Tip has too much power; Jack Pumpkinhead will make the better assistant.

Medusa-like, she decides to change Tip into a marble statue, whereupon Tip and Jack run off with her "elixir of life" and have dazzling
adventures.

  With her power to make men hard and to create new
life, Mombi is a fantastic version of "Mommy" and a grim version
of the "eternal feminine." Her elixir of life is the symbolic equivalent
of woman's reproductive power—and Tip's stealing of this power
and his successful creation of the talking sawhorse and crotchety
gump bears witness to the dominant culture's convictions about
which gender should "own" creativity. But Tip's playfulness also
has a metaphysical aspect. To understand this metaphysic we must
construct a brief genealogy of the child at play.

  According to Romantic myth children represent that
portion of humanity still unspoiled by civilization. Closer to nature,
the Romantic child shares nature's splendor while the civilized adult
possesses "embers" of the child's sophistry and jouissance. This
Romantic rendering of childhood has lost its conceptual power, and
we have adopted Freud's descriptions of infantile sexuality and
Piaget's notions of the child's rational development. But according
to Walter Benjamin even Freud's and Piaget's myths of childhood
must be replaced, for children represent something more urgent
than untapped sexual ferocity or the undeveloped capacity for logical
thinking. While Piaget focuses on what is gained as the infant
becomes youth and Freud on the loss of the child's polymorphous
perversity, Benjamin sees only the child's creativity: for him the
child is the best revolutionary. As children grow up, what is lost
is their active, irascible power of improvisation and change. Child's
play can be characterized by its peculiar creativity, its power to
seize upon the shards of culture: to use the fragments of used-up
life that society rejects, and organize these fragments in a completely
new way. "In using these things [children] do not so much imitate
the words of adults as bring together, in the artifacts produced in
play, materials of widely differing kinds in a new intuitive relationship."[21]

  According to Benjamin, children are always transforming
what is around them, and this transformation has "revolutionary
power." As Susan Buck-Morss explains in her analysis of Benjamin,

children's cognition is "tactile and hence tied to action." Children refuse to accept an object's given meaning, but instead get "to know objects by laying hold of them and using them in a manner that changes their meaning." Although Lévi-Strauss emphasizes that the bricoleur acts in a world already "pre-constrained," and that bricolage has no revolutionary power since the elements that the bricoleur collects evoke an older mythos, Benjamin does not recognize this preconstraint. He believes that the bricoleur's power carries a disruptive initiative and agrees with Valéry who says that "children are absolute *monsters* of activity. You might say they're only conscious of all the things around them in so far as they can *act* on them, or through them, in no matter what way: the action, in fact, is all."[22] For Benjamin, the "triumph of cognition" Piaget celebrates in the adult signals the child's "defeat as revolutionary subject." However, the presence of children speaks eloquently in every generation about a new potential for emancipatory activity. "In children, the capacity for revolutionary transformation [is] present from the start," Benjamin explains, and each generation is "endowed with a *weak* Messianic power."[23] Since this emancipatory power is reborn in every generation, by stripping history of its "metaphysical pretensions," we can redefine history as "the begetting of children, and as such, it [is] always a return to beginnings."[24] While Benjamin's conflation of the values of reproductive labor and child's play seems underanalyzed, his discussion of the potentially revolutionary value of the play impulse will help us understand what Ozma's loss of his/her ludic capacity means.

Ozma's crossing of genders would be no more than a piece of clever textual legerdemain if it were not for a subplot that brings Benjamin's vision of the revolutionary child and a feminist vision of women's empowerment together. Baum's text is simultaneously preoccupied with finding Ozma and with discovering a way for Tip and his comrades to conquer a woman's army that has taken over the Emerald City. On the road to the Emerald City Tip meets Jinjur, who has assembled a female "army of revolt" because "the Emerald City has been ruled by men long enough." Since this army is a heavily caricatured version of suffragist protest, Tip's task is simple, for Jinjur's "army" tires quickly of power;

they prefer the ease of conspicuous consumption to the nitty-gritty of battle. While Jinjur does reapportion the usual division of labor by making househusbands of the men and taking her army of women to the streets, her revolutionary compatriots remain lovers of pretty objects, narcissistic self-adorners: "the City glitters with beautiful gems, which might far better be used for rings, bracelets and necklaces; and there is enough money in the King's treasury to buy every girl in our Army a dozen new gowns," Jinjur says. "So we intend to conquer the City and run the government to suit ourselves" (p. 81). With Ozma's return this period of wanton governance comes to an end: "At once the men of the Emerald City cast off their aprons. And it is said that the women were so tired eating of their husbands' cooking that they all hailed the conquest of Jinjur with joy . . . the good wives prepared so delicious a feast for the weary men that harmony was immediately restored in every family" (pp. 276–77). While Baum trivializes Jinjur's revolutionary desire, the persistence of this "feminist" plot is worth exploring.

    The Land of Oz is organized around this battle between opposing genders—a battle over who owns creativity and who owns political power. Once the division of reproductive labor is renegotiated in men's favor, the situation of female power in Baum's text remains volatile—the division of labor that makes male homoeroticism the source of reproductivity is threatened by Jinjur and her army. But when this army is overpowered and the text's anxiety about female powerfulness could come to an end, the narrative begins to struggle once more with an unrest which is only resolved through Tip's transformation. Why is this unrest so persistent?

    First, Baum's manner of dealing with his revolutionary subplot is complicated by an even better story: Baum's mother was a suffragist who campaigned forcefully for women's rights. Not only does "Mombi's" covert alliance with the female rebels become clearer, but knowing that Baum has an ongoing concern with issues of women's empowerment invites us to rewrite his text in new terms.

    If in Baum's terms to play is to be capable of revising one's culture by appropriating and reshaping reproductive and political power, then from the point of view of the dominant sex/

gender system, women's play is among those dangerous sign systems that must be repressed. In Baum's story, women's rebellious energy is coterminous with women's playfulness, and both impulses get excised simultaneously.

Fredric Jameson's notion of a "political unconscious" helps us see how this excision is coded in *The Land of Oz*. Jameson explains that Marxist (and I would add feminist) criticism encourages the rewriting of old hegemonic forms, since these forms can now "be grasped as a process of the reappropriation and neutralization, the cooptation and class transformation . . . of forms which orginally expressed the situation of 'popular,' subordinate, or dominated groups."[25] Such revision is not just permissible, but necessary,

since by definition the cultural monuments and masterworks that have survived tend necessarily to perpetuate only a single voice in this class dialogue, the voice of a hegemonic class, they cannot be properly assigned their relational place in a dialogical system with the restoration or artificial reconstruction of the voice to which they were initially opposed, a voice for the most part stifled and reduced to silence, marginalized, its own utterances scattered to the winds, or reappropriated in their turn by the hegemonic culture. (p. 85)

In Baum's story these marginalized voices keep speaking; we see traces in his text of a "permanent struggle" between coexisting genders that is also an index of ongoing cultural revolution. Although the text's ideology of male dominance acts as a "strategy of containment" repressing what the dominant culture deems unthinkable, *The Land of Oz* gives us moments in which "the coexistence of various modes of production" and division of labor "become visibly antagonistic" (p. 95). In Jameson's view any text is a "field of force in which the dynamics of sign systems of several distinct modes of production can be registered and apprehended" (p. 98). *The Land of Oz* in particular offers a place for examining male appropriation of women's creativity. Baum's "innocent" text has a political dimension that coincides with its repression of women's playfulness; at the same time, because it dwells on the revolutionary potential of women, their violence and anger at cultural disenfranchisement, and works out a way to recode and to reappropriate that anger, the text covertly acknowledges its own repressiveness. If Baum is intent on disenfranchising women, why does he give power back to Ozma? *The Land of Oz* is organized around a battle between genders over who owns creativity. Given Baum's misogyny, the forces of patriarchy are bound to win, but this is oddly difficult, for each separate victory leads to another compulsive male anxiety about defeat. The "unconscious" of Baum's text knows that women continue to represent, in real life and in fiction, a deprived cultural force whose repression must be ideologically coded again and again if women are to be kept in their "place." Thus Baum finally contains women's revolutionary impulses within a girl child who is empty of both the revolutionary desires of Jinjur and the playful desires of Tip. Ozma has no yearning for "otherness." She has been this "other" already; she has inhabited both genders.

While the power of Baum's story seems at first to be its fantasied creation of a child who, like Tiresias, controls both roles at once, its real meaning is political; Baum makes it seem "natural" for women to give up the revolutionary power of transformation and play. By making continuity between male and female "zones" a *fait accompli,* Baum structures his story so that woman's desire disappears.

At the end of *The Land of Oz* the continuum between masculine and feminine identity is addressed and then repressed; as this continuum vanishes, the lives of two very different children are mapped onto one another—possessed and not possessed by the same person. As the text simultaneously breaks the taboo forbidding men and women to perceive themselves as similar, and reinstates that taboo, we find ourselves at that odd point in the territory of gender described by Lacan in "the famous parable of the two doors":

A train arrives at a station. A little boy and a little girl, brother and sister, are seated in a compartment face to face next to the window through which the buildings along the station platform can be seen passing as the train pulls to a stop. "Look," says the brother, "we're at Ladies!"; "Idiot!" replies his sister, "Can't you see we're at Gentlemen?"[26]

When Jane Gallop quotes this parable in *The Daughter's Seduction,* she expands Lacan's meaning and explains it in more detail:

Because of the rule of the signifier over the signified, the two words "Ladies" and "Gentlemen," in the illustration above, constitute, by their very installation, the two doors, although, in some mythical prehistory prior to the signifier's arrival, the doors are identical. Similarly, it is not the biological given of male and female that is in question in psychoanalysis . . . but the subject as constituted by the pre-existing signifying chain, that is, by culture, in which the subject must place himself.[27]

We return to an initial problem in our discussion of emancipatory strategies, to the fact that although sex/gender systems are socially constructed, they are no less potent for this constructedness. To know that we are controlled, our vision altered by the signifying chain, does not mean we can remove ourselves from its meanings "merely by knowing that the second rest room exists somewhere outside" our field of vision. Nor is this division and alienation from this "other" room one we can tolerate. In telling the parable of the two doors Lacan is not just describing a structural *fait accompli* that insures society's successful partitioning of masculine and feminine fields of possibility into different locales. Instead he is describing a set-piece, a tragedy; he wants to acknowledge our inevitable situation of desire for the other and irrevocable inscription within that place of longing and conflict in which hostilities never cease because the signifier mediates our removal from the real. We must endure the constant perversion of our "needs" by the signifier's bludgeonings. As Gallop explains, "Desire is that portion of the pre-articulated need which finds itself left out of the demand—the demand being the register of ethical discourse" (p. 11).

In neither Lacan's nor Gallop's terms is it possible to struggle successfully against "the cultural constructs of male-dominated society" because the subject who struggles cannot, as Gallop says, "consider as illusory the entire structure which makes the realms of Gentlemen and Ladies appear defined and absolute. . . . That effort would place the feminist as observer in some sort of floating position outside the structure, a position of omniscience" (p. 12).

If we can neither float beyond the signifying structure (be Tip and Ozma at once) nor act willfully to "overthrow" the signifier's reign (revolt successfully with Jinjur) then what are our options? According to Gallop, "if patriarchal culture is that within which the self originally constitutes itself, it is always already there in each subject as subject. Thus how can it be overthrown if it has been necessarily internalized in everybody who could possibly act to overthrow it?" (p. 114). We are stuck forever in the situation of Ozma's world—in which brown hands are opposed to white hands, swarthy skin to golden fragility, Tip's playful transformations to Ozma's inert maxims. Or are we?

One of the terms missing from Lacan's story, though incipiently present in Gallop's, is a theory of play—and an examination of the ways in which play can help psyches work, either collectively or individually, to transform the conditions of their socialization.[28] To see what this absence means I propose a playful examination of Gallop's text. Her heady rhetoric in *The Daughter's Seduction* suggests one way to begin to "overthrow" some forms of "necessity."

At the beginning of *The Daughter's Seduction* Gallop describes her narrative strategy in a passage both tumultuous and enticing. She promises to enact a new kind of critical transgression:

In a manner analogous to the dialogue between psychonanalysis and feminism, each chapter of the book stages the encounter between texts of at least two authors. This method is a way of getting more out of the texts read, something that goes beyond the boundaries which an author might want to impose upon his or her work. The notions of integrity and closure in a text are like that of virginity in a body. They assume that if one does not respect the boundaries between inside and outside, one is "breaking and entering," violating a property. (pp. xii–xii)

In Lacan's parable the little boy and little girl are stuck in a form of verbal propriety; to overthrow the division of labor and language instilled by their society is impossible. The young lady who looks out the train window is blinded by the signifiers that surround her; she can look at the door marked "Gentlemen," but she can never cross its threshold with propriety or be a man herself. But in *The*

Daughter's Seduction Gallop posits another kind of relation to the father's game. She reserves for herself the action of "breaking and entering," of going into the wrong parables, peeping in forbidden windows, throwing open the wrong doors. Gallop's delightful trespass, her transgression of the sacrosanct space of "the two doors," disrupts the internalized boundaries of "patriarchal culture" and begins to envision "a different economy" in which feminist theorists seize the license to play.

As long as the fallacies of integrity and closure are upheld, a desire to penetrate becomes a desire for rape. I hope to engage in some intercourse with these textual bodies that has a different economy, one in which entry and interpenetration do not mean disrespect or violation because they are not based upon the myth of the book's or the self's or the body's virginal wholeness. But rather upon the belief that, if words there be or body there be, somewhere there is a desire for dialogue, intercourse, exchange. (p. xiii)

Gallop takes on the stereotypical male role of raping, penetrating, and then she playfully revises that role, refusing the sadism of these stereotypes. But even if this playfulness is effective in *The Daughter's Seduction,* why should it be necessary to "theorize" it?

When a description of women's writing as "play" is left out of feminist theory, when we take the weight of patriarchy—its force and inevitability—too seriously, we miss a great deal of what goes on in women's texts. Our inherited sex/gender system is dangerous for women. But it is also a system that women writers have been working to deconstruct. To understand how play contributes to this deconstruction, we need to move from the metaphysics to the politics of play.

In *Eros and Civilization: A Philosophical Inquiry into Freud,* Marcuse contends that we must rescue aesthetic experience from marginality and proposes Schiller's explication of the play impulse as an operational base. Schiller describes play as an impulse mediating between sensuous and form-giving or rational experience. This mediation is neceessary because, for Schiller, the "sensuous impulse" (which is essentially passive and receptive), is always overpowered by the "form-impulse," (which is essentially "active, mastering, domineering)."[29] Culture grows out of this antagonism. As Marcuse says, "instead of reconciling both impulses by making sensuousness rational and reason sensuous, civilization has subjugated sensuousness to reason in such a manner that the former, if it reasserts itself," does so savagely and invites reason to grow tyrannical and "impoverish" or "barbarize" sensuousness (pp. 186–87). For Marcuse these impulses can only be reconciled through the work of the "play impulse."

As metaphysic, Schiller's ideas are less than systematic, but as a phenomenology of play that might lead to a politics, these ideas are worth pursuing.[30] Schiller, according to Marcuse, is the first philosopher to attempt to find a sensuous solution to a political problem. Schiller wants to negotiate men's and women's liberation from "inhuman existential conditions." He asks that we "pass through the aesthetic," since it is his view that "beauty . . . leads to freedom" (Marcuse, p. 187; Schiller, p. 71). This theory is old; what is new about Schiller's system is that play becomes the medium of this liberation, and play is not playing with something or for something—it is the very rhythm of existence free from constraint. Schiller is enough of a realist to recognize that "such constraint *is* the reality"; his insistence that "man is free when the 'reality loses its seriousness' " is entirely provisional (Marcuse, p. 187; Schiller, p. 71). Still, his description of play as the lightening of strain, as a way of making light and volatile that which is oppressive and heavy, takes us back to the themes of chapter 3, to the woman writer's need to return the letter "to the air," to capitalize on the "animality of the letter."

Kristeva's model of the text as that site where law, reason, and custom are challenged by the body's dense music has affinities with Schiller's description of the emancipatory value of sensuousness. As we have seen, for Kristeva it is the social violence of *"Geist"* that the play impulse must resist. Like Schiller, she describes the text as a place where what is repressive and cumbersome becomes light: in Marcuse's paraphrase of Schiller, "man is free when the 'reality loses its seriousness' and when its necessity 'becomes light' *(leicht)*" (p. 187). For Kristeva, the function of the text is also to "lift" the repression that weighs on the text's participation in social struggle (p. 27).

Moreover, in "Psychoanalysis and the Polis," Kristeva suggests that critics and psychoanalysts should indulge their playfulness frequently in order to give the work of analysis more volatile power. "The wise interpreter" must "give way to delirium":

The dimension of *desire,* appearing for the first time in the citadel of interpretive will . . . opens up time, suspends Stoic suicide, and confers not only an interpretive power but also a transforming power to these new, unpredictable signifying effects which must be called *an imaginary.* I would suggest that the wise interpreter give way to delirium so that, out of his desire, the imaginary may join interpretive closure, thus producing a perpetual interpretive creative force.[31]

We have seen that when Jane Gallop "gives way to delirium" her prose takes on, or appears to take on, a transformative power. How transformative this power is depends not just on Gallop's playfulness, but on her audience's.

There is always a moment in history when those discourses obtain a general consensus not so much because they interpret the situation correctly (i.e., in accordance with the exigencies of the moment and developments dictated by the needs of the majority) but rather because they correspond to the essentially utopian desires of the majority. Such political interpretation interprets *desires;* even if it lacks reality, it contains the truth of desires. It is, for that very reason, utopian and ideological.

Yet, as in analysis, such an interpretation can be a powerful factor in the mobilization of energies that can lead social groups and masses beyond a sadomasochistic ascesis to change real conditions. Such a mobilizing interpretation can be called revolution or demagogy. By contrast, a more objective, neutral, and technocratic interpretation would only solidify or very slowly modify the real conditions.[32]

It is in this dimension that writers like Cixous give us extra delight. Placing Cixous' ribald fictions in the context of carnival gave us a new way to evaluate her textual politics. If we ignore Cixous' playfulness and call her pronouncements philosophically rigid rather than ludic we not only miss the best parts of her revisionary ethic, but miss the chance to participate in such an ethic ourselves.[33] For

Cixous, women's relation to philosophy must be insoucient: "am I in philosophy? I do not think so. I have a relationship to philosophy, but it is one of dialogue." It is also a relationship of cultivated delirium:

> I would be capable of carrying on a philosophical discourse, but I do not. I let myself be carried off by the poetic word. Is it a mad word? Does it say something? I must say that my steed or my barge and my poetic body never do forget the philosophical rigor. So what is happening? Philosophy is like an accompaniment, but humorous. . . . I take it into account but precisely as that from which I can take my distance.[34]

When we fail to notice the uses of play in women's writing, or gloss over the woman writer's openness to the ceremonious madness of words, we may see little intellectual value in Gallop's bravura or Cixous' lighthearted appropriation of what the dominant culture regards as weighty and serious.

Cixous and Kristeva are not the only theorists who use Schiller's ideas "as an accompaniment." While Gadamer does not admit the political value of play, he does direct our attention to the buoyancy, the to-and-fro rhythm that characterizes "gaming":

> Now I contend that the basic constitution of the game, to be filled with its spirit—the spirit of buoyancy, freedom and the joy of success—and to fulfill him who is playing, is structurally related to the constitution of the dialogue in which language is a reality.[35]

But Winnicott goes even farther than Gadamer in explaining how this "spirit of buoyancy" does political work. He suggests that parents let their children play because parents want to relieve "the strain inherent in objective perception." Winnicott is quite explicit about how this "strain" motivates not only play, but social transformation.

For Winnicott the play state represents a withdrawal from the rational world that allows the creation of an "alternative" world:

> To get to the idea of playing it is helpful to think of the *preoccupation* that characterizes the playing of a young child. The content does not matter. What matters is the near-withdrawal state, akin to the *concen-*

tration of older children and adults. The playing child inhabits an area that cannot be easily left, nor can it easily admit intrusions.[36]

The arena of play has a curious liminal status. It exists neither inside nor outside, neither bound by social rules nor free from them. "This area of playing is not inner psychic reality. It is outside the individual, but it is not the external world." "The area of playing" is, in fact, the place where the opposition between a reality which is "objectively perceptible and objectively knowable" and a delirous inner reality breaks down:

Into this play area the child gathers objects and phenomena from external reality and uses these in the service of some sample derived from inner or personal reality. Without hallucinating the child puts out a sample of dream potential and lives with this sample in a chosen setting of fragments from external reality.

The child "lives with" its wishes, its dreaminess, as if dreams were real, and it is this "living with" that gives play both its buoyancy and its potential for transformation. In play the child experiences a continual slippage, a to-and-fro motion between the world that restricts desire and desire itself. "In playing, the child manipulates external phenomena in the service of the dream and invests chosen external phenomena with dream meaning and feeling."

According to Winnicott, play has political implications because this slippage beween "dream" and "external reality" can move "reality" itself in new directions. "There is a direct development from transitional phenomena to playing, and from playing to shared playing, and from this to cultural experiences." Sometimes we are able to interpolate what happens in play into the shared solidarity of everyday life.

In this chapter I have juxtaposed the dominant culture's need to repress women's playfulness with the power of the feminist critic at play. I have also established a theoretical matrix in which it is possible to conceive of play as a way of making light and volatile what is repressive, of returning "the letter to the air." Theorists like Kristeva and Winnicott help us to see play as a way of unburdening oneself of the dominant tradition, of lightening the weight of custom and making it open to change. But how do these ideas apply to women's writing? To make something "light" can also mean to trivialize it, to fail to take seriously the weight of what confounds us.[37] It is time to consider how we might incorporate a theory of play into the practice of feminist criticism.

The theatre was full—crammed to its roof: royal and noble were there: palace and hotel had emptied their inmates into those tiers so thronged and so hushed. Deeply did I feel myself privileged in having a place before that stage; I longed to see a being of whose power I had heard reports which made me conceive peculiar anticipations. . . . She was a study of such nature as had not encountered my eyes yet: a great and new planet she was: but in what shape? I waited her rising.[38]

In *Villette* Lucy's encounter with Vashti is an occasion of tumult and grandeur. Vashti is "light," she "rises," but her volatility spells disaster:

She rose at nine that December night; above the horizon I saw her come. She could shine yet with pale grandeur and steady might; but that star verged already on its judgment day. Seen near, it was a chaos—hollow, half consumed: an orb perished or perishing—half lava, half glow. (p. 233)

What kind of game is Brontë playing here? Vashti may "rise," she may "lift the repression that weighs heavily on this moment of struggle," but her character is too punishing to be described as "playful" or lighthearted.

If Vashti is not "playful" in this conventional way, can we include her character in the dialectic of play I have outlined above? Before arguing that we can, I want to present a counter-argument. Vashti enters the novel as Lucy Snowe's double and opposite; Lucy is not only inwardly repressed, she is outwardly constrained; her revolutionary impulses are projected onto Vashti "whose release of 'hunger, rebellion and rage' sets the theatre literally alight with its revolutionary force." As Mary Jacobus comments in "The Buried Letter: Feminism and Romanticism in *Villette*," "Vashti is a female version of the central Romantic protagonist, the satanic rebel and fallen angel whose damnation is a function of divine tyranny."[39]

Jacobus argues that this displacement of rebellious energy is barely successful. "*Villette* can only be silent about the true nature and origin of Lucy's oppression; like Charlotte Brontë's letters, it never questions the enshrining of marriage within Victorian sexual ideology, nor pursues its economic and social consequences for women." Jacobus adds that what Brontë cannot say outright in *Villette* is "inscribed in its sub-text—in the 'discursive' activity of Lucy's (over-)heated imagination, and in the agitated notation and heightened language which signal it" (pp. 46–47). But this subtext has, for Jacobus, conservative power. She says that "Charlotte Brontë's own mistrust" is the force that "erupts in *Villette* with the fire that flames out during Vashti's performance." "The drive to female emancipation" is "fuelled by revolutionary energy," although this desire has an "ultimately conservative aim—successful integration into existing social structures" (p. 57).

In calling Vashti's scene "the flaming out" of Brontë's mistrust, Jacobus misses one other important arena of interpretation. Vashti may not be "playful" in the most euphoric sense of the word, but she permits Brontë to set up an "area of playing." What the double text does is to establish a space where Lucy (and Brontë) can play with forbidden impulses. This play both admits and refuses "integration into existing social structures" until Lucy Snowe herself becomes a double figure who can echo Vashti's body language and say to Ginevra: "I am a rising character."

How does Vashti's story set up a new space of ebullience in Brontë's novel? Lucy's response to Vashti is ambivalent: "It was a marvellous sight: a mighty revelation. It was a spectacle low, horrible, immoral" (p. 234). Lucy's imagination is thrown into contradiction, but Dr. Graham's response is simply vacuous: "*impressionable* he was as dimpling water. . . . Her agony did not pain him, her wild moan—worse than a shriek—did not much move him; her fury revolted him somewhat, but not to the point of horror. Cool young Briton!" (pp. 236–37).

Distanced from Graham, Lucy recognizes his insipidity and blindness. While her heart is drawn "out of its wonted orbit" by Vashti's presence, Graham judges Vashti: "He judged her as a woman, not an artist: it was a branding judgment." This judgment collapses under the burden of Lucy's feeling. Vashti's presence "disclosed power like a deep, swollen winter river thundering in cataract, and bearing the soul, like a leaf, on the steep and steeply sweep of its descent" (p. 235). The gap between Graham's and Lucy's responses makes a change in the novel's games. According to Gadamer,

there is an ultimate sense in which you cannot have a game by yourself. In order for there to be a game, there always has to be, not necessarily literally another player, but something else with which the player plays and automatically responds to his move with a counter-move. Thus the cat at play chooses the ball of wool because it responds to play, and ball games will be with us forever because the ball is freely mobile in every direction, apearing to do surprising things of its own accord. (*Truth and Method,* p. 95)

When Graham does not offer Lucy anything like this mobility, Vashti does. Around midnight, during Vashti's death scene, Lucy is completely enthralled. At the moment when the actress refuses to die, the chaos Vashti contains in her body breaks into the theatre:

Just then a stir, pregnant with omen, rustled behind the scenes—feet ran, voices spoke. What was it? demanded the whole house. A flame, a smell of smoke replied.
"Fire!" rang through the gallery. "Fire!" was repeated, reechoed, yelled forth. (p. 237)

Lucy's fantasy of Vashti is spilling over, affecting the frame of the story. Lucy sees Vashti as "a fierce light, not solar—a rushing, red, cometary light—hot on vision and to sensation," and suddenly this rushing light feeds, or seems to feed, on the theatre; it does "surprising things of its own accord." The first thing it does is to further separate Graham and Lucy, and in so doing, to provide Lucy with a more important partner than the doctor.

Lucy's first response to the fire is to follow Graham's orders. "I would not have moved to give him trouble, thwart his will, or make demands on his attention" (p. 237). But Graham breaks away from her:

While Graham was speaking, a young girl who had been very quietly and steadily clinging to a gentleman before us, was suddenly struck from her protector's arm by a big butcherly intruder, and hurled under the feet of the crowd. (p. 237)

Graham and Lucy are now physically as well as emotionally separated—he rushes to save the young girl and lifting her up discovers that " 'She is very light . . . like a child!' "

What has been "lightened" by this child's appearance? The role of acquiescent, good little woman that has been weighing Lucy down, constricting her movements, remains part of Lucy's character to the end. But in this scene Vashti's fire accelerates a transformation; Lucy begins to split off part of herself, to work with it, and to repudiate it. The terror and attraction Lucy felt for Vashti now has a more immediate manifestation. The fainting girl is the gothic impulse domesticated; she is Paulina *Home*—an allegorical concentration of her society's fantasies about what it means to be a good girl.

To say that Polly's appearance brings an emotional "buoyancy" to Brontë's text would be wrong—Lucy gets depressed as soon as Dr. John's interest in Paulina becomes evident. But in bringing Polly back into the text Brontë has set up an arena for playing with conventional definitions of womanhood. The text moves back and forth between what Polly represents, what Vashti represents and what Lucy must do to seize Vashti's fire.

The most remarkable evidence of the splitting in Lucy's text that Vashti's "rising" accentuates comes in the scene where Lucy is appointed, soon after this accident, to be Polly's caretaker. Graham, still concerned for her health, sends Lucy to Polly's room because Polly's servants cannot speak English. "You can at least direct their movements, and thus spare her some pain. She must be touched very tenderly" (p. 239).

Polly grows lighter and lighter, and Lucy's duty is to bring her down to earth. What follows is a disturbing creation scene in which the hallucinatory doubling of both Vashti/Lucy and Polly/Lucy flares out and becomes the demonic undercurrent of Lucy's interactions with Polly:

The chamber was a room shadowy with pale-blue hangings, vaporous with curtainings and veilings of muslin; the bed seemed to me like snow-drift and mist—spotless, soft, and gauzy. Making the women stand apart, I undressed their mistress. . . . I received a general impression of refinement, delicacy, and perfect, personal cultivation. (p. 240)

Lucy drifts through this natal chamber of mist and "snow"—a reference to Lucy's name that intensifies this scene's specularity:

The girl was herself a small delicate creature, but made like a model. As I folded back her plentiful yet fine hair, so shining and soft, and so exquisitely tended, I had under my observation a young, pale, weary, but high-bred face. The brow was smooth and clear; the eyebrows were distinct but soft, and melting to a mere trace at the temples. . . . Her skin was perfectly fair, the neck and hands veined finely like to petals of a flower; a thin glazing of the ice of pride polished this delicate exterior, and her lip wore a curl. (p. 240)

The doubling between Lucy and Polly is clearest here; Lucy seems to be giving birth to a little ice maiden who has come, half flower, half wraith, to take Lucy's place in the story with Graham Bretton. In the following chapter Lucy plays out the emotions she feels for Graham, and finally rejects his conventionality: "He wanted always to give me a role not mine."

In the "area of playing" Vashti's fieriness creates, Lucy acquires a strange volatility; her character is put into play in a new way and begins "to do surprising things of its own accord." In a scene where she rejects the opportunity to act as go-between between Graham and Polly, Lucy is replicating Vashti's rebellious energy. She is beset by M. Paul:

"Petite chatte, doucerette, coquette!" sibilated the sudden boa-con-strictor; "vous avez l'air bien triste, soumise, rêveuse, mais vous ne l'êtes pas: c'est moi qui vous le dis: Sauvage! la flamme à l'âme, l'éclair aux yeux!"

"Oui; j'ai la flamme à l'âme, et je dois l'avoir!" retorted I, turning in just wrath; but Professor Emanuel had hissed his insult and was gone. (p. 290)

Later, on the way home with Ginevra, Vashti's explosiveness rocks the carriage:

After listening for a while with assumed stoicism, my outraged sense of justice at last and suddenly caught fire. An explosion ensued: for I could be passionate too; especially with my present fair but faulty associate, who never failed to stir the worst dregs of me. (p. 293)

By setting up a new space of "preoccupation and concentration" in the character of Vashti, Brontë has provided an "area of playing" in which Vashti's alternative world can be partially internalized not only by Lucy, but by the reader. As Winnicott suggests, this space is neither "inner psychic reality" nor "the external world," but a space in which the player "lives with" an array of objects representing both "dream potential" and external constraints. Under these conditions Lucy comes to look less and less like Polly Home and more like a "rushing, red cometary light," a force capable of changing the course of the game.[40] As Richard Sennett comments:

Through self-distanced play the child learns that he can work and rework rules, that rules are not immutable truths but conventions, under his control. . . . Parents teach obedience to rules; play teaches that rules themselves are malleable, and that expression occurs when rules are made up, or changed.[41]

Sennett's description of the "self-distance" of play should remind us that the very tidiness of this analysis (the convenient appearance of metaphors of lightness and "rising" in Brontë's text, the symmetry of her use of fire imagery) can work against what I want to say. The perfection of these metaphors teaches us that Brontë's text is ornately coherent; that its plot has a conventional logic we can trace and then name. But these structuring operations are also my own sleight of hand; they can repress the processes pervading the text that give it its buoyancy. We must not reduce the buoyancy in Brontë's text to a set of rules nor should we, in general, deal with women's texts as if they were structures in which puzzles are sturdily set to be solved by critics or heroines. Instead, the text is troubled by its own metaphors, and troubled by the symbolic structures it has inherited. Its response to these structures is not to become a "sleeping body," but a puzzled and mischievous body which tries to put these structures in process, to challenge and tease them into the fact or facsimile of a new game.

If we fail to see how disturbed and disturbing the locus of play can be, we will gloss over the cracks, flaws, and inequities, the "madness" of ideology that form the basis and create the need for play. If playfulness does offer the woman writer a way of making the "weight" of the tradition lighter, this is because "the area of play" allows the player to formulate a dialectic that may look "finished" to the critic's eye, but is actually an adventure of shreds and patches, a way of taking risks that only the glee of the wandering sentence, the "animality" of the letter, or the anger of the "honey-mad woman" can hope to discover.

EIGHT

Emancipatory Strategies

The writings of Bakhtin, Derrida, Foucault, Kristeva, and Lacan have become a kind of technology we apply to literary texts, and while these theorists have provided systems that are indispensable, they can also blind us to alternative paradigms for describing what goes on in women's writing. In the preceding chapters I have both worked with these theories and developed new constellations of meaning that will illuminate women's writing in provocative ways. Metaphors such as "honey-mad women," or "the animality of the letter," or "women at play," are useful because they address moments of pleasure in women's writing and point toward moments of oral glee neglected by Anglo-American critics. These metaphors may not do their work for everyone, but I am not attempting to fashion them into a technology. Instead, I want to emphasize our need to multiply the paradigms available to the feminist critic.[1] In "starring" moments of liberation, tracing private "zones of reading" in women's texts, I have begun a public narration of women's emancipation from dominant codes.[2] In this chapter the multiplication of paradigms continues. I want to discuss some contemporary theories of emancipation in order to explore their usefulness for the feminist critic and to explore, in more detail, several contemporary challenges to the concept of "emancipatory strategies."

No starring of the texts of "honey-mad women" would be complete without mention of Emily Dickinson, whose poems are buoyant, playful, and filled with the sound of bees.[3] In "I taste a liquor never brewed" the speaker identifies with the honey bee's power of gathering:

> Inebriate of Air—am I—
> And Debauchee of Dew—
> Reeling—thro endless summer days—
> From inns of Molten Blue—
>
> When "Landlords" turn the drunken Bee
> Out of the Foxglove's door—
> When Butterflies—renounce their "drams"—
> I shall but drink the more!

The poem builds to a crescendo of election and ecstasy:

> Till Seraphs swing their snowy Hats—
> And Saints—to windows run—
> To see the little Tippler
> Leaning against the—Sun—[4]

In playing so freely the bee (and the poet), gather an extraordinary power, but in other poems Dickinson treats this power with ambivalence. In "The Soul has Bandaged moments" Dickinson constructs a sober vision of female creativity in which manic self-construction is followed by depression. She contrasts the soul's passivity with its moments of "Escape— / When bursting all the doors— / She dances like a Bomb, abroad, / And swings upon the Hours." The soul may experience delirium, and this delirium may give the poet access to an ecstasy like the bee "delirious borne." But if such glimpses of freedom allow the soul to "Touch Liberty—then know no more, / But Noon, and Paradise," they offer a fool's paradise only. The soul in flight is vulnerable to

> retaken moments—
> When, Felon led along,
> With shackles on the plumed feet,
> And staples, in the Song,
>
> The Horror welcomes her, again   (P. 521)

In Dickinson's poem honey-mad bliss lasts only a moment and leaves the poet open to agony; her music is "shackled" and "stapled," her lyrics turn gothic. While Dickinson's verse flows with a sense of pleasure and empowerment, she is skeptical about emancipation. In "We—Bee and I—live by the quaffing" the dangers and temptations of greedy orality are comically glossed.

> While runs the Rhine—
> He and I—revel—
> First—at the vat—and latest at the Vine—
> Noon—our last Cup—
> "Found dead"—"of Nectar"—
> By a humming Coroner—
> In a By-Thyme!   (P. 230)

Is this a danger for the feminist critic as well? Should we give in to the ecstasy of inventing delirious names for ourselves and our heroines, or will these new names cast women into an abyss of madness and melancholy where we have foundered before? Dickinson's verse makes it imperative to address the negative side of the "honey-mad woman" paradigm, to confront this association of honey madness with the pleasures that lead to delirium.

> Come slowly—Eden!
> Lips unused to Thee—
> Bashful—sip thy Jessamines—
> As the fainting Bee—
>
> Reaching late his flower,
> Round her chamber hums—
> Counts his nectars—
> Enters—and is lost in Balms.   (P. 211)

Does the archetype of the "honey-mad" woman writer invite a return to hysteria, to the "powers of the weak"?

When Gilbert and Gubar presented the "madwoman in the attic" as an archetype to describe, among other tribulations, the nineteenth-century woman writer's anxiety of authorship, suddenly texts we thought we had understood came to life: they were nourished by this archetype in new ways. But "the madwoman in the attic" also opened the question of the social efficacy of women's hysteria, of how politically effective—and how inevitable—women's madness might be.

In celebrating the archetype of the honey-mad woman, I have also associated women and madness, and promoted another kind of female delirium. I have chosen a figure that foregrounds the woman writer's happy orality, her playfulness, and reminds us of the propensity women writers have to seek situations of buoyancy and volatility. In focusing on honey madness and play, I have not focused on mindless activities, but on play as a form of praxis, on a politics of pleasure that involves struggle as well as ecstasy.

In *Eros and Civilization* Marcuse contrasts Prometheus, the wily trickster who creates culture at the "cost of perpetual pain," with Orpheus/Narcissus, the pleasure seeker and lover of fulfillment, who possesses "the voice which does not command but sings."[5] A culture must follow the path of pain or of pleasure, Marcuse says, and he condemns those cultures that follow Prometheus. This suffering god may perform superhuman deeds, but Prometheus' actions also "promote and strengthen [mundane] reality; they do not explode it." In contrast, Orpheus and Narcissus "do explode" this reality; like Dickinson's honey bee, these pleasure gods awaken and liberate "potentialities that are real in things animate and inanimate . . . real but in the un-erotic reality suppressed" (p. 165).

Marcuse's opposition of cultural icons who promote productivity through pain with those who promote productivity through pleasure remains too simple. Marcuse ignores those systematic features of everyday life that distort vision, inhibit freedom, prevent men and women from entering into dialogue; he forgets that Prometheus is also a rebel who tries to overcome such distortions. While my espousal of women writers' "honey-mad" moments has an affinity with Marcuse's affirmation of cultural icons that encourage narcissistic or orphic gratification, in proposing that we shift the focus of feminist theory from "Promethean" artists and heroines to those "orphic" writers who invest in the letter's animality and invent new language games, I am not proposing that we make Marcuse's choice. Instead of setting up an opposition between two iconographies, I have pointed to a missing term in feminist criticism and spoken about the responsibility feminist theorists have to discover a dialectic of pleasure as well as of pain in women's texts, an "orphic" gratification that does not repress, but redresses and preserves women's struggles.

Thus when Dickinson's speakers read their own powerfulness as a mood swing in a manic-depressive cycle, when they associate full-throated ease with death ("Her—'last Poems[1]— / Poets—ended— / Silver—perished—with her Tongue— / Not on Record—bubbled other, / Flute—or Woman— / So divine" (P 312), these oppositions reinvent an ecstatic twittering machine that offers neither closure nor exit from the poem's predicaments. If Marcuse's analysis in *Eros and Civilization* is equally nondialectical, there are other ways to think about the positive uses of delirium. For example, in Mary Oliver's "The Roses" we encounter a landscape that "dances like a bomb" but does not explode, because the speaker is exercising her capacity to play, to amble back and forth between law and desire. Sitting in a landscape of summer fecundity, speaking from amidst the burgeoning flora of *carpe diem,* Oliver's speaker satisfies desire without making herself one of the tradition's metaphors.

> One day in summer
> when everything has already
> been more than enough
> the wild beds start
> exploding open along the berm
> of the sea; day after day
> you sit near them; day after day
> the honey keeps on coming
> in the red cups and the bees
> like amber drops roll
> in the petals; there is no end,
> believe me! to the inventions of summer,
> to the happiness your body
> is willing to bear.[6]

Oliver is responding to several layers of poetic tradition. In celebrating the female poet's glad productivity, she is replying to Dickinson, unfolding the ecstatic moments in Dickinson's glossolalia without collapsing these moments into their depressive phase. While the bees who flit through Dickinson's meadows are masculine (following the poetic tradition in which "male" bees penetrate "feminine" flowers), Oliver makes their penetration neuter, innocent. The bees become "like amber drops" that neither impregnate nor overpower. Rolling on the petals, the bees give themselves over to the poet's will: they are coaxed into simile.[7]

The dominant tradition states that rosebuds must be gathered, time march onward, and bees "o'erbrim their clammy cells." In *carpe diem* the period of creativity is brief, and gratification depends less on woman's pleasure than on the male poet's capacity to blend metaphors of male desire and female fertility. The payoff for Oliver's readers and speakers is a pleasure in simultaneously resisting this tradition and finding another story. Where Marvell threatens his female interlocutors with worms and hurrying chariots, Oliver promises her reader moments of plenty: "there is no end, / believe me! to the inventions of summer, / to the happiness your body / is willing to bear."

The metaphors in this poem are satisfying, but do they justify the presentation of the honey-mad woman as a general image for the woman writer's endeavor? "Honey" evokes the sweeter side of women's texts, but "madness" is associated with a marginality at odds with a feminist vision. In multiplying "madwomen in the attic" with "honey-mad women," do we reinstate hysteria and delirium as permanent attributes of feminist theory?

The first emancipatory strategy that I want to address in this chapter is the strategy of delirium. In "Psychoanalysis and the Polis" Kristeva acknowledges the stigma attached to delirium, which she defines as "a discourse which has supposedly strayed from a presumed reality. The speaking subject is presumed to have known an object, a relationship, an experience that he is henceforth incapable of reconstituting accurately." But she explains that when we admit delirium into our critical repertoire, we do not enter the cloud of unknowing:

we normally assume the opposite of delirium to be an objective reality, objectively perceptible and objectively knowable, as if the speaking subject were only a simple knowing subject. Yet we must admit that, given the cleavage of the subject (conscious/unconscious) and given that the subject is also a subject of desire, perceptual and knowing apprehension of the original object is only a theoretical, albeit undoubtedly indispensable, hypothesis.[8]

Kristeva suggests that we seek delirium in some active way, "that the wise interpreter give way to delirium" in order to make this "cleavage" productive:

More importantly, the system Freud calls perception-knowledge . . . is always already marked by a *lack;* for it shelters within its very being the nonsignifiable, the nonsymbolized. This "minus factor," by which, even in perception-knowledge, the subject signifies himself as subject of the desire of the Other, is what provokes, through its insistence on acceding to further significations, those deformations and displacements which characterize delirium.[9]

One of the uses of delirium is to turn this "minus factor" into a "minus factory"—to find metaphors that push the unspoken into speech.

　　　　And yet Kristeva's discourse could have another effect; it could push us toward the recognition that there is no solid epistemological ground for any mode of speech or representation, that this "minus factory" can only produce the existential vertigo of Paul de Man's description of the "madness of words" in *Deconstruction and Criticism,* or Roland Barthes' of the "free play of the signifier" in *The Pleasure of the Text.* Barthes defines writing as an achingly negative delirium: "The language I speak *within myself* is not of my time: it is prey, by nature, to ideological suspicion; thus, it is with this language that I must struggle. I write because I do not want the words I find: by subtraction."[10] We slip with astonishing speed from the happiness of Marcuse's reconstructed Orpheus to the zero-sum writing defined by de Man:

To read is to understand, to question, to know, to forget, to erase, to deface, to repeat—that is to say, the endless prosopopoeia by which the dead are made to have a face and a voice which tells the allegory of their demise and allows us to apostrophize them in our turn. No degree of knowledge can ever stop this madness, for it is the madness of words.[11]

According to de Man, writing and reading are acts of erasure that can neither be affirmed nor defamed. "What *would* be naive is to believe that this strategy, which is not *our* strategy as subjects, since we are its product rather than its agent, can be a source of value and has to be celebrated or denounced accordingly."[12] Once we have admitted the "madness of words," how can we claim that language adds a dimension of freedom to women's lives? How can we talk about the woman writer's emancipatory strategies?

To answer this question I will give way once more to my own obsession with theory—an obsession fully in evidence in earlier chapters. In moving my dialogue in the direction of theories of emancipation (especially theories invented by men), I risk another form of slippage, for I may plummet from the madness of words to their grim rationale. But it is my conviction that within this rationale it is possible to work out another calculus of mischief. In the pages that follow the multiplication of theories that support the possibility of emancipation, verges on the vertiginous. This vertigo will leave me open to the charge that I have bitten the hard fruit of theory, like the fallen Lizzie in Christina Rossetti's "Goblin Market" and jeopardized my own voice, placed it under erasure. In "Goblin Market" Lizzie loses herself in "the haunted glen" where "wicked quaint fruit-merchant men" give her fruits that feel "like honey to the throat / But poison in the blood."[13] She sucks this fruit with the knowledge that its fecundity may destroy her own:

> She dropped a tear more rare than pearl,
> Then sucked their fruit globes fair or red.
> Sweeter than honey from the rock,
> Stronger than man-rejoicing wine,
> Clearer than water flowed that juice;
> She never tasted such before,
> How should it cloy with length of use?
> She sucked and sucked and sucked the more
> Fruits which the unknown orchard bore;
> Then flung the emptied rinds away
> But gathered up one kernel stone,
> And knew not was it night or day
> As she turned home alone.   (ll. 127–40)

Using male theory and finding—as I do—so much oral pleasure in it, may not be in keeping with either the woman-centered playfulness of the last chapter or the pleasure seeking of the honey-mad woman who is my paradigm. When the goblin men bid Lizzie "taste / In tones as smooth as honey" (ll. 107–8) and she does, her body loses its fire and vigor; the cost of her pleasure is speechlessness.

But perhaps we can find a milder index of the dangers of men's theories for the honey-mad critic. Instead of proposing a plunge from the boundlessness of honey-mad women toward the rectifying "frame" of such theories, I want, instead, to bring male theory into the frame of my text, and to remind the reader that there is another sister in "Goblin Market." As Lizzie starts to pine away, her sister Laura decides that she, too, will risk the temptations of the goblin merchants to find her sister's cure. The goblin men torment Laura cruelly, and she returns from their wrangling covered, head to foot, in their juices. Upon entering Lizzie's room, she cries out to her sister:

> "Did you miss me?
> Come and kiss me.
> Never mind my bruises,
> Hug me, kiss me, suck my juices
> Squeezed from goblin fruits for you,
> Goblin pulp and goblin dew.
> Eat me, drink me, love me;
> Laura, make much of me;
> For your sake I have braved the glen
> And had to do with goblin merchant men."   (ll. 465–74)

Laura has gathered the forbidden fruit, which covers her body but has not been absorbed, and this "pulp" becomes an antidote to the goblin spell itself: "She kissed and kissed her with a hungry mouth. / Her lips began to scorch, / That juice was wormwood to her tongue, / She loathed the feast: / Writhing as one possessed she leaped and sung."

In filling this chapter with writhing male voices—and openly reveling in the fact that I have "had to do with goblin merchant men"—I would like to argue, as Laura implicitly does, that this gathering of male texts can also represent a feminist harvest. The descriptions of the "emancipation debates" that follow (whose most vocal contemporary proponents are Jürgen Habermas and Jean François Lyotard), may read like goblin texts—but it is my conviction that these theories of emancipation can be useful to the feminist critic, can provide, in their application to women's texts, a useful homeopathy for phallocentric inquiry.

EMANCIPATORY DISCOURSE

We already possess, in Sartre's *What Is Literature,* a theory of literature as emancipatory praxis. For Sartre, the writer's obligation to be "socially committed" is central to the literary act; each writer must view language as a medium of change, a means of action. "Each word is a path of transcendence; it shapes our feelings, names them, and attributes them to an imaginary personage who takes it upon himself to live them for us."[14] The writer's task is to communicate better values and to impel us to live in the direction of those values. After reading a Hemingway or a St.-Exupéry, we must follow their example, "plunge things into action," for the "density of being" these writers convey can only be measured for the reader by the multiplicity of "practical relations which they maintain with the characters. . . . Thus the world and man reveal themselves by *undertakings.* And all the undertakings we might speak of reduce themselves to a single one, that of *making history"* (p. 233).

Sartre's prose is driven and exhilirating, but his view that the literary text can emancipate the reader into action has long been discredited. In *Writing Degree Zero* Roland Barthes responds to Sartre's passionate belief in emancipatory discourse by attacking Sartre's view of "free" speech. Language is not the easy communicative medium Sartre imagines, but "a corpus of prescriptions and habits . . . an abstract circle of truths outside of which alone the solid residue of an individual *logos* begins to settle."[15] Language is not the site of decision, the willful "locus of a social commitment," but "merely a reflex response involving no choice"; language informs and inscribes us; we do not exist outside it, hence can never regard ourselves as "pure freedom, as an unconditioned activity."[16]

To speak of emancipation has become not only un-
fashionable, but epistemologically suspect. In an interview published
in *Diacritics* Lyotard suggests that intellectuals should not cling to
nineteenth-century myths of liberation, but devote themselves to
finding "passages" between "phrase universes." "What is gained"
in this "passage" from a libertarian game model to a model asserting
that we can only disrupt one "phrase universe" by entering the
constraints of another, is the ontological purity that comes from
refusing to recognize the subject's transcendence. "Briefly, I have
schooled myself in the *Philosophy Untersuchungen*," Lyotard says,
"in order to purge myself of the metaphysics of the subject (still
present, in my opinion, in the *Tractatus*)." He finds this purgation
exhilirating:

Desolating my culture fecundated me. Thereafter, it seemed to me that
"language games" implied players that made use of language like a
toolbox, thus repeating the constant arrogance of Western anthropo-
centrism. "Phrases" came to say that the so-called players were on the
contrary situated by phrases in the universes those phrases present,
"before" any intention. Intention is itself a phrase, which doubles the
phrase it inhabits, and which doubles or redoubles the addresser of that
phrase.[17]

Lyotard speaks with gusto of the "ruin of subject-systems," those
"great narratives" of Western thought—"the liberal, the Marxist,
the capitalist, the Christian, the speculative." His own special language game, or "phrase universe," consists of "desolating" these
"great narratives," and he asks us to join this sortie:

Interviewer: What do you feel to be the pedagogical responsibilities of
those of us still engaged in "classical" university teaching? What alternatives can you propose to the great Enlightenment narrative of education
as emancipation?

Lyotard: Whether it be in the "classical" university or in the supple-
mentary institutions to which you allude, the pedagogical task, once
stripped of its trappings, that of the great narrative of emancipation,
can be designated by one word: an apprenticeship in resistance. Resistance against the academic genres of discourse. . . . against the great
narratives themselves, against the way thought is treated in the new

postmodern technologies insofar as they express the most recent application of capitalist rules to language, resistance against every object of thought which is given to be grasped through some "obvious" delimitation, method, or end.[18]

Our condition requires the vigilant remembrance that "language cannot be mastered." Language, goes the postmodern refrain, "is something that I do not manipulate; in a way it comes to me from elsewhere; it does not come from me" (pp. 98–99).[19]

　　To return to Barthes' early schema, the freedom of the woman writer, when it occurs, is wonderful, but this moment comes rarely—is strained, blind, subdued—because we write within the limits of a language which speaks with the pervasive voice of social norms and so fills the horizon of the writer that she or he cannot see beyond society's terms. What we call "style" offers little additional leverage; it designates a purely inward limit, a process "indifferent to society," closed in on itself, bodily, erotic, secretly indiscreet. If language is a voice turned toward the writer's social context, and style a voice turned toward his or her "personal and secret mythology," then writing is always a "personal utterance" bounded by history. "Writing as Freedom is therefore a mere moment," Barthes says.[20]

　　After *Writing Degree Zero,* after *Blindness and Insight,* after *The Postmodern Condition,* how can feminist critics talk about literature as emancipation? We can describe the text's delirium, but how do we celebrate its liberating power once we have realized its power to name and constrain us? Adorno offers one sort of answer. Recognizing that words remain "concepts" whose imprecision is an inadequate substitute for things themselves, Adorno insists that language is *always* delirious; it has already strayed "from a presumed reality." But Adorno does not share de Man's skepticism about the word's lack of emancipatory power. Concepts can still "achieve what the concept prevents," for the flaw in each concept "makes it necessary to cite others; this is the font of the only constellations which inherited some of the hope of the name."[21]

　　For Adorno, as for Kristeva, the madness of words is a positive madness. Writing is not a form of erasure but a recurring homage to inventiveness and to "outwardness"; language itself offers to reconstruct, again and again, the possibility of representation. In philosophy this need expresses itself in the form of delirium:

A truth that cannot plunge into the abyss . . . of madness—will at the bidding of its certainty principle turn analytical, a potential tautology. Only thoughts that go the limit are facing up to the omnipotent impotence of certain accord; only a cerebral acrobatics keeps relating to the matter. (p. 34)

This acrobatics is risky, since "a cognition that is to bear fruit will throw itself to the objects à fond perdu. The vertigo which this causes is an index veri" (p. 33). The best philosophical writing is not erasure, but a combination of cogency and playfulness, and emancipation is never an absolute moment or process, but a continual and vigilant introduction of "free" energy into the "bound" energy of statements or texts. "Mobility is of the essence of consciousness; it is no accidental feature. It means a doubled mode of conduct: an inner one, the immanent process which is the properly dialectical one, and a free, unbound one like a stepping out of dialectics" (p. 31).

This stepping in and out of dialectics, this buoyant to-and-fro motion occurs where it is least expected. In the conclusion to The Archaeology of Knowledge Foucault makes this playful self-accusation:

You have tried to reduce the dimensions proper to discourse, ignore its specific irregularity, hide what initiative and freedom it possesses, and make up for the imbalance that it sets up within the language (langue): you have tried to close this openness. Like a certain form of linguistics, you have tried to dispense with the speaking subject.[22]

Foucault acknowledges that his task in The Archaeology of Knowledge has been to "cleanse [history] of all transcendental narcissism" (p. 203), and that the specificity of this task lends his discourse a false sense of closure. But in thus accusing himself, Foucault opens his own text to other meanings; he acknowledges that his own language does not work in quite the way he has described it, that, in fact, we are in need of a theory of language that addresses the spirit of Sartre's utopian desire to unlimit the language, as well as Barthes' (or Foucault's) sense of the writer's restricted musicality. But Foucault admits that his own task has been to reduce or mask whatever freedoms language possesses. To this end, Foucault refuses all models of emancipation even as he invents a new language game that works toward freeing "the history of thought from its subjection to transcendence."

Thus my first defense of emancipation is that although "phrase universes" may preexist, even the strongest proponents of the limits of these universes describe ways of going to the edge, of inventing new rules and descriptions that transform the burden of what we believe. Foucault's and Lyotard's strategies are exactly "strategies"; their words have an emancipatory bent that expresses their desires to free us from systems they consider regressive.

My second defense of emancipation as "strategy" is that these new language games are neither random, nor do they promise the "erasure" of other systems. To return to Adorno, "the unregimented thought has an elective affinity to dialectics, which as criticism of the system recalls what would be outside the system; and the force that liberates the dialectical movement in cognition is the very same that rebels against the system" (p. 31). Delirium, the discourse that has "strayed from a presumed reality," moves us toward a dialectic that can be political as well as cognitive. Its mobility reveals the recurring responsiveness of thought to what is "inside" the system as well as its potential openness to what is "outside."

Third, despite Lyotard's insistence that notions of emancipation are necessarily wedded to the "transcendental subject," we may argue, as Coward, Ellis, and Kristeva do, that emancipation should be described as an explosive protest brought about by a "split subject" who simultaneously gives into and resists the burden of the sociolect. When we speak of "action" or emancipation, we do not necessarily mean that this action emanates from a unified psyche. If the Cartesian subject has disappeared, this does not mean that praxis is finished. Instead, our definition of what it means to act as split subject must change, and texts themselves can be located as sites where this divided subject enacts a divided mode of historical struggle. As Frank Lentricchia suggests in *Criticism and Social Change,* even though we are defined by a past, a language, and a repetitious need to act from the unconscious, we must recall that "the act so deconstructed, to reveal forces within it beyond the consciousness of the active subject, is [not the same as] the act cancelled, called back, inserted into the fatality of history."[23]

Finally, the "great narratives of liberation" have not been overturned or "ruined," as Lyotard suggests. Instead, these naratives have reinvented themselves and become less dependent on the transcendental subject, more attuned to the text as a theater of struggle. We can ground a final argument in favor of "emancipatory strategies" in an analysis of the ways emancipatory narratives have persisted—even among poststructuralists—in contemporary literary and aesthetic theory. These emancipatory narratives can be useful to the feminist critic in locating points of agitation or change in women's texts. Moreover, these narratives demonstrate variety as well as tenacity and can be divided into seven categories, namely, into theories of: 1) dialogue, 2) the dialogic, 3) semiotic intervention, 4) rational critique, 5) absence or dissonance, 6) cultural revolution, and 7) utopian projects or aims. After examining these narratives we will ask what is missing: what does feminist theory still have to fill in?

1. *A Theory of Dialogue.* While in chapter 5 I argued that the simple process of dialogue can lead to the invention of an abnormal discourse, Gadamer's emancipatory theory of dialogue is nevertheless the only narrative of emancipation that does not stress the importance of going beyond normal linguistic competence. Rorty and Gadamer defend conversation as a communicative mode that helps us "break free from outworn vocabularies and attitudes." Words may construct character ("what is most characteristic of our humanity is that we are dialogical or conversational beings in whom 'language is a reality' "[24]), but for Gadamer, language is a mysterious object which conceals itself from us with benignity—the constructive capacity of language is not dangerous. We can allow ourselves to come so close "to this universal mystery of language that is prior

to everything else, that we can entrust ourselves to the object that we are investigating to guide us safely in the quest." Language makes each speaker vatic:

While we live wholly within a language, the fact that we do so does not constitute linguistic relativism because there is absolutely no captivity within a language—not even within our native language. . . . even . . . stammering is the obstruction of a desire to speak and is thus opened into the infinite realm of possible expression. Any language in which we live is infinite in this sense, and it is completely mistaken to infer that reason is fragmented because there are various languages. Just the opposite is the case. Precisely through our finitude, the particularity of our being, which is evident even in the variety of languages, the infinite dialogue is opened in the direction of the truth that we are.[25]

Gadamer's theory almost fails to qualify as an "emancipatory" theory because he is not concerned with overcoming forces of distortion, domination, or constraint. However, for Gadamer conversation, interpretation, and word play do represent an overcoming of cultural and temporal boundaries. In "successful conversation" both conversants

come under the influence of the truth of the object and are thus bound to one another in a new community. To reach an understanding with one's partner in a dialogue is not merely a matter of total self-expression and the successful assertion of one's own point of view, but a transformation into a communion, in which we do not remain what we were.[26]

Practice: We find a feminist analysis with Gadamerian overtones in Naomi Scheman's "Anger and the Politics of Naming." For Scheman, conversation also has radical power. "One's discovery of anger can often occur not from focusing on one's feelings, but from a political redescription of one's situation."[27] Scheman invents a politics of naming that disposes of Gadamer's mystification of language, but recognizes that the hermeneutic "bestowing or withholding of a name can be personally and politically explosive. To see that some state of affairs counts as oppression or exploitation, or that one's own feelings count as dissatisfaction or anger is already to change the nature of that situation or those feelings."[28] Gadamer is hardly the intellectual precursor Scheman would name as her model, but his theories help to frame the emancipatory potential that Scheman finds in feminist acts of naming.

2. *A Theory of the Dialogic.* For Mikhail Bakhtin, the act of renaming is not as powerful as the "struggle among sociolinguistic points of view." The dialogic tendency of languages to interact with one another is the source of textual liberation.

Thus Bakhtin's theory of the "dialogic" is more agonistic than Gadamer's theory of dialogue. Any dominant discourse is inherently flawed, for it can only come into dominance by repressing other discourses, a repression not easy to overcome despite the fact that "the generative forces of linguistic life" are subject to opposing tendencies: the "forces that struggle to overcome the heteroglossia of language" are at war with "forces that unite and centralize verbal-ideological thought."[29] Discourse is, then, an arena of permanent struggle in which any language that seems "unitary" is always embattled, at work "defending an already formed language from the pressure of growing heteroglossia." The literary text is the place where this work of preserving cultural hegemony is undone. For Bakhtin the novel is, especially, the "carrier" of a plural, decentralizing tendency in which the "dialogic orientation of a word among other words" can create new and significant artistic potential in discourse"—can become the source of verbal and political emancipation.

This process—experimenting by turning persuasive discourse into speaking persons—becomes especially important in those cases where a struggle against such images has already begun, where someone is striving to liberate himself from the influence of such an image and its discourse by means of objectification, or is striving to expose the limitations of both image and discourse. The importance of struggling with another's discourse, its influence in the history of an individual's coming to ideological consciousness, is enormous. One's own discourse and one's own voice, although born of another or dynamically stimulated by another, will sooner or later begin to liberate themselves from the authority of the other's discourse. (p. 348)

Practice: In exploring Emily Brontë's transition from sampler to poem to novel, we have seen that the novel can become an arena for the woman writer's struggle with "another discourse." Bakhtin's work has been appropriated by a number of feminist critics who are interested in this dialogue between hegemonic and nonhegemonic discourses, including my own work on Eudora Welty's *The Golden Apples,* " 'Because a Fire Was In My Head': Eudora Welty and the Dialogic Imagination." In addition, Bakhtin's theories intersect with Elaine Showalter's description of "dominant" and "muted" discourse in "Feminist Criticism in the Wilderness" and give us a methodology for analyzing the subversive interactions of dominant and muted discourses in women's writing.

3. *A Theory of Semiotic or Alinguistic Intervention.* For Julia Kristeva, language has a preverbal resonance that neither Bakhtin nor Gadamer sees. She says that spoken and written language contain elements "heterogeneous to sense and signification." Words may represent the dominant culture's repressions, but they are also electric; they carry within them the prelinguistic jolt of emotion that accompanied their learning. Words have vestiges of a preoedipal energy that intrudes into postoedipal identity; they have the capacity to signify something other than what they say.[23]

Because the subject in language is not a unified "I" but a network composed of the multiple effects of syntax at war with desire, writing can offer a moment when the subject disrupts conventional linguistic practice with the alinguistic pulse of desire; the result is the insertion within society of "a practice that it censors; to communicate what it cannot understand or hear; and thus to reconstitute the cohesion and harmony of a social discourse, inherently ruptured." The stuttering and multilanguagedness that are, for Gadamer, aspects of the word's everyday life, represent for Kristeva a polynomia dangerous to traditional practice: "a kind of asymbolic memory of the body" that finds its way into the symbolic.

Thus Kristeva is not concerned with the conversational dimension of speech. The cost of communicative competence is always repression. Once the subject is introduced into the universe of symbols via the repression of unconscious drives, these drives do not disappear: instead, the subject who possesses language is a divided subject who is implicitly heterogeneous and disunited, whose identity is always in crisis, who is both "structure and process simultaneously." The subject is not just the bearer of a static ideology, but a contradiction capable of activating practice.

Practice: The Kristevan emphasis on the split subject who is able to shatter the parameters of the social text has been useful to feminist critics who want to talk about textual disruption and change. Feminist analyses based on Kristeva's theories are legion, but good examples are Alice Jardine's analysis of Virginia Woolf in "Pre-Texts for the Transatlantic Feminist," and Toril Moi's analysis of Woolf in *Sexual/Textual Politics.*

4. *A Theory of Critique.* While Kristeva defines emancipatory moments as the irruption of the asymbolic or alinguistic into the symbolic, for Habermas emancipation is always the product of communicative reason. As rational beings we are responsible for evaluating social inequality and protesting injustice. We must overcome, through communicative interaction, both systematic distortions and asymmetrical distributions of power:

Like Kristeva (and unlike Gadamer), Habermas argues that social structures are always implicit forms of violence.

The human species secures its existence in systems of social labor and self-assertion through violence, through tradition-bound social life in ordinary-language communication, and with the aid of ego identities that at every level of individuation reconsolidate the consciousness of the individual in relation to the norms of the group.[31]

But Habermas argues that it is not possible to begin repairing this violence merely by "musicating" ordinary language. The prelinguistic gusto Kristeva defines as the subversive component of literary texts is already part of the distortion of everyday life:

Ordinary language is its own metalanguage. It acquires this unique function in virtue of its ability to incorporate into its own dimension even the non-verbal life expressions through which it itself is interpreted. . . . All ordinary language allows reflexive allusions to what has remained unstated.[32]

Alert to "those systematic features of contemporary society that inhibit, distort, or keep such dialogue from being concretely embodied in our everyday practises," Habermas insists that we must practice a form of communicative reason that will engage in "a dialectic that takes the historical traces of suppressed dialogue and reconstructs what has been suppressed."[33] This dialectic will inevitably contain both a critical and a utopian (or unattainable) element. As Thomas McCarthy comments: "Whereas Gadamer speaks of 'the dialogue that we are,' Habermas speaks of the dialogue that is not yet but ought to be. Whereas Gadamer is moved by respect for the superiority (*Überlegenheit*) of tradition, Habermas is motivated by the anticipation of a future state of freedom."[34] At the same time, Habermas shares with Bakhtin and Kristeva the conviction that transformation only happens through a process of what he calls "decentration":

A devaluation of the explanatory and justificatory potentials of entire traditions took place in the great civilizations with the dissolution of mythological-narrative figures of thought, in the modern age with the dissolution of religious, cosmological, and metaphysical figures of thought. These *devaluative shifts* appear to be connected with socio-evolutionary transitions to new levels of learning.[35]

Practice: Habermas' positing of an "emancipatory interest" in his early work has been influential in shaping my project. In addition, his belief in communicative reason is shared (albeit in a form less conservative and Kantian) by those feminists who want to affirm consciousness raising as a powerful source of feminist critique. For example, although de Lauretis' descriptions of semiotic intervention look very different from Habermas' descriptions of communicative reason, her affirmations of self-consciousness as an activity falling somewhere "between instinct and reason" (*Alice Doesn't,* p. 182) and Catherine MacKinnon's description of consciousness raising as progressive activity in "Feminism, Marxism, Method, and the State" share with Habermas an implicit belief in the efficacy of dialogue among equals that takes the form of an impassioned critique of those oppressive structures of institutions and dominant forms of consciousness that have become habitual.

5. *A Theory of Dissonance or Absence.* Several theories of emancipation focus on what remains marginal and unstated in speech

rather than focusing on its practical surfaces. For example, although Pierre Macherey talks about the text's multivoicedness, he also insists that dialogue is a form of "opulence." The text's multivocality is less a form of historical struggle than evidence that the text is possessed by its own gorgeous helplessness.[36] This helpless text is not emancipatory in and of itself, but is in need of a critic who will measure "the *distance* which separates the *various* meanings" (p. 79). Nor is this silence something temporary to be remedied; there is no word of "communicative reason" that the critic can supply. Instead, amidst its welter of meanings, the text's silent "center" connotes an inscription of "otherness" "through which the text maintains a relationship with that which it is not, that which happens at its margins" (p. 79).

This blindness to diversity, this impotence of the text to thematize its multiple voices and meanings, is founded in the text's relation to an ideology that is always repressive. As a story designed to efface contradictions, "ideology's essential weakness is that it can never recognise for itself its own real limits: at best it can learn of these limits from elsewhere, in the action of a radical criticism" (p. 133). The text cannot enter into a dialogue with its own ideology—this would be another way of getting caught up in a given culture's illusions. Instead, the text shows us ideology "in a non-ideological form," for by giving ideological content a spatial location something extraordinary happens. The work has a doubling effect which reveals the insufficiency of ideological constructs, "revealing difference and discordances, or a significant incongruity." Literature, then, "challenges ideology by using it"; it confronts ideology with itself.

Eagleton's variations on Macherey's theories in *Marxism and Literary Criticism* are motivated by the recognition that Macherey avoids the historical and material implications of what he sees. Eagleton also makes the text's relation to ideology—its dissonance with itself—the center of an emancipatory theory, but he argues that the text is not as "opulent" or as "helpless" as it seems. Instead, the text puts ideology to work; it makes the unsaid visible, makes silences speak. "An ideology exists because there are certain things which must not be spoken of," and it is the critic's re-

sponsibility to theorize these silences, to make them sound.[37] Of
course, this is difficult because the unconscious can only say what
it wants in a "softened, distorted, perhaps unrecognisable form" so
that "breaks in the text" become "places where an interpretation
has prevailed which is ego-alien even though a product of the
ego."[38] The critic's practice is emancipatory when she or he looks
at the mechanisms that produce gaps in an ideological discourse.

   Practice: The feminist analysis that makes Eagleton's
and Macherey's theories most useful to the feminist critic, that
shares their convictions about the relation of texts to ideology while
extending this analysis into a zone of homoerotic politics they
ignore, is Eve Sedgwick's *Between Men: English Literature and
Male Homosocial Desire.* For Sedgwick, it is male homosocial
desire mediated through the traffic in women that is the invisible
glue making social structures cohere. "The sexually pitiable or
contemptible female figure is a solvent that not only facilitates the
relative democratization that grows up with capitalism and cash
exchange, but goes a long way—for the men whom she leaves
bonded together—toward palliating its gaps and failures" (p. 160).[39]
Feminist texts that focus on absences, lacunae, or distortions as
sites of revealed abjection or of revolutionary activity share Macherey's and Eagleton's assumptions about the transformative potential
of making invisible ideologies visible.

6. *A Theory of Cultural Revolution.* For Jameson in *The Political
Unconscious,* the text is a collective activity, a sublime field of
force that does not depict one cultural voice or ideology at work,
but several, simultaneous voices. Jameson describes the text as "a
symbolic move" in a "strategic confrontation between classes."[40]
He is not interested—as is Sartre—in the ways a particular text
reflects the symbolic and "purely individual" solution of its writer,
nor is he interested—as is Macherey—in the text's nonideological
margins. Instead, the text is engaged in epic work—its contradictions
chart "the irreconcilable demands and positions of antagonistic
classes" (p. 85). Thus while Jameson celebrates, as does Eagleton,
the text's productive dissonances, and while he argues that these
dissonances require a critic's presence to be fully productive, the

text occupies a larger field of force; it emerges in a context that is "crisscrossed and intersected" by impulses so various they cannot be made homologous or described under a single rubric. The text bears witness to numerous "impulses from contradictory modes of cultural production" which are not present serially, but all at once. This means that every text, at least potentially, contributes to a moment of "cultural revolution"—a moment "in which the coexistence of various modes of production becomes visibly antagonistic, their contradictions moving to the very center of political, social, and historical life."

Despite this crisis rhetoric, Jameson wants to displace the concept of cultural revolution from those punctual moments in history when change takes center stage and a particular historical practice seems—retrospectively—to have originated. For Jameson cultural revolution does not consist of a moment or series of moments that occur in "transition periods" in which "a radical restructuration" seems to be taking place. Instead, its "moment" is a dynamic, diachronic event which has been happening for some time in what Jameson calls "a kind of metasynchronicity" in which particular social formations argue with and attempt to overcome other social formations, each pursuing their own dynamic, each moving within a semiautonomous time scheme.

Just as overt revolution is no punctual event either, but brings to the surface the innumerable daily struggles and forms of class polarization which are at work in the whole course of social life that precedes it . . . so also the overtly "transitional" moments of cultural revolution are themselves but the passage to the surface of a permanent process in human societies, of a permanent struggle between the various coexisting modes of production. (p. 97)

For Jameson the textual object must always be restructured by its readers "as a field of force" in which these struggles can be read, a field "in which the dynamics of sign systems of several distinct modes of production can be registered and apprehended"—not only as form, but as content. That is, unlike the practice of "traditional formal analysis," Jameson invites us to study the text as a field of energy which reveals the collective enterprise of "the human race" to create and to escape from its own "political unconscious":

The literary structure, far from being completely realized on any one of its levels tilts powerfully into the underside or *impense* or *non-dit,* in short, into the very political, unconscious, of the text, such that the latter's dispersed semes—when reconstructed according to this model of ideological closure—themselves then insistently direct us to the informing power of forces or contradictions which the text seeks in vain wholly to control or master (or *manage,* to use Norman Holland's suggestive term). (p. 49)

What most differentiates Jameson from Eagleton/Macherey is his desire to find in the text a promise, a future. His vision of the text as an " 'utterance' in an essentially collective or class discourse" (p. 80) is a refusal to see the text as "thin"—its productivity happening only in lacunae or absences. An Hegelian at heart, Jameson asks us to "take dialectical thought to be the anticipation of the logic of a collectivity which has not yet come into being" (p. 286). He finds in even the most diabolic of cultural documents "the hope of the name":

Any Marxist analysis of culture . . . can no longer be content with its demystifying vocation to unmask and to demonstrate the ways in which a cultural artifact fulfills a specific ideological mission . . . but must seek . . . to project its simultaneously utopian power as the symbolic affirmation of a specific form of collective unity. (p. 291)

Practice: To apply Jameson's ideas to women's writing, we might think about the ways in which Ruby Fisher's incipient desire for a story of her own is at war with the stories her culture has constructed to contain her. Welty's text defines a desire on Ruby's part for a "cultural revolution" which is neither fully formed nor articulated and is in serious danger of never achieving articulation. Similarly, Bishop's "In the Village" maps the struggle between the father's word and a form of maternal discourse that is perceived by its speakers and listeners as dangerous—but that is seeking a new form of social incorporation, of communicative being. However, neither of these utopian visions are fleshed out in Welty's or Bishop's texts. As Jameson suggests, these texts tilt "powerfully" into the "*non-dit,* in short, into the very political unconscious" of gender asymmetry.

7. *A Theory of Utopian Aims.* For a number of French, English, and American feminists the only viable emancipatory strategy is the act of abandoning—or destroying—the practices of the dominant culture. In "The Straight Mind" Wittig argues that women must not "forget the material (physical) violence that they directly do to the oppressed people, a violence produced by the abstract and 'scientific' discourses as well as by the discourse of the mass media. I would like to insist on the material oppression of individuals by discourses."[41] Response to this oppression must be a transformation of everything, beginning with language. Wittig refuses to use the name "women" to describe lesbian subjects: the term is too redolent with past repression. Janeway echoes this refusal in *The Powers of the Weak:*

The ruled cannot deny their subjugation to the tyrant unless and until they are willing to deny the whole body of social mythology in which his legitimacy is embodied. Making such a denial requires both courage and intellectual force. It is possible, as we shall see, but hard and rare. The alternative is the dark alley of apathy, alienation.[42]

Practice: Since Wittig's novels are the best examples of her brand of guerilla warfare, let me add to my happiness in reading these novels the perception that not only Wittig, but numbers of feminist critics, have benefited from or invented their own versions of the utopian rhetoric of transformation we find in Wittig's and Janeway's works. This rhetoric has inspired us to look for ideas or hopes outside a common mythology. But while this rhetoric is invaluable, it should not overshadow our response to an accumulation of "other" emancipatory strategies in women's texts. The need to isolate a single emancipatory strategy as the only one appropriate to woman writers, or to argue that since only two of the theories outlined above have been invented by women, only two of these theories will be epistemologically defensible, limits our ability to understand women's texts.

Women writers use a range of emancipatory responses
to overcome the constraints of the tradition—the choice of response
depends upon the writer's context and her historical era. In addition,
women writers use emancipatory responses I have not named. (I
have, because of my own pleasure in theory, limited my descriptions
to theories that are extensively rationalized and philosophically based.)
For example, we can turn to Nancy Miller's "Emphasis Added:
Plots and Plausibilities in Women's Fiction" to understand the
function in women's writing of reiterations of male maxims that,
in other contexts, have been inimical to women's needs, or to
Cixous' description of the poetics of excess to understand why
women writers have begun to flood the market with words. It is
part of our business as feminist critics to rediscover the libertarian
potential of women's texts and to excavate our own radical past.
To do this we must continue to employ and invent a wide range
of emancipatory paradigms. In conclusion, I want to investigate a
simple emancipatory strategy that the narratives outlined above do
not name: the strategy of "combining and covenanting," of asking
women's "works" to exert a new constellating power.

COMBINING AND COVENANTING

Although in Rebecca Harding Davis' *Life in the Iron
Mills* we discover an extreme skepticism about the representational
capacity of language, at the end of the novella—awkwardly, yet
determinately—Davis positions a place for the image to stay; she
tries to create a space beyond negativity for housing "the combined
power of action" her prose has released. I want to conclude this
chapter with an analysis of Davis' work, and to point out that
although each of the theories outlined above offers useful ways for
thinking about the work done by women's texts, at the same time,
each theory is incomplete. Many of these theories share with theories
of the avant-garde a reliance on textual moments of rupture or
crisis that, while they appeal to a postmodern sensibility, cannot
help to explain the textual power of a work like Davis' *Life in the
Iron Mills*.

In "Feminism in an International Frame," Gayatri Spivak responds to academic avant-garde tactics by arguing that while they may, in principle, seem radical, in practice, they are not. "The 'political' energy of avant-garde production, contained within the present academic system, leads to little more than the stockpiling of exegeses, restoring these texts back to propositional discourse," she explains. In contrast,

the power of a *Les Guérillères* or *Tell Me a Riddle* (to mention a non-French text)—distinguishing them from the "liberated texts" supposedly subverting "the traditional components of discourse," but in fact sharing "all the components of the most classic pornographic literature" . . . is what they talk *about,* their *substantive* revision of, rather than their apparent *formal* allegiance to, the European avant-garde. This differential will stubbornly remain in the most "deconstructive" of readings.[43]

We need to acknowledge emancipatory strategies that do more than disrupt the existing sociolect, to acknowledge the emancipatory potential of those texts involved in a "substantive revision" of their culture even when that revision involves some complicity with older power structures. (Linda Singer pursues this line of argument in "Value, Power, and Gender" when she asks how we can "counteract the tendency of the dominant class to assimilate and contain feminine resistance through existing codes." Her suggestion is that "one possibility for the weak might be to prevent hasty dismissal of their actions by pursuing the unexpected appropriation of some of the tactics and strategies of the strong.")[44]

What is at stake here is not just the woman writer's imitation of traditional structures of domination, but a question these theories of dialogue or rupture do not address—the question of how we can account for a text's structuring of "what is to be preserved." Benjamin's theory of revolutionary transformation offers one place to begin. Unlike other Frankfurt theorists, Benjamin believes that ordinary culture can be transformed from an ideology into "a revolutionary tool." Commodities can be made into "dialectical images" in a two-stage procedure whose first moment is deconstructive. This moment involves the recognition that the conservative impetus which gives objects exchange value also prevents them from having "revolutionary use-value."[45] A cultural apparatus has to be "blown apart"—exploded by negative dialectics—and the sequences of bourgeois history usurped by a depatterning of history and by a refutation of the idea of progress. Within this explosive dialectic, no species of objects should have "pre-eminent cognitive value." "Revelation could be sparked," Susan Buck-Morss explains in her analysis of Benjamin, "by children's books, furniture, gaslight, political cartoons, photographs, travelogues, gestures, physiognomies, fashions, as well as philosophical treatises and historical events" (p. 56).

Benjamin argues, however, that this negative moment must be offset by a positive one in which objects coalesce in new constellations of meaning. He argues that such constellations can illuminate the revolutionary potential of the present. Thus deconstruction, semiotic intervention, dialogism, and the energy of the avant-garde fulfill only the first half of Benjamin's project. A deconstructive euphoria may be "based self-consciously on an epistemology that claims to be both anti-ideological and politically radical" but this disruptive project is always inadequate. In Buck-Morss's reading of Benjamin, we are in trouble as long as there is

no image of the present moment of revolutionary possibility to arrest thought. In the absence of this "vanishing point," deconstructionists "decentre" the texts as a series of individualist and anarchist acts. Changes appear eternal, even while society remains static. The revolutionary gesture of deconstruction (the form of interpretation most in vogue in our own given-present) is thus reduced to the sheer novelty of interpretations: fashion masquerades as politics. (p. 58)[46]

We do not have to join Buck-Morss in her condemnation of deconstructive politics to see that she has a point. The text should provoke some new constellation of meaning if its explosive politics are to have staying power. If the image of the honey-mad woman, or the madwomen in the attic, or the mermaid and the minotaur, or "Alice Doesn't," have this constellating power for feminist theorists, how and where do these constellating images emerge in literary texts? To understand this dimension of textuality, I want to turn once more to the philosophy of Hannah Arendt.

In *On Revolution* Arendt explains that power structures can have a positive dimension; she invites us to consider the ways in which power is constellated among individuals:

In distinction to strength, which is the gift and the possession of every man in his isolation against all other men, power comes into being only if and when men join themselves together for the purpose of action, and it will disappear when for whatever reason, they disperse and desert one another. Hence, binding and promising, combining and covenanting are the means by which power is kept in existence; where and when men succeed in keeping intact the power which sprang up between them during the course of any particular act or deed, they are already in the process of foundation, of constituting a stable worldly structure to house, as it were, their combined power of action.[47]

How might a woman's text "house" this collective power? We need to grant that power may not just be something we are subject to, but a force that women and men create through mutual sharing and participation. For Arendt power, "like freedom, equality, speech, and action—is essentially intersubjective and communicative; it comes into existence only in the mutual creation of a public space in between individuals."[48] This communicative founding of power is also a feminist goal. As Joan Kelly says in the introduction to *Women, History and Theory:*

I believe all feminist work emerges out of the spirit and reality of collectivity. Mine has. When women are scattered and cannot work together, a condition that originated with the early modern state, women suffer a loss in position and in the possibility of feminist expression. When some connection among women exists, even if it is only a literary one (as it was among the participants in the *querelle de femmes*) it creates an impressive tradition of feminist thinking.[49]

Kelly echoes Virginia Woolf's insistence that nineteenth-century novelists could not have written without the kinds of "binding and promising" implicit in the eighteenth-century emergence of women's voices. But how does this collective impulse find an image, an objective correlative, in texts themselves? How do we describe the structuring in women's writing of what is to be preserved??

In *Life in the Iron Mills,* Davis' primary impulse is deconstructive. But the novella ends with a constellating gesture that will return us to the question of content and collectivity. The educated, wealthy men who visit the mill workers at the beginning of *Life in the Iron Mills* use language to avoid confronting the material differences between their own conditions and those of the workers; the visitors use several rhetorical modes to dissemble economic distances that would otherwise be unbearable. First, Mitchell, gentleman, amateur gymnast, and armchair philosopher, says he despises "nothing, in heaven, earth, or hell, but one-ideaed men"; as proof, he quotes scripture freely and tosses maxims into the air like so much confetti:

Why, May, look at him! *"De profundis clamavi."* Or, to quote in English, "Hungry and thirsty, his soul faints in him." And so Money sends back its answer into the depths through you, Kirby! Very clear the answer, too!—I think I remember reading the same words somewhere:—washing your hands in Eau de Cologne, and saying, "I am innocent of the blood of this man. See ye to it!"[50]

Davis makes us conscious of this class's dependence on words. Mitchell's easy responses protect him from horror. He bestows generous words upon the poor, but refuses them money or friendship. When he encounters the korl worker, Wolf, who has sculpted a breath-taking statue out of iron scraps, Mitchell is eloquent in protesting Wolf's lot in the very moment that he washes his hands of all action:

Mitchell was leaning against a brick wall. He turned his head indolently, and looked into the mills. There hung about the place a thick, unclean odor. The slightest motion of his hand marked that he perceived it, and his insufferable disgust. That was all. May said nothing, only quickened his angry tramp.

"Besides," added Mitchell, giving a corollary to his answer, "it would be of no use. I am not one of them."

"You do not mean"—said May, facing him.

"Yes, I mean just that. Reform is born of need, not pity. No vital movement of the people's has worked down, for good or evil; fermented, instead, carried up the heaving, cloggy mass. Think back through history, and you will know it. What will this lowest deep—thieves, Magdalens, negroes—do with the light filtered through ponderous Church creeds, Baconian theories, Goethe schemes? Some day, out of their bitter need will be thrown up their own light-bringer,—their Jean Paul, their Cromwell, their Messiah."

"Bah!" was the Doctor's inward criticism. However, in practice, he adopted the theory; for, when, night and morning, afterwards, he prayed that power might be given these degraded souls to rise, he glowed at heart, recognizing an accomplished duty. (pp. 38–39)

Dr. May's theology has no more value than Mitchell's maxims. These men use language to evade responsibility: "Something of a vague idea possessed the Doctor's brain that much good was to be done here by a friendly word or two: a latent genius to be warmed into life by a waited-for sunbeam." More direct and sympathetic than Mitchell, Dr. May can exclaim: "Do you know, boy, you have it in you to be a great sculptor, a great man? . . . A man may make himself anything he chooses. God has given you stronger powers than many men,—me, for instance" (p. 37). The doctor's magnanimity touches Wolf to the core. "Make yourself what you will. It is your right," the doctor urges. "Will you help me?" Wolf's question is useless. The wealthy, well-educated men turn away; their ideology protects them from harm. Still, Wolf believes their belief system; when he overhears a minister speak to his congregation in "burning, light-laden words" the reader is reminded of the distance between Wolf's world and their middle-class values. The minister describes

the incarnate Life, Love, the universal Man: words that become reality in the lives of these people,—that lived again in beautiful words and actions, trifling, but heroic. Sin, as he defined it, was a real foe to them; their trials, temptations, were his. His words passed far over the furnace-tender's grasp, toned to suit another class of culture; they sounded in his ears a very pleasant song in an unknown tongue. . . . In this morbid, distorted heart of the Welsh puddler he had failed. (p. 49)

In *Life in the Iron Mills* Davis wants us to consider how completely out of touch with Wolf's material reality this ordinary language is; she insists on the ordinary word's inadequacy, its cruelty, its capacity to reify, and in reifying to maim listeners of all classes. The minister's sermon repeats his culture's "regime of truth"; by deconstructing its language Davis shows us the terror and oppression that are this culture's base.

In deconstructing popular doxae Davis is also attempting to limit the authority of the politically powerful discourses of her day; she dramatizes their inadequacy. We learn about Wolf's arrest and conviction through Dr. May as he reads the police report to his wife from a page in the daily news. " 'Charge, grand larceny. Sentence, nineteen years hard labor in penitentiary.'—Scoundrel! Serves him right! After all our kindness that night! Picking Mitchell's pocket at the very time!" His wife responds with sharp words about the lower classes' ingratitude, "and then they began to talk of something else." Speech is revealed as a mode of evasion. "Nineteen years!" the narrator says. "How easy that was to read! What a simple word for Judge Day to utter!" (pp. 50–51).

Davis points to the ease with which well-to-do men and women create figures of speech, and contrasts this glibness with the laborious speech and the wage labor of the iron workers. The language of the upper and middle classes is a subterfuge, a means of mediating the enormous distances between rich and poor. As the mill owner's son says contemptuously to his friends, "I have no fancy for nursing infant geniuses. I suppose there are some stray gleams of mind and soul among these wretches. The Lord will take care of his own; or else they can work out their own salvation. I have heard you call our American system a ladder which any man can scale. Do you doubt it? Or perhaps you want to banish all social ladders, and put us all on a flat table-land,—eh, May?" (p. 34). These orderly sentences elide everything that matters.

Wolf's carvings lack this finesse and completeness. The minute they are finished, Wolf destroys them. "The few hours for rest he spent hewing and hacking with his blunt knife, never speaking, until his watch came again,—working at one figure for months, and, when it was finished, breaking it to pieces perhaps, in a fit of disappointment" (pp. 24–25).

Nor is this shattering Wolf's work alone; from the beginning of Davis' Life in the Iron Mills we see a similar dispersion

of metaphor in the body of Davis' narrative. The narrator does not
trust mimesis. She insists on breaking those images that conform
too quickly to the expected reality. In the opening descriptions of
the mill town the streets are overcrowded; as they fill with neglected,
angry laborers, inside one of their cottages the narrator finds "a
little broken figure of an angel pointing upward from the mantel
shelf; but even its wings are covered with smoke, clotted and black"
(p. 12). The narrator introduces death into her signifying device;
she is stunned by the unbearable lightness of speech, its inability
to express the misery she sees. Meanwhile the river, "dull and
tawny-colored," rushes past the town, and the narrator remembers:

When I was a child, I used to fancy a look of weary, dumb appeal upon
the face of the negro-like river slavishly bearing its burden day after
day. Something of the same idle notion comes to me to-day, when from
the street-window I look on the slow stream of human life creeping
past, night and morning, to the great mills. (p. 12)

In describing this stream of life, these "masses of men . . . breathing
from infancy to death an air saturated with fog and grease and
soot, vileness for soul and body" (p. 12), she insists that her own
metaphor describing the "slavish river" does not work:

My fancy about the river was an idle one: it is no type of such a life.
What if it be stagnant and slimy here? It knows that beyond there waits
for it odorous sunlight—quaint old gardens, dusky with soft, green foliage
of apple-trees, and flushing crimson with roses,—air, and fields, and
mountains. (p. 13)

Like Wolf, Davis breaks her own metaphors, and this assault on
the communicative value of words is necessary not only because
words are inadequate to tell her story, but because the language
she wants is implicated in abuse and violence. Wolf's silence promises
another kind of power, a repressed force of thought and energy
that will not find its way into common parlance.

 If Wolf's silence indicates the repressed, alinguistic force
of thought, the disallowed energy that cannot find its way into
words, the statue of the korl woman (Wolf's urgent attempt to
communicate) emerges from the bowels of Davis' story like the

return of the repressed: "Mitchell started back, half-frightened, as, suddenly turning a corner, the white figure of a woman faced him in the darkness,—a woman, white, of giant proportions, crouching on the ground, her arms flung out in some wild gesture of warning" (p. 31). This eloquent expression of spiritual hunger, this statue of one idea, is initially shrouded by the upper classes' irrelevant talk. Without this talk, the statue's message is overpowering: "There was not one line of beauty or grace in it: a nude woman's form, muscular, grown coarse with labor, the powerful limbs instinct with some one poignant longing. One idea: there it was in the tense, rigid muscles, the clutching hands, the wild, eager face, like that of a starving wolf's" (p. 32).

Davis' book enforces a skepticism about the power of representation, but the novel also sets about "structuring what is to be preserved" in the figure of the korl woman.[51] Wolf dies before he has a chance to break this image, and the narrator also refuses to break the korl woman as she has broken her own rhetorical flourishes. The statue represents a kind of desperate excess, a delirious call for help, but in the end its call and its wildness are preserved.

Davis' story ends late at night, when the narrator is alone in her library—or almost alone:

Nothing remains to tell that the poor Welsh puddler once lived, but this figure of the mill-woman cut in korl. I have it here in a corner of my library. I keep it hid behind a curtain,—it is such a rough, ungainly thing. Yet there are about it touches, grand sweeps of outline, that show a master's hand.

The statue represents "unfinished work." "Its pale, vague lips seem to tremble with a terrible question. 'Is this the End?' they say,— 'nothing beyond?—no more?' " (p. 64). Language is once more fragmented, brought into crisis.

In preserving the rough blasphemy of the protesting figure Davis attacks the word's powers of representation and brings the expressive resources of language into disharmony, but she also summons up new expressive resources, for her text equates the writer's power of representation with the latent musicality of the korl woman. For Kristeva the idea of freedom is a nonidea since the subject must "produce a new thesis in order to ensure social communication."[52] But clearly there are instances where such communication works toward transforming the reigning sociolect and supporting those who wish to transform it; any thesis produced to ensure a new form of communication might not be entirely revolutionary, but it could be emancipatory.[53]

Davis presents this tableaux: "The deep of the night is passing while I write. The gas-light wakens from the shadows here and there the objects which lie scattered through the room" (pp. 64–65). These objects are dimly outlined since "they belong to the open sunlight," and summon up happy thoughts of the day to come. But a new "letter" has been added to this dailiness, another fragment added to the "half-moulded child's head," the statue of Aphrodite, the "bough of forest leaves": "homely fragments" which fill the room. The boundary separating the middle-class woman's permitted passions from the darker machinations of the korl woman has been crossed and the text opened to another sense of place. Davis' book ends drenched in sentiment, but she also holds open the dream of a miraculously cosmic and undistorted reciprocity— the hand of the statue points to the east, where "in the flickering, nebulous crimson, God has set the promise of the Dawn" (p. 65). The statue of the korl woman is a figure for the terrible silence within speech, for the blasphemous exclusion of those who need it most. At the same time, the statue holds open a faith in representation as the text asks us to contemplate the statue's imagined revery as one source of liberation: What must I do to be saved? What must we do to be free? Where in language does our freedom lie?

Where indeed? While my own text places itself in a delirious relation to the work of feminist theorists who focus on women's silence, helplessness, or exclusion, and while I have been made euphoric by women who revise the tradition to accommodate their own voices, as my project comes to an end, it is tempting to ignore Davis' final representational strategy and follow Wolf's lead by breaking my own archetype. For I have asked my readers to feel satisfied—even satiated—with the creative delirium of the woman writer, the ecstasy of the honey-mad woman. And yet, *Life in the Iron Mills* teaches us that the jubilation of discovering a new language game should be rationalized against the risks of its regressive orality. In her depiction of white Southern childhood in *Killers of the Dream,* Lillian Smith also describes the political dangers of pleasurable speech.

We were petted children, not puritans. Sugar-tit words and sugar-tit experiences too often made of our minds and manner a fatty tissue that hid the sharp rickety bones of our souls. *Honey, sugar, sweetie* were milk names that still cling to our middle-aged vocabulary.[54]

What do the somber lessons of *Life in the Iron Mills* or the obfuscating lessons of Southern segregationists have to tell us about the woman writer's pleasure in language, about the fate of the honey-mad woman as metaphor?

Davis' text has informed us that language is civil and therefore dangerous. Her text suggests that the language of honey-mad women, like the words of Mitchell or Dr. May, can be obsequiously oriented toward middle-class pleasures. We hear these warnings from all sides. Rogue-gentlemen like Mandeville—and Derrida—have ordained the honey hive as source and seat of civilization, while poets like Sylvia Plath explore the accurate severity of this analogy in poems about women or workers who are honey-mad. In Plath's "The Swarm," the worker bees, filled with angry elation, "argue, in their black ball" while underneath their muttering "the man with grey hands stands under the honeycomb / Of their dream, the hived station." This swarm is easily controlled, its speech co-opted, as the man carries the hive to "a new mausoleum / An ivory palace." The founding of modern civilization on mob violence and patriarchal restraint finds its objective correlative in the act of beekeeping: "O Europe," the poem ends, "O ton of honey."[55] Elsewhere, Plath's speakers choose to inhabit the persona of the queen who abandons the hive, but the choice exacts a terrible cost. As the queen flies away, lifted up by her "lion red body, her wings of glass," she becomes a ghost of her former self, a woman without country or creed.[56] To claim country and language is to eviscerate this self again, to give into the demands of the worker bees, this queen's hungry children: "I am no source of honey / So why should they turn on me?"[57] In "Women in the Beehive" Derrida connects these metaphors with a feminist politics. For him the honey-mad woman is already implicated in the processes she tries to escape:

As much as women's studies has not put back into question the very principles of the structure of the former model of the university, it risks to be just another cell in the university beehive. . . . On the other hand, the effort to put back into question the structural principles . . . which construct the university law, the academic law, that is to say, in the end, the social law in general . . . one has the impression that the questioning of this principle is unequally developed in comparison to those studies which we could call "positive."[58]

I am not so confident that these questions have been "unequally developed." In our dalliance with the productive uses of decon-struction and negativity, we often ignore a text's efforts at com-munication. Such ignorance may lead us toward Kristeva's tempting conclusion in *Revolution in Poetic Language* that works of art do not need to represent a "progressive ideology" since "the text fulfills its ethical function only when it pluralizes, pulverizes, 'musicates' these truths, which is to say, on the condition that it develops them to the point of laughter."[59] What I have begun to argue in this final chapter is that we must also make room in a theory of emancipatory strategies for the "positive ideology" of content and the intersubjective dimension of collective dreams.

If this dimension of textuality has a dangerous affinity with Habermas' affirmation of communicative reason in *The Theory of Communicative Action,* we should not reject a text's efforts at communication out of hand.

For Habermas,

communicative reason does not simply encounter ready-made subjects and systems; rather, it takes part in structuring what is to be preserved. The utopian perspective of reconciliation and freedom is ingrained in the conditions for the communicative sociation of individuals; it is built into the linguistic mechanism of the reproduction of the species.[60]

Habermas' faith in a built-in "linguistic mechanism" is suspect because he makes the desire for emancipatory strategizing part of a program of intersubjective freedom that he believes women and men inevitably strive for. But we do not have to believe in a built-in "linguistic mechanism" to recognize that a theory of emancipation will have to take into account the ways in which texts attempt— and occasionally succeed—in taking an active role "in structuring what is to be preserved." This structuring will inevitably be subject to the limits of a hegemonic language, but if we only focus on the constraints of such hegemony, we miss the potency—and the efficacy—of the woman writer's desire to open up within language a site of unconstrained communication.

So, just as Rebecca Harding Davis saves her korl woman, just as Laura saves Lizzie, just as Chloe continues to cherish Olivia, I want to make room, both inside and outside the hive, for my honey-mad woman to stay. For in this moment of "making room" we discover in the korl woman another version of the honey-mad woman; in her "starving wolf's face" we see hunger explode into rational raving. This raving, in turn, has helped to create a nexus of women "combining and covenanting," "acting and speaking together." As Arendt suggests:

The polis, properly speaking, is not the city-state in its physical location; it is the organization of the people as it arises out of acting and speaking together, and its true space lies between people living together for this purpose, no matter where they happen to be. . . . This space does not always exist, and although all men are capable of deed and word, most of them—like the slave, the foreigner, and the barbarian in antiquity, like the laborer or craftsman prior to the modern age . . . do not live in it. . . . To be deprived of it means to be deprived of reality, which, humanly and politically speaking, is the same as appearance. To men the reality of the world is guaranteed by the presence of others, by its appearing to all; "for what appears to all, this we call Being," and whatever lacks this appearance comes and passes away like a dream, intimately and exclusively our own but without reality.[61]

Arendt's discussion of the polis brings to mind another question I have not yet addressed, and that is the question of how this communicative discourse becomes public, how it enters history. As Dale Spender explains in Man Made Language, "our foremothers may have generated similar meanings to our own but as a muted group without access to the production of legitimated language their meanings may also have remained invisible."[62] Olsen develops this idea at length in *Silences,* but I would respond to Olsen and Spender with Gilbert and Gubar's insistence in "Sexual Linguistics" that we must take seriously "the possibility that women have already entered history."[63] Davis' korl woman has become a potent figure for feminist thought in the last decade—and who is to say that her fiction did not "enter history" in its own time by setting in motion alternative readings of nineteenth-century class and gender struggle?

The strength of feminist theory may lie in its recognition that there is a reality outside of Arendt's political reality, a reality that is still finding speech. But we need to recognize that honey-mad women, women mad for emancipatory language, have begun the process of describing this reality; we have built the cognitive and emotional foundations for constructing a community of speaking women guaranteed by the presence of "others" who speak.

Notes

1. Honey-Mad Women

Epigraph: Webster, "Pornography and Pleasure," p. 49.

1. Kristeva, "Oscillation Between Power and Denial," in Marks and de Courtivron, eds., *New French Feminisms* (hereafter *NFF*), pp. 165–66.

2. Howells, *A Modern Instance*, p. 9.

3. *Ibid.*

4. Oliver, *American Primitive*, p. 3. Further references to this work will be cited in the text.

5. For example, in Alicia Ostriker's review of Oliver's latest book of poems, *Dream Work*, Ostriker praises Oliver's recent emphasis on suffering and devalues her jubilant primitivism: "*Dream Work* . . . is an advance on her earlier writing in two ways, which are probably connected. Formally, her verse feels increasingly confident, smoother, and thus bolder. . . . At the same time she has moved from the natural world and its desires, the 'heaven of appetite' that goes on without much intervention or possibility of control, further into the world of historical and personal suffering" (see Ostriker, "Natural Facts," p. 150).

6. Clark and Holquist, *Mikhail Bakhtin*, pp. 301–2. See also Bakhtin's *Rabelais and His World*, esp. pp. 278–302.

7. Chopin, *The Awakening*, p. 56. Further references to this work will be cited in the text.

8. Bakhtin, *Rabelais and His World*, p. 317. (This translation has been slightly modified by Clark and Holquist, *Mikhail Bakhtin*, p. 303.) Bakhtin adds that "there is an ancient tie between the feast and the spoken word. . . . Prandial speech is a free and jocular speech. . . . The popular-festive right of laughter and clowneries, the right to be frank, was extended to the table" (pp. 283–84). Further references to this work will be cited in the text.

9. This is not to suggest that biology is scriptive destiny, but that Irigaray's metaphor of the "two lips speaking together" has its own poetic justice. In a world of overinflated phallic metaphors, her word play seems particularly liberating—a metaphor the feminist critic can play with and celebrate.

10. Barthes, *The Pleasure of the Text*, p. 17. Further references to this work will be cited in the text.

11. Irigaray, "When Our Lips Speak Together," p. 76. Further references to this work will be cited in the text.

12. Jehlen, "Archimedes and the Paradox of Feminist Criticism," p. 76.

13. Benveniste, Problems in General Linguistics, p. 226.

14. Chomsky, Cartesian Linguistics, p. 29.

15. Ibid., p. 20.

16. Derrida, "La parole soufflé," in Derrida, Writing and Difference, pp. 177–78. Further references to this work will be cited in the text.

17. Derrida, "Force and Signification," in Derrida, Writing and Difference, p. 9.

18. Ibid., p. 11.

19. Wittig, Les Guérillères, pp. 112, 114. Further references to this work will be cited in the text.

20. Edmond Jabès, Le livre des questions, p. 23. Further references to this work will be cited in the text.

21. Derrida, "Edmond Jabès and the Question of the Book," in Derrida, Writing and Difference, p. 70.

22. Gauthier, "Is There Such a Thing as Women's Writing?" Marks and de Courtivron, eds., NFF, pp. 162–63.

23. Leclerc, Parole de femme, as quoted by Madeleine Gagnon in Marks and de Courtivron, eds., NFF, p. 179.

24. Cixous, "The Laugh of the Medusa," in Marks and de Courtivron, eds., p. 260. Further references to this work will be cited in the text.

25. Chawaf, "Linguistic Flesh," in Marks and de Courtivron, eds., NFF, p. 177–178.

26. Gaudin et al., Feminist Readings (Yale French Studies), p. 10.

27. For an explication of this thesis, see also Gilbert and Gubar's "Sexual Linguistics," esp. pp. 523–31.

28. In "Sexual Linguistics" Gilbert and Gubar move very quickly from describing women's fantasies "about a utopian linguistic structure" to affirming the idea that "the very fact that one can metaphorize the mouth as a womb, the Word as the child of female power, implies that women need not experience any ontological alienation from the idea of language as we know it" (p. 537). This affirmation begs too many questions, and is especially problematic because it fixes us in the mirrorland of psycholinguistics. Their critique of Lacan (p. 536) takes a more promising direction.

29. In their attempt to find a point of congruence between French and Anglo-American feminist theory, Gilbert and Gubar argue in "Sexual Linguistics" that the "female linguistic fantasy . . . has been increasingly important since the turn of the century" (p. 523). I agree, but rather than stressing women's new "fantasy" of the sentence, I want to insist on the enactment of these "new" sentences over several centuries.

30. Showalter, "Feminist Criticism in the Wilderness," p. 185.

31. One problem I have not taken up in this set of essays is the split between white American and Afro-American feminist criticism. This difference is essential. As others have pointed out, one of the dangers of overplaying the Franco-American divide is that it obliterates other oppositions and imposes imaginary affinities between feminists of similar nationalities but different races. On this debate, see especially Barbara Smith's "Towards a Black Feminist Criticism," and Deborah McDowell's "New Directions for Black Feminist Criticism" in Showalter's The New Feminist Criticism. On the tendencies of

"American" feminists, see Gilbert's introduction to Cixous and Clement's *The Newly Born Woman.* According to Gilbert, "American feminists . . . have difficulty imagining for themselves the French feminist's thieving and flying, her utopian body, her desirous fantasizing and guilty shuddering" (p. x). (However, for an example of Gilbert's "thieving and flying" see her essay "The Second Coming of Aphrodite.") On the problem of combining approaches, see Jardine, "Pre-Texts for the Transatlantic Feminist": "American feminists find themselves facing a new version of the anxiety of influence. Caught between the predominantly American feminist's 'know thyself!' . . . and the French women's discovery that there is no more self to know, she often feels obliged to opt for one camp over the other" (p. 224). For an essay that crosses both racial and national boundaries see Homans, "Her Very Own Howl." Finally, for an essay that excavates the Afro-American/white American feminist divide, but uses a euphoric word play resembling the inventiveness of the French feminists at their best, see Spillers' "Interstices: A Small Drama of Words."

32. See, for example, Silverman's "Histoire d'O," or Jacobs' *"Now Voyager,"* or Kolodny's assertion in "Dancing Through the Minefield" that "what unites and repeatedly invigorates feminist literary criticism, then, is neither dogma nor method but an acute and impassioned *attentiveness* to the ways in which primarily male structures of power are inscribed (or encoded) within our literary inheritance" (p. 162). In "Feminist Criticism in the Wilderness," Showalter insists on distinguishing between feminist critique and "gynocriticism"—whose "subjects are the history, styles, themes, genres, and structures of writing by women; the psychodynamics of female creativity . . . the evolution and laws of a female literary tradition" (pp. 184–85).

33. A number of feminist critics have already begun to explore women's pleasure in language. See especially Ostriker's *Stealing the Language,* and Gilbert and Gubar's "Sexual Linguistics." Most of these discussions limit the scope of such inventiveness to the twentieth century. (Ann R. Jones' fine essays on Renaissance poetry by women offer exceptions.) In *The Madwoman in the Attic* Gilbert and Gubar describe the potency of women's revisions of male culture in their opening chapters (see especially p. 44). But the central burden of their book lies in its analysis of the crushing weight of patriarchy—and women's strategies of survival when they were acted "upon" by patriarchal culture. "What was the effect upon women writers of that complex of culture myths summarized by Woolf as Milton's bogey? Surrounded by 'patriarchal poetry,' what strategies for artistic survival were they able to develop?" (p. 213) I am indebted, here and elsewhere, to their analysis, but I want to redirect our vision to include moments of emancipation and empowerment. Gilbert and Gubar feel the same dialectical need, but since they have defined the nineteenth century as a time of frustration and revisionary anger, the twentieth century must become the site of women's new-found self-expression. By localizing women's experience of verbal empowerment in the twentieth century, they split in half what is actually a chaotic, dynamic dialectic of change. This splitting leads to the utopian tone of Gilbert's essay on *The Awakening,* a novel that she asks to usher in a new age of feminist self-transformation (see her "The Second Coming of Aphrodite").

34. There are delightful exceptions, including Kolodny's call for a "playful pluralism" in "Dancing Through the Minefield" (p. 161), Gilberts' extravagant reading of *The Awakening* ("The Second Coming of Aphrodite"), and Chessman's reading of Gertrude Stein in *The Public Is Invited to Dance: Representation, the Body, and Dialogue in Gertrude Stein.*

35. Miller, "The Text's Heroine," p. 53.

36. De Lauretis, *Alice Doesn't*, p. 185–86. Further references to this work will be cited in the text. Although I am restricting my comments to *Alice Doesn't*, a more complex view of the relation between language and woman's creativity emerges in de Lauretis' "Feminist Studies/Critical Studies: Issues, Terms, and Contexts." Here she describes the feminist critical text as a more freewheeling space in which women not only address themselves as subjects, but experiment with unmasking themselves and with masquerade as ways of bringing different desires into "political consciousness" (p. 17).

37. De Lauretis' description of women's self-consciousness is very moving. But Joan Kelly reminds us in "Early Feminist Theory and the *Querelle des Femmes*" in *Women, History, and Theory*, that the "new" habit of consciousness raising could not work without changes in economic and political conditions. Earlier feminist thinkers also effected this "habit change" within themselves and their cohorts, but theorists like Pisan, Marinella, or Astell "had few or no connections with the movements for social change that periodically erupted and were suppressed. Such movements were isolated and/or short lived, confined to classes of people whose powers were not yet fed by the productive forces of the age. It would take the French Revolution and the industrialization of Europe and North America before social theory and practice would cohere, bound by democratic movements that were broad enough to aim at transforming the entire stature of hierarchical society" (p. 68).

38. Alicia Ostriker traces a similar plot in *Stealing the Language*. See especially the chapter "Thieves of Language," also in Showalter's *Feminist Criticism*. On the reinvention of women's orality, see also Michie's *The Flesh Made Word*, pp. 131–138.

39. Adorno, *Negative Dialectics*, p. 23. Further references to this work will be cited in the text.

40. Gauthier, "Is There Such a Thing as Women's Writing?" in Marks and de Courtivron, eds., *NFF*, p. 163.

41. I have spelled out this position in some detail in " 'Because a Fire Was in My Head': Eudora Welty and the Dialogic Imagination."

42. Dinnerstein, *The Mermaid and the Minotaur*, p. 73.

43. *Ibid.*

44. For an essay that explores this and other feminist issues in playful detail see Donna Haraway's "A Manifesto for Cyborgs."

45. Cixous, "An Exchange with Hélène Cixous," in Conley, *Hélène Cixous*, p. 138.

46. This is Coward and Ellis's excellent (if somewhat politicized) synopsis of Lévi-Strauss' ideas from *Language and Materialism*, p. 19. See also Lévi-Strauss' *From Honey to Ashes*. Note, in addition, that while Coward and Ellis fully hyphenate the term "honey-mad-women" to signify a unified mythological entity, I have unsutured "woman" from Lévi-Strauss' version of honey-madness and invented for the honey-mad-woman (*"la fille folle de miel"*) a more playful and fluid persona.

47. Coward and Ellis, *Language and Materialism*, p. 19.

48. Showalter, "Feminist Criticism in the Wilderness," p. 193.

49. Black, *Models and Metaphors*, p. 239. This passage is quoted in Turner, *Dramas, Fields, and Metaphors*, p. 30. Turner also quotes Nisbet, *Social Change and History*, who explains that metaphors function almost invisibly in our analytical speech. When words like "growth" or "development" are applied to social phenomena (as in "the growth of the city-state" or "the role of developing nations in the world economy"), they

bring with them associations of organicism and continuity that foreground some attributes of social formations while blocking our perception of others (Nisbet, p. 6; Turner, p. 24).

50. Turner, *Dramas, Fields, and Metaphors*, p. 31.

51. Turner, *Dramas, Fields, and Metaphors*, p. 30.

52. Black, *Models and Metaphors*, p. 241. Also quoted in Turner, *Dramas, Fields, and Metaphors*, p. 26. In *The Woman and the Demon* Nina Auerbach takes on this project of renegotiating older "conceptual archetypes." She focuses on metaphor's volatility and discounts its powers of limitation. Thus she emphasizes the life that exists within metaphors feminist theorists may have discarded too quickly. "The mythologies of the past as well have become stronger endowments than oppressions. When properly understood, the angel in the house, along with her seemingly victimized Victorian sisters, is too strong and interesting a creature for us to kill" (p. 12).

2. The Bilingual Heroine: From "Text" to "Work"

1. De Lauretis, *Alice Doesn't*, p. 35. Further references to this work will be cited in the text.

2. Brontë, *Jane Eyre*, p. 105. Further references to this work will be cited in the text.

3. Heidegger, "The Origin of the Work of Art," in *Poetry, Language, Thought*, p. 44. Further references to this work will be cited in the text.

4. Silverman, "*Histoire d'O*: The Construction of a Female Subject," p. 325. Further references to this work will be cited in the text. De Lauretis also quotes Silverman in *Alice Doesn't*, p. 150.

5. In *Shirley* Brontë retreats from her use of French as a form of abnormal discourse. Here it is the men—the mill owners—who speak French, and the narrator who keeps herself busy translating the dialect spoken by the workers into "legible English." Clearly Brontë is aware of the revolutionary possibility of dialect as counterlanguage, but by keeping the women and the workers in separate spheres (by making Shirley into a baronial "lord of the manor") and by translating and thus homogenizing the rough-hewn linguistic differences of the workers and mill owners, Brontë avoids the transformative possibility of a second language. What we see in this novel is the work of repression: Brontë is drawn to the disruptive possibility a second language offers, but in *Shirley* she seems frightened of the similar plights shared by workers and women, and invents labyrinthine language and plot devices to keep these similarities constantly in view even as she tries to present these similarities as oppositional.

6. Hardy, *Jude*, p. 41. Further references to this work will be cited in the text.

7. Homans' "Her Very Own Howl" is both an example and a critique of this "solution." She explains that in Toni Morrison's *Sula* "what finally expresses [Nel's] woman-identified self is of necessity nonrepresentational" (p. 193). But Homans' conclusion does not condone this "separatism in language" wholeheartedly. "Those novelists who, like the French critics, question the possibility that language can represent women, are all 'American' in the sense that they do so, after all, by representing their skepticism about representation. In effect, they displace unrepresentability from the structure of language to a thematics of language" (p. 205). My project differs from Homans' in the following way. She asserts that Morrison's image of "unrepresentability" "radically questions the compatibility of genuine female self-expression and the use of ordinary (to say nothing of literary or lyrical)

discourse" (p. 194), while I want to discover moments when normal and "abnormal" discourse gain this expressive capacity.

    8. Brontë, *Villette*, p. 442. Further references to this work will be cited in the text.

    9. Rorty, *Philosophy and the Mirror of Nature*, p. 320.

    10. Keats, "The Fall of Hyperion," in *Selected Poems and Letters*, p. 235, ll. 13–15. Further references to this work will be cited in the text by line number.

    11. Keats, *Letters*, p. 384.

    12. Other feminist critics have described such a "liberating multilanguagedness" in women's texts. See, for example, Gilbert and Gubar's "Sexual Linguistics," p. 528 (on Christina Stead's *The Man Who Loved Children*), Donna Haraway's "A Manifesto for Cyborgs," p. 94 (on Cherrie Moraga's *Loving in the War Years*), and Dianne Hunter's "Hysteria, Psychoanalysis, and Feminism" (on Bertha Pappenheim—Freud's and Breuer's "Anna O."). Hunter, in particular, equates Pappenheim's multilanguagedness with an alienation from male significations and a regression to prepatriarchal semiosis. While her analysis is persuasive in the case of Bertha Pappenheim, I find other strategies of linguistic doubling at work in *Villette*.

    13. Coleridge, "The Nightingale," in *The Complete Works*, ll. 97–98.

    14. Adorno, *Negative Dialectics*, p. 53.

    15. Gilbert and Gubar, *The Madwoman in the Attic*, pp. 401–2. Further references to this work will be cited in the text.

    16. Jacobus, "The Buried Letter: Feminism and Romanticism in *Villette*, p. 57. While my reading of *Villette* differs from Jacobus' in many respects, my analysis has not just been enriched—it has been enabled by her analysis. For another excellent, revisionary reading of *Villette* that celebrates Lucy's creativity, see Brenda Silver's "The Reflecting Reader in *Villette*."

    17. Coleridge, "Kubla Khan," *The Complete Works*, ll. 46–54.

    18. Jehlen, "Archimedes and the Paradox of Feminist Criticism," p. 79. Further references to this work will be cited in the text.

    19. Weiskel, *The Romantic Sublime*, p. 57.

    20. Keats, *Selected Poems and Letters*, p. 279.

    21. Eliot, *Mill on the Floss*, p. 217. Further references to this work will be cited in the text. See also Mary Jacobus' "The Question of Language: Men of Maxims and *The Mill on the Floss*," pp. 212–16, for a suggestive reading of this passage.

    22. Keats, *Selected Poems and Letters*, p. 265.

    23. James treats bilingualism somewhat differently in *The Golden Bowl* and *The Tragic Muse*. In *The Tragic Muse* Miriam Rooth's bilingualism is a sign of her self-control in a theater world slightly to one side of the constraints of patriarchy. In *The Golden Bowl* the Prince and Charlotte believe that their knowledge of Italian (which is also a marker of their social class), keeps the secret of their affair safe from the shopkeeper who wants to sell them the golden bowl. The shopkeeper "penetrates" their language game, and in this gesture James repudiates the notion of a sacrosanct, authoritative discourse safely insulating class from class.

    24. Homans, *Women Writers and Poetic Identity*, p. 12. Further references to this work will be cited in the text. While I find myself in partial disagreement with some of Homans' postulates, her readings of nineteenth-century women poets in the context of their male contemporaries remain a powerful analysis of the limitations nineteenth-century women writers encountered when they took up the pen.

25. Coleridge, "The Nightingale," in *The Collected Works*, ll. 98–109.
26. Coleridge, "The Rime of the Ancient Mariner," in *The Complete Poetical Works*, vol. 1, gloss to ll 131–34.
27. Coleridge, "Dejection: an Ode," in *The Complete Poetical Works*, vol. I. epigraph. Further references to this work will be cited in the text as line numbers.
28. Wordsworth, "Nutting," in *Selected Poems and Prefaces*, ll. 54–56.
29. In describing bilingualism as a "language game" I want both to distinguish this practice from what other feminist critics have said about literary women's "double-voiced discourse" and to establish a continuum with such double-voicedness. In *The Madwoman in the Attic* Gilbert and Gubar suggest that "Austen was indisputably fascinated by double-talk, by conversations that imply the opposite of what they intend, narrative statements that can only confuse, and descriptions that are linguistically sound, but indecipherable, or tautological" (p. 127). In "Pre-Texts for the Transatlantic Feminist" Jardine explains that because woman can never experience herself as other than her mother, this "has combined with that culture's constant denial of her ability to write through its designation of her, *with* her mother, as The Other. Doubly Other, then, the woman who writes translates this at least double message. She experiences a kind of double vision . . . a difficult and double practice" (p. 229).
30. Barthes, *Sade, Fourier, Loyola*, p. 7. Further references to this work will be cited in the text.
31. Wordsworth, *The Prelude*, in *Selected Poems and Prefaces*, Book 7, ll. 679–685. Further references to this work are all from book 7 and will be cited as line numbers.
32. Bakhtin, "Discourse in the Novel" in Bakhtin, *Dialogic Imagination*, p. 367.
33. This commentary on *The Prelude* (ll. 384–99) is designed to add a missing voice to Geoffrey Hartman's interesting reading of this same passage in "The Unremarkable Wordsworth." Mary Jacobus has also written a response to Hartman's essay in which she describes "an alternative profession for The Romantic daughter" in *Romanticism, Writing, and Sexual Difference*. See especially "Splitting The Race of Man / In Twain': Prostitution, Personification, and *The Prelude*."
34. Cixous, "La Venue à l'écriture," p. 37. This passage is cited in Duren, "Cixous' Exorbitant Texts," p. 46.
35. Cixous, "La Venue à l'écriture," p. 37.
36. Barthes, "From Work to Text," pp. 74–75. Although I am calling for a renegotiation of the idea that women's writing does "work," I do not feel dogmatic about whether we use the term "text" or "work" to describe women's "works" and use both terms throughout, with the understanding that "text" should never be understood in my own "text" as a return to Barthes' "Text," but as a piece of writing that does "work" in the way I have described.
37. *Ibid.*, p. 80.
38. Lentricchia, *Criticism and Social Change*, p. 11. Jerome McGann, in *The Romantic Ideology*, also insists on an affirmation of "work," as opposed to "text." In McGann's analysis, however, the "text" is not affirmed as that impassioned site of heterogeneous practice that Barthes describes in "From Work to Text." If such heterogeneity is anathema to McGann, it is because he sees Barthes' plurally read and written texts as staging grounds for the ideological interests of late capitalism. For McGann, "the most imperative task now facing the world of literary criticism" involves the effort "to return poetry to a human form—to see that what we read and study are poetic *works* produced

and reproduced by numbers of specific men and women" (p. 160). Whether or not this notion of "human" poetry produced by "specific men and women" can accommodate Kristeva's notion of the poetic language produced by a split subject, McGann does not say.

39. Cixous, "The Laugh of the Medusa," p. 257.

3. The Animality of the Letter

1. Melville, *Moby-Dick*, p. 494. Further references to this work will be cited in the text.

2. De Lauretis, *Alice Doesn't*, p. 13. Further references to this work will be cited in the text.

3. Derrida, "Structure, Sign, and Play," in Derrida, *Writing and Differences*, p. 279. Further references to this work will be cited in the text.

4. See de Lauretis, *Alice Doesn't*, pp. 12–36.

5. Oliver, "Humpbacks," in Oliver, *American Primitive*, p. 60. Further references to this work will be cited in the text.

6. Silverman, *"Histoire d'O,"* p. 325. Further references to this work will be cited in the text.

7. Kristeva, "Interview," p. 166. Also quoted in de Lauretis, *Alice Doesn't*, p. 95. In describing Roeg's film *Bad Timing*, de Lauretis adds that "it is just in the split, in that non-coherence between registers of time and desire, that figural and narrative identification are possible for me, that I can pose the question of my time and place in the terms of the film's imaging" (p. 102). Once again nonrepresentability is what distinguishes "woman's time" from every other. That these moments are important in women's writing and experience I will not deny. (See, for example, Yaeger, " 'A Language Which Nobody Understood.' ") My quarrel is with those critics who would make this nonrepresentability woman's only or primary space of "self-identification." On empowering use of male texts and images as a space of women's self-representation, see Heilbrun, *Reinventing Womanhood*.

8. See Kolodny, "Dancing Through the Minefield," for an elaboration of this project.

9. Not everyone argues that these structures are permanent. For Kolodny, in "Dancing Through the Minefield," the feminist critic's "overriding commitment is to a radical alteration . . . in the nature of that experience" (p. 159), while in *Man Made Language*, a book devoted to describing sexism in speech, Spender tells a touching anecdote of trying to collect data on "women's speech" in a situation in which Spender had already pointed out to a group of women speakers that they had been outvoiced by male colleagues. Suddenly aware of their own silence, the women began to speak out, and Spender's data on women's aphasia disappears. In addition, see Munich, "Notorious Signs, Feminist Criticism and Literary Tradition."

10. Stevens, "The World as Meditation," in *The Collected Poems of Wallace Stevens*, pp. 520–21.

11. Foucault, *The Archaeology of Knowledge*, p. 117.

12. Anouilh, *Antigone*, p. 3.

13. Racevskis, *Michel Foucault and the Subversion of Intellect*, p. 58. Further references to this work will be cited in the text.

14. Foucault, *The Order of Things*, p. 322.

15. Foucault, "Truth and Power" in Foucault, *Power/Knowledge*, p. 131.

16. Foucault, "The Discourse on Language," in Foucault, *The Archaeology of Knowledge*, p. 229.

17. Foucault, *The Archaeology of Knowledge*, p. 128.

18. Bakhtin, *Rabelais and his World*, p. 423. Iswolsky's translation has been slightly modified by Clark and Holquist, *Mikhail Bakhtin*, p. 317.

19. Foucault does not deny that such moments exist; the question is whether or not we can locate them. In *The History of Sexuality* (vol. 1), he explains that "where there is power, there is resistance, and yet, or rather consequently, this resistance is never in a position of exteriority in relation to power. . . . Their existence [power relations] depends on a multiplicity of points of resistance; these play the role of adversary, target, support or handle in power relations. These points of resistance are present everywhere in the power network. Hence there is no single locus of the great Refusal, no soul of revolt, source of all rebellions or pure law of the revolutionary. . . . But this does not mean that they are only a reaction or rebound, forming with respect to the basic domination an underside that is in the end always passive, doomed to perpetual defeat. . . . it is doubtless the strategic codification of these points of resistance that makes a revolution possible" (95–96). There is even space in Foucault's theory, then, for "emancipatory strategies."

20. Bové, "Intellectuals at War: Michel Foucault and the Analytics of Power," p. 50. Further references to this work will be cited in the text.

21. This way of thinking is becoming quite common. In a flier for *Theory in the Classroom* Vincent B. Leitch explains (albeit with less proscriptive force than Bové) that "the main job of deconstructive pedagogy is to suspend the oppressive forces of discursive language—to loosen, baffle or lighten their power."

22. Dodgson, *Alice in Wonderland*, p. 18. Further references to this work will be cited in the text.

23. Heidegger, *Introduction to Metaphysics*, p. 131.

24. Heidegger, "Language," in Heidegger, *Poetry, Language, Thought*, p. 198.

25. Empson, *Some Versions of Pastoral*, pp. 272–73.

26. Foucault, *The Archaeology of Knowledge*, pp. 210–11.

27. *Ibid.*, p. 49.

28. Arendt, *The Human Condition*, pp. 190–91. Further references to this work will be cited in the text.

29. Malcolm X, *Autobiography*, p. 171. Further references to this work will be cited in the text.

30. Rich, "The Burning of Paper Instead of Children," in *Adrienne Rich's Poetry*, p. 47. Further references to this work will be cited in the text.

31. For a discussion of the complications and historical distortions involved in applying Derrida's ideas directly to political subversion and historical change, see "No Words Apart," McClintock and Nixon's response in *Critical Inquiry* (1986) 13:140–154 to Derrida's "Le Dernier Mot du Racisme" in *Critical Inquiry* (1985) 12:290–299.

32. Derrida, "Outwork," in Derrida, *Dissemination*, p. 5.

33. *Ibid.*

34. Derrida, "Edmond Jabès and the Question of the Book," in Derrida, *Writing and Difference*, p. 72. The quotations are from Jabès *Le livre des questions*, p. 68.

35. *Ibid.*, pp. 72–73.

36. Barthes, "The Spirit of the Letter," in *The Responsibility of Forms*, p. 98. Further references to this work will be cited in the text.

37. Welty, "A Piece of News," pp. 22–23.

38. *Ibid.*, p. 23.

39. For a description of Arendt's impact on another feminist thinker see Minnich's "Hannah Arendt: Thinking as We Are."

4. Alice Can

1. De Lauretis, *Alice Doesn't*, p. 34. Further references to this work will be cited in the text.

2. Showalter, "Feminist Criticism in the Wilderness," pp. 184–87. Further references to this work will be cited in the text.

3. Welty, "A Piece of News," p. 21. Further references to this work will be cited in the text.

4. Brand, *The Essential Wittgenstein*, p. 32.

5. Barthes, *Writing Degree Zero*, p. 10. Further references to this work will be cited in the text.

6. For an excellent analysis of *Writing Degree Zero* see Susan Sontag's introduction to Barthes' *Writing Degree Zero* and Kristeva's "From One Identity to Another," in Kristeva, *Desire in Language*.

7. See, for example, Gubar's " 'The Blank Page' and Female Creativity": "just as important as the anxiety the male pen produces in the would-be woman writer is the horror she experiences at having been defined as his creation. Indeed, this problem seems to explain the coherence of nineteenth- and twentieth-century writing by women. . . . The woman artist who experiences herself as killed into art may also experience herself as bleeding into print" (pp. 247–48). I am not suggesting that these conclusions are absent from the story Gubar analyzes, Dinesen's 'The Blank Page,' but asking how much territory the feminist critic's generalizations should try to account for. Lipking goes to greater extremes in his search for a theory of women's writing than Gubar. Lipking, in "Aristotle's Sister: A Poetics of Abandonment," tries to define a woman's poetics as "the poetics of abandonment": "Abandoned women know that the world can shift too fast to be imitated, that the harmony of art is made to be broken. Hence their poetics obeys another law of nature, the unsatisfied craving of children who cry to be held" (p. 78). Lipking claims to be writing with the voice of Aristotle's sister, but he more nearly speaks with the voice of a Virgilian patriarch: "Arms and the man I sing."

8. Rich, "Sibling Mysteries," in Rich, *Dream of a Common Language*, p. 47. Further references to this work will be cited in the text.

9. Barthes, *The Pleasure of the Text*, p. 47.

10. This is a more aggressive version of the poetics of the literary woman involved in "revisionary struggle" that Gilbert and Gubar define in *Madwoman*. "Frequently . . . she can begin such a struggle only by actively seeking a *female* precursor who, far from representing a threatening force to be denied or killed proves by example that a revolt against patriarchal literary authority is possible" (p. 49). Gubar takes this to another extreme in " 'The Blank Page' and Female Creativity." "The blood on the royal marriage sheets seems to imply that women's paint and ink are produced through a painful wounding, a literal influence of male authority" (p. 256). In both these examples Gilbert and Gubar

imply that women are overpowered by male language and that the only hope for pleasurable productivity is through the obliteratation of male discourse.

11. Irigaray, "When Our Lips Speak Together," pp. 69–70.

12. Cixous, "An Exchange with Hélène Cixous," in Conley, *Hélène Cixous: Writing the Feminine*, p. 138.

13. Oliver, "Mussels," in Oliver, *Twelve Moons*, p. 4. Further references to this work will be cited in the text.

14. Gilbert and Gubar, *The Madwoman in the Attic*, p. 93. Further references to this work will be cited in the text.

15. De Beauvoir, *The Second Sex*, p. 78.

16. Gilbert and Gubar, *Madwoman*, p. 94.

17. Jehlen, "Archimedes and the Paradox of Feminist Criticism," p. 76.

18. Bishop, "In the Village," in *The Collected Prose*, p. 251. Further references to this work will be cited in the text.

19. Lemaire, *Jacques Lacan*, p. 51.

20. *Ibid.*

21. Robert Giroux, "Introduction," in Bishop, *The Collected Prose*, p. x.

22. Moss, "A Long Voyage Home," p. 110.

23. Kelly, *Post-Partum Document*, p. 167. Further references to this work will be cited in the text.

24. Heidegger, "The Origin of the Work of Art," in Heidegger, *Poetry, Language, Thought*, p. 46.

25. *Ibid.*, p. 26.

26. Bernstein, *Beyond Objectivism and Relativism*, pp. 82–86.

27. Bakhtin has a valuable discussion in *The Dialogic Imagination* of what it means for language itself to be "imaged." He divides this imaging into three modes. First, "hybridization" is mixing "two social languages within the limits of a single utterance" (p. 358). For Bakhtin these hybrid words are filled with "potential for new world views" (p. 360). This hybridization is at work in Bishop's "In the Village." Next Bakhtin describes stylization, or the "dialogized interrelation of languages" that allows a writer to highlight some aspects of discourse while leaving others as background. This creates a feeling within a text for the boundaries of language—"compels one to sense physically the plastic [and limited] forms of difference languages" (p. 364). This stylization is at work in Welty's "A Piece of News." Finally, Bakhtin describes the advantages offered by straightforward dialogue—a strategy with which Oliver and Rich experiment.

28. Bakhtin, "Discourse in the Novel," in Bakhtin, *The Dialogic Imagination*, p. 358.

5. Writing as Action: *A Vindication of the Rights of Women*

Epigraph: "An Exchange with Hélène Cixous," in Conley, *Hélène Cixous*, p. 157.

1. Donovan, *Feminist Theory*, p. 10. See also Wollstonecraft's *A Vindication*, "Observations on the State of Degradation to which Woman is Reduced by Various Causes," pp. 52–77.

2. For the differences between Fuller and Wollstoncraft, see Donovan, *Feminist Theory*, p. 176. It is worth noting that Bertha Pappenheim, the multilingual Anna O.,

translated Wollstonecraft's *A Vindication*. See Diane Hunter's "Hysteria, Psychoanalysis, and Feminism: The Case of Anna O.," p. 104.

3. Marquerite Duras, "Interview," in Marks and de Courtivron, eds., *New French Feminisms* (hereafter *NFF*), p. 174.

4. Poovey, *The Proper Lady and the Woman Writer*, pp. 67–68.

5. Gauthier, "Is There Such a Thing as Women's Writing?" in Marks and de Courtivron, eds., *NFF*, pp. 162–63.

6. Jardine, "Gynesis," p. 57. In "Pre-Texts for the Transatlantic Feminist" Jardine does, however, define two resources for the "female writing subject" who is both excluded from dominance and forced to conform. First, she can employ a discourse that focuses on decentering the subject. Second, she can "assume the symbolic armor . . . name the law and attack it using the same laws. Multiplicity, polyphony, genitality, rejection of time, rhythm, repetition—and violence—are then consciously encoded at the level of the fiction. As *technique*, this is most often the case with *explicitly* feminist productions" (p. 231). This second resource is employed by Wollstonecraft.

7. See Miller's "Emphasis Added" for another example of the emancipatory functioning of repetition in women's texts.

8. Olsen, *Silences*, epigraph, p. xi.

9. Olsen is not the only one to theorize about women's silences, nor is the variety of silence she describes the only kind we see figured in women's texts. For other observations about women's silence, almost any feminist critic will do, but see especially Gilbert and Gubar in *The Madwoman in the Attic*, p. 127, or Heilbrun and Stimpson in "Theories of Feminist Criticism: A Dialogue," p. 62. Heilbrun and Stimpson discuss "the presence of absence" in literature by women, the "hollows, centers, caverns within the work—places where activity that one might expect is missing . . . or deceptively coded" (p. 62). Showalter develops this idea in her observation in "Feminist Criticism in the Wilderness" that our consciousness of gender has allowed us to "see meaning in what has previously been empty space. The orthodox plot recedes, and another plot . . . stands out in bold relief." (p. 204). There is a contrast in the criticism between theorists who describe this silence as a productive space and those who find, as Sarah Kofman does (in *The Enigma of Women*, pp. 36–97), that the narcissistic woman is silenced in order for men to speak in her place. Frequently these contrasting views work together, as in Susan Gubar's " 'The Blank Page' ": "Blankness there is an act of defiance, a dangerous and risky refusal to certify purity" (p. 259).

10. McCullers, *The Ballad of the Sad Cafe*, p. 71. Further references to this work will be cited in the text.

11. Rousseau, *Émile*, p. 339.

12. Wollstonecraft, *A Vindication*, p. 86. Further references to this work will be cited in the text.

13. Other feminist critics have described similar moments in women's texts. See, for example, Ann Rosalind Jones, in "Assimilation with a Difference": "Speaking out of silence, entering the terrain of male discourse from the margins, Pernette and Labé take over its central position as speakers and appropriate its rituals for their own ends. Their women's situations and women's voices do more than modify poetic style. They rewrite the rules of the game" (p. 153).

14. Blake, "Visions of the Daughters of Albion," in *The Poetry and Prose of William Blake*, plate 1, ll. 6–10. Further references to this work will be cited in the text.

15. Bakhtin is especially eloquent in arguing that discourse "always wants to be heard . . . it always is in search of responsive understanding, and does not stop at *the most proximate* understanding but makes its way further and further away (without limits)." It is in the nature of language to ask for a response, "for discourse (and, therefore, for man) nothing is more frightening than the *absence of answer.*" Bakhtin, quoted in Todorov, *Mikhail Bakhtin,* p. 111.

16. See my essay on *The Awakening,* " 'A Language Which Nobody Understood,' " for an application of these same principles in another context.

17. Gadamer, *Truth and Method,* p. 347.

18. For a wide-ranging discussion of female/male dialogics see Dale Spender, *Man Made Language,* especially ch. 3, "The Dominant and the Muted."

19. Arendt, *The Human Condition,* p. 246. Further references to this work will be cited in the text.

20. Habermas, *Knowledge and Human Interests,* pp. 314–15.

21. Rorty, *Philosophy and the Mirror of Nature,* pp. 370–71. Further references to this work will be cited in the text.

22. Since feminist historians have devoted a great deal of energy to explicating such historical moments, it would be useful for feminist literary critics to make more use of their insights. See, for example, Joan Kelly's essay on "Early Feminist Theory and the *Querelle de Femmes*" in Kelly, *Women, History and Theory.* "Even their sexual politics appear conservative to our time . . . largely reactive to what the misogynists said. Yet the way beyond that resistance to misogyny had to lie through it. . . . The greatest achievement of the early feminist theorists was to set that dialectic in motion. They were limited to a battle of pens, but in that battle they exposed the male bias of learning and its misogynous intent" (p. 94).

23. I am restricting my comments to Rorty's reflections in *Philosophy and the Mirror of Nature.* A more complex view of language emerges in such later essays as "Habermas and Lyotard on Postmodernity."

24. Gadamer, "The Scope and Function of Reflection," in Gadamer, *Philosophical Hermeneutics,* p. 32.

25. Giegel, "Reflexion und Emanzipation," quoted in Habermas, *Theory and Practice,* p. 30.

26. Bakhtin, "Discourse in the Novel," in Bakhtin, *The Dialogic Imagination,* pp. 270–71. Further references to this work will be cited in the text.

27. De Lauretis, *Alice Doesn't,* pp. 18–19.

28. Eagleton, *The Rape of Clarissa,* p. 56. Further references to this work will be cited in the text.

29. De Lauretis, *Alice Doesn't,* pp. 160–61.

30. *Ibid.,* p. 20.

31. Bakhtin, "Discourse in the Novel," in Bakhtin, *The Dialogic Imagination,* p. 294.

32. Rousseau, *Émile,* p. 326, quoted in Wollstonecraft, *A Vindication,* p. 79.

33. Rousseau, *Émile,* p. 332, quoted in Wollstonecraft, *A Vindication,* p. 82.

34. *A Vindication* is dedicated to a man and addressed to men as citizens with the political power to change things. It is in this sense that women are Wollstonecraft's "objects."

35. Williams, *Marxism and Literature,* p. 126.

36. Fuller, *Woman in the Nineteenth Century*, p. 166. See also Fuller's description of Wollstonecraft, pp. 75–78.

6. The Novel and Laughter: *Wuthering Heights*

1. Cixous, "The Laugh of the Medusa," in Marks and de Courtivron, eds., *New French Feminisms*, p. 260. Further references to this work will be cited in the text.

2. Scholes and Kellogg, in *The Nature of Narrative*, set the Anglo-American tone for condemning the novel. They say that a novel-centered view of narrative "cuts us off from the narrative literature of the past and . . . from the literature of the future" (p. 8). But their critique of the novel emphasizes its "imperfection" and condemns its moments of struggle. While Bakhtin discovers productivity precisely in dialogic, unfinished moments of novelization, for Scholes and Kellogg the novel is a form that fails because it fails to "conquer." "In its instability the novel . . . is capable of greater extremes than other forms of literary art, but pays the price for this capability in its capacity for imperfection. The least formal of disciplines, it offers a domain too broad for any single work to conquer, and it continually provokes literary compromise and subterfuge" (p. 16).

3. Kristeva, *Revolution in Poetic Language*, p. 191.

4. Brontë, *Wuthering Heights*, p. 55. Further references to this work will be cited in the text. Miller, in *Fiction and Repetition*, is one of a number of critics who read the opening chapters of *Wuthering Heights* with high seriousness. "The second chapter gives additional examples of Lockwood's ineptness as a reader of signs or as a gatherer of details into a pattern. . . . His errors are a warning to the over-confident reader" (p. 44). I would suggest that this reading of the novel's opening, persuasive though it is, is also gender-based. For Miller, Lockwood is an example "of how not to do things with signs," but he is also "the reader's representative in the novel" (p. 58). In my reading of Brontë Lockwood is especially the male reader's representative in the novel.

5. Dodgson, *Alice in Wonderland*, p. 77.

6. Bakhtin, "From the Prehistory of Novelistic Discourse," in Bakhtin, *The Dialogic Imagination*, p. 55. On the woman writer and parody, see also Gilbert and Gubar, *The Madwoman in the Attic*, p. 80.

7. Kristeva, *Revolution in Poetic Language*, pp. 224–25. A number of post-structuralist theorists privilege laughter. See, for example, Derrida's assertion in *Writing and Difference*, pp. 254–62, that laughter represents something beyond names and theory. For Derrida laughter cannot be harnessed for systematic (or political?) ends; for Kristeva laughter always participates in the production of a more radical politics; it does the "work" Derrida condemns via some of the very mechanisms he describes.

8. Woolf, *A Room of One's Own*, p. 68. Further references to this work will be cited in the text.

9. Habermas, *Theory and Practice*, p. 25.

10. Brownstein, *Becoming a Heroine*, p. xv. Further references to this work will be cited in the text.

11. Jehlen, "Archimedes and the Paradox of Feminist Criticism," p. 92. Further references to this work will be cited in the text.

12. Of all these critics Jehlen's theory of the novel's relation to individualism is the most detailed. "The novel . . . is organically individualistic: even when it deals with several equally important individuals, or attacks individualism itself, it is always about the unitary self versus the others. Moreover, it is about the generation, the becoming, of that

self. I want to suggest that this process may be so defined as to require a definition of female characters that effectively precludes their becoming autonomous, so that indeed they would do so at the risk of the novel's artistic life" ("Archimedes and the Paradox of Feminist Criticism," p. 89).

13. Van Ghent, *The English Novel*, p. 6.

14. *Ibid.*, pp. 6–7.

15. In *Fiction and Repetition*, Miller does not emphasize this dramatic interaction of "warring social formations" in *Wuthering Heights*, but he does describe the way in which "each character in *Wuthering Heights* seems to be an element in a system, defined by his or her place in the system, rather than a separate, unique person" (p. 57). Miller's description of the novel's undecidability, its incompatible readings, its signs beneath signs, represents something more than a brilliant poststructuralist analysis. These incompatibilities are also the effect of the competing social formations Brontë depicts and refuses to bring into ideological closure.

16. Bakhtin, "Discourse in the Novel," in Bakhtin, *The Dialogic Imagination*, p. 331. Further references to this work will be cited in the text.

17. Lukacs and Bakhtin disagree about the value of this "homelessness." Lukacs' *Theory of the Novel* begins with a dream about "those ages when the starry sky is the map of all possible paths. . . . The world is wide and yet it is like a home" (p. 29). The epic is Lukacs' ideal form since the epic always assumes that the human spirit can find a home anywhere—"it does not yet know that it can lose itself" (p. 30). Thus Lukacs' description of the novel as an expression of "this transcendental homelessness" is couched in a tone of regret. The genius of Bakhtin's theory is that Bakhtin takes Lukacs' negative reading and finds the novel's deconstructive energy, its strength, in this "homelessness."

18. "Interruptibility" operates as another theme in feminist criticism. Donovan, in *Feminist Theory*, comments that "in the domestic sphere, while women have been able to carve out a separate space of their own . . . they nevertheless even there were continually at their masters' beck and call. The fundamental 'interruptibility' of women's projects may also have contributed to women's sense of personal vulnerability to environmental influence. . . . The resulting consciousness would be one of flexibility, of relativity, of contingency" (p. 173). I do not want to deny the negative effects of such distracting life rhythms, but to suggest that the woman writer's response to interruption may be more emancipatory than we have seen.

19. Derrida, *Of Grammatology*, p. 18.

20. Brontë sampler, the Parsonage in Haworth.

21. Bakhtin, "Discourse in the Novel," in Bakhtin, *The Dialogic Imagination*, p. 343.

22. Brontë "The Philosopher's Conclusion," pp. 80–81. Further references to this work will be cited in the text with line numbers.

23. A number of feminist critics have discussed the relation of muse to woman poet. See Gilbert and Gubar, *The Madwoman in the Attic*, p. 49, and Jardine, "Pre-Texts for the Transatlantic Feminist," p. 230.

24. For a different account of how women bend the rules of lyric, see Ann Rosalind Jones' essays. Jones cautions us "not to overestimate the room for maneuver available to women." However, since "men as writers and as readers" have such centrality in "the sixteenth-century literary system, "every woman poet recognized the necessity of winning men over to her side as mentors and as critics" ("Surprising Fame," p. 80). This

strategic power implies a greater control over verse than I have discovered in Brontë. Jones' caution to other feminist critics is sound: "Prohibitions on women's intercourse with the literary world were not as paralyzing as they were intended to be. Their effect was not to silence women but to provoke them into complex forms of negotiation and compromise" ("Surprising Fame," p. 92). For Brontë *Wuthering Heights* is such a form of negotiation.

25. For an extended analysis of the relation of female poets to a male literary tradition see Homans' *Women Writers and Poetic Identity*. Homans' discovery that Brontë "defends herself from the danger of becoming a feminine object by aligning her poetic self with the stage in feminine development in which the mother is rejected in favor of a turn toward masculine objects, but that turn cannot become an identity" (p. 107), is a useful psychological precis of the plot of "The Philosopher's Conclusion." Homans also finds that Emily Brontë has more freedom to work through the contradictions inherent in gender asymmetry in *Wuthering Heights*.

26. In *The Madwoman in the Attic* Gilbert and Gubar argue that "most Western literary genres are, after all, essentially male—devised by male authors to tell male stories about the world" (p. 67). I am challenging this hypothesis and arguing that there are genres—and genres with genres—that are useful to different women at different times. For readings that stress the continuity of Brontë's poems and *Wuthering Heights*, see Juliet Mitchell's "*Wuthering Heights*: Romanticism and Rationality" in Mitchell, *Women: The Longest Revolution* and Dorothy Van Ghent's chapter on *Wuthering Heights* in Van Ghent, *The English Novel*.

27. This devaluation of the novel is, of course, one voice in an old debate. See Gilbert and Gubar, *The Madwoman in the Attic*, pp. 131–32, on Austen's defense of the novel in *Northanger Abbey*.

28. Brontë *Jane Eyre*, pp. 71–72; Woolf, *A Room of One's Own*, pp. 140–41.

29. Kristeva, *Revolution in Poetic Language*, p. 224. Further references to this work will be cited in the text.

30. Kristeva, *Revolution in Poetic Language*, p. 224.

31. Jameson, *The Political Unconscious*, p. 151.

32. My project here is not to quarrel with Gilbert and Gubar's notion of the "anxiety of authorship," which I find useful in talking about the beginning of *Wuthering Heights*. Instead, I want to quarrel with the single paradigm they invent for working out this anxiety, and to suggest that this anxiety itself changes shape in the course of Brontë's novel.

33. Gallop, *The Daughter's Seduction*, p. 147. Further references to this work will be cited in the text. See also Cixous and Clements, *The Newly Born Woman*, p. 150–57.

34. Both Bakhtin and Kristeva are concerned with demythologizing existing verbal structures, but Bakhtin does not account for the way in which the unsymbolized is brought into speech. Since Kristeva does, this chapter moves from Bakhtin's dialogics to her semiotics. Although both Bakhtin and Kristeva agree on the importance of the body as the site of transgression, they differ in their schematization of the unconscious. For Bakhtin, the unconscious does not exist; it is a conservative notion encouraging us to view social and external problems as internal and "curable." For Kristeva, writing can only be revelatory because poetic language is a form of speech marked by the unconscious. Bakhtin sees a break between "official" and "unofficial" language; the deeper the rift, the harder it is for internal, unofficial speech to pass into dominant discourse. But he continues to politicize Freud's model—the id is not stuck in "mindless" revolt but represents a

speaking voice which is "other" than the dominant culture's. This voice can disrupt official discourse and enter into dialogue. But in Brontë's text where a voice cries out: "let me in, let me in," but is unable to come in, Bakhtin's model falls short, and we need to turn to Kristeva and to Jameson for a vision of the text's "political unconscious."

35. Van Ghent, The English Novel, p. 157.

36. Mitchell, "Wuthering Heights: Romanticism and Rationality," in Mitchell, The Longest Revolution, p. 129.

37. Van Ghent, The English Novel, p. 153.

38. Gilbert and Gubar, The Madwoman in the Attic, p. 293–94.

39. I am indebted to Toril Moi for this reading of Heathcliff from her discussion of Madwoman in the Attic, at the panel on "The Future of Marxist and Feminism and The Problem of History" on December 29 at the 1983 meeting of the Modern Language Association.

40. Jameson, The Political Unconscious, p. 128.

41. Eagleton, Myths of Power, p. 101.

42. Miller, Fiction and Repetition, p. 63.

43. Eagleton, Myths of Power, p. 102.

44. Kristeva's notion of a "practice text" is wonderfully applicable to this aspect of Wuthering Heights, although Kristeva has developed this model to account for subversive strategies in avant-garde literature. See her section in Revolution in Poetic Language on "Practice," pp. 195–234. See also Coward and Ellis, Language and Materialism, pp. 147–52.

7. Toward a Theory of Play

1. Benjamin, "The Storyteller," in Benjamin, Illuminations, p. 102.

2. Bakhtin, Rabelais and His World, p. 21. Further references to this work will be cited in the text.

3. Cixous, "The Laugh of the Medusa," p. 252. Further references to this work will be cited in the text.

4. For another reading of Cixous' writing that locates it in the carnival mode and identifies carnivalesque writing with écriture feminine, see Mary Russo's "Female Grotesques: Carnival and Theory," p. 7. For an inventory of Cixous' inventions of new language games, see Conley's Hélène Cixous.

5. This strategy is not new with Cixous, although she describes it with a new bravado. In chapter 2 we saw that by attacking the word in its physical incarnation Jane Eyre also began to attain a new power over language itself. The word is literally debased when Jane throws it into the fire; it is demoted from transcendental signifier to carnal sign.

6. O'Brien, "Feminist Theory and Dialectical Logic," p. 147.

7. Many feminist critics valorize but do not theorize play. In Jacobus' review of Gilbert and Gubar's The Madwoman in the Attic, she comments that plot and author become "a form of tight lacing which immobilizes the play of meaning in the texts whose hidden plots they uncover. . . . Their book . . . reenacts endlessly the revisionary struggle, unlocking the secrets of the female text again and again with the same key" (pp. 518–19). In Sexual/Textual Politics Toril Moi makes a similar point about Showalter's A Literature of Their Own. "Showalter wants the literary text to yield the reader a . . . firm perspective from which to judge the world. Woolf, on the other hand, seems to practise what we

might now call a 'deconstructive' form of writing. . . . The free play of signifiers will never yield a final, unified meaning that in turn might ground and explain all the others. It is in the light of such textual and linguistic theory that we can read Woolf's playful shifts and changes of perspective. . . . Through her conscious exploitation of the sportive, sensual nature of language, Woolf rejects the metaphysical essentialism underlying patriarchal ideology" (p. 9). In both instances feminist critics are criticized for not being playful enough, but while Moi's analysis of Woolf is a step in the right direction, beyond this we have no developed theory of what play means for the woman writer. There are feminist texts which seem implicitly opposed to such a theory. In *Alice Doesn't* de Lauretis not only suggests that play excludes women, but protests that "language, of which we have no mastery, for it is indeed populated with the intentions of others, is finally much more than a game" (p. 2).

   8. Arendt, *The Human Condition*, pp. 127–28.

   9. Singer, "Value, Power, and Gender," p. 24.

   10. Geertz, "Deep Play," pp. 23, 26.

   11. Freud, *Beyond the Pleasure Principle*, pp. 10–11.

   12. Clifton, "Admonitions," in Clifton, *Good Times*.

   13. Eagleton, *Walter Benjamin*, p. 148.

   14. Wittig, *Les Guérillères*, pp. 85–86.

   15. Gadamer, *Truth and Method*, pp. 95–96. Further references to this work will be cited in the text.

   16. Baum, *The Land of Oz*, p. 264. Further references to this work will be cited in the text.

   17. Also cited in Bernstein, p. 121; for a telling analysis of Gadamer's analysis of play see Bernstein, pp. 118–25.

   18. Milton, *Paradise Lost*, book 7, ll. 449–52, 463–69.

   19. Brontë *Villette*, p. 220.

   20. Austen, *Northanger Abbey*, p. 10. Further references to this work will be cited in the text. Compare these scenes with Wordsworth's descriptions of play in books 2 and 5 of *The Prelude*.

   21. Benjamin, *One Way Street*, p. 53. This passage is also quoted in Buck-Morss, "Walter Benjamin," part 2, p. 84. My discussion of Benjamin is indebted to Buck-Morss for her detailed analysis.

   22. Valéry, *Idée Fixe*, p. 36. Quoted in Buck-Morss, "Walter Benjamin," part 2, p. 86.

   23. Benjamin, *illuminations*, p. 245. This passage is also quoted in Buck-Morss, "Walter Benjamin," part 2, p. 87.

   24. Buck-Morss, "Walter Benjamin," part 2, p. 87.

   25. Jameson, *The Political Unconscious*, p. 86. Further references to this work will be cited in the text.

   26. Lacan, "The Agency of the Letter in the Unconscious or Reason Since Freud," in Lacan, *Ecrits*, p. 152.

   27. Gallop, *The Daughter's Seduction*, pp. 11–12. Further references to this work will be cited in the text.

   28. Jardine gives one version of this absence in "Pre-Texts for the Transatlantic Feminist." "What becomes 'free play' with the primarily erotic boundaries of the mother's body, of death, in men's texts, is more difficult to 'hear' in writing by women—especially in the United States where women writers are working primarily at providing the narratives,

identities, origins, history and desires we have never had access to" (p. 229). I have argued that this play is invisible not because of the woman writer's experience of the oedipal trauma of the mother's unavailability, but because we have not developed a way of conceptualizing, hence organizing, this aspect of the Anglo-American woman writer's (or critic's) inscription. Gallop does theorize one playful movement in "Quand nos lèvres s'écrivent" when she describes Lacan's theory of metaphor as the "loophole" in his system. But this loophole is momentary. "For as soon as the metaphor becomes a proper noun, we no longer have creation, we have paternity" (p. 81).

29. Marcuse, *Eros and Civilization*, p. 186. Further references to this work will be cited in the text. For this and other quotations from Schiller, Marcuse cites Schiller, *The Aesthetic Letter*, J. Weiss, tr. (Boston: Little, Brown, 1845). Since Marcuse has made his own "minor changes and interpolations in this translation, I will continue to cite Marcuse as source of this quotations in my text, as well as Schiller. Here, Marcuse refers the reader to p. 53 of *The Aesthetic Letters*. I turn to Marcuse rather than Huizinga because I want to go beyond Huizinga's transcendental and apolitical notion of play as "a significant function—that is to say, there is some sense to it. In play there is something 'at play' which transcends the immediate needs of life and imparts meaning to the action. All play means something" (*Homo Ludens*, p. 1).

30. If we are to understand the radicalism of Schiller's ideas we need to distinguish them from Hegel's, since for Hegel art is also the realm of "free" negativity. However, this "freedom" means that nature gives itself over to *"Geist."* Hegel writes, in *On Art, Religion, Philosophy,* that "not only has art at command the whole wealth of natural forms in the brilliant variety of their appearance, but also the creative imagination has power to expatiate inexhaustibly beyond their limit in products of *its own"* (p. 27). For Hegel, nature is the realm of necessity and uniformity, while the mind, especially in its aspect of imagination, is the locus of a "caprice and lawlessness" that resists not only nature, but "the regulative activity of thought." For Hegel art liberates us from the solid and the real—it heals the schism between abstract thought and the world. "Art liberates the real import of appearances from the semblance and deception of this bad and fleeting world and imparts to phenomenal semblances a higher reality, born of mind. The appearances of art, therefore, far from being mere semblances, have the higher reality and the more genuine existence in comparison with the realities of common life," p. 31. For Hegel art is not a form of praxis, but a way of reaching after *"Geist."* But for Schiller, the "bad and fleeting world" is the world we must save. "Sensuousness must triumphantly maintain its province, and resist the violence which spirit *(Geist)* would fain inflict upon it by its encroaching activity" (Marcuse, p. 191; Schiller, p. 63).

31. Kristeva, "Psychoanalysis and the Polis," p. 81.

32. *Ibid.,* p. 86.

33. This is also my critique of Moi's discussion of Cixous in *Sexual/Textual Politics.* Moi reads the language games of French feminists like Cixous and Irigaray with such seriousness that their appropriations of patriarchal myth spell "closure and unity" to her, while their attempts to rewrite the body lapse into "essentialism" (pp. 116, 143). Moi affirms Kristeva's vision, on the other hand, because "it is one in which the hierarchical closure imposed on meaning and language has been opened up to the free play of the signifier" (p. 172). Too often, this celebration of a poststructuralist theory substitutes in feminist theory for a more concrete valorization of playful moments in women's texts— moments not characterized by the random play of the signifier, but by complicated attempts to lighten the weight of oppressive social formations. For a reading of Cixous and Kristeva

that urges this concretion and also reverses the terms of Moi's analysis of Kristeva and Cixous, see Spivak's "French Feminism in an International Frame."

34. Cixous, "An Exchange with Hélène Cixous," in Conley, *Hélène Cixous*, p. 152.

35. Gadamer, "Man and Language," in Gadamer, *Philosophical Hermeneutics*, p. 66.

36. Winnicott, *Playing and Reality*, p. 51. Through the end of the next paragraph, all quotes are from p. 51 of this text.

37. It is my contention that the repression or excision of woman's playfulness necessarily results in this trivialization. This unbearable lightness of being becomes Ozma's fate. When the time comes for Ozma to relinquish Tip's playful capacities, she becomes a floating wonder—the plaything of others: "Her eyes sparkled as two diamonds, and her lips were tinted like a tourmaline. All down her back floated tresses of ruddy gold, with a slender jeweled circlet confining them at the brow. Her robes of silken gauze floated around her like a cloud, and dainty satin slippers shod her feet." (Baum, *The land of Oz*, p. 270). As the nut-brown complexion disappears, with it goes Tip's confident voice: " 'I hope none of you will care less for me than you did before. I'm just the same Tip, you know; only—only—' 'Only you're different!' said the Pumpkinhead; and everyone thought it was the wisest speech he had ever made" (p. 271). Now Ozma is at a loss for words, and her sentences are completed by her "son," Jack Pumpkinhead.

38. Brontë *Villette*, p. 233. Further references to this work will be cited in the text.

39. Jacobus, "The Buried Letter," p. 46. Further references to this work will be cited in the text.

40. Lucy Snowe is outwardly a conformist at the end of *Villette*—although she is a self-supporting conformist with a career. But the storm at the end of *Villette* should also remind us of the internal storms that rack Lucy's being throughout the novel. Brontë's staging of this scene at the end suggests that something of Vashti's violence and murderousness survives in the storm, and that this storm continues to be coterminous with Lucy's hidden rage, making Lucy's desire for independent selfhood "implicitly" complicitous in Paul's disappearance. Thus I read the end of *Villette* as another turn in the novel's psychomachia, its vale of feminist soul-making that Paul's marriage to Lucy would inevitably censor.

41. Sennett, *The Fall of Public Man*, pp. 321–22. See also Donovan on Carol Gilligan in *Feminist Theory*. Donovan praises Gilligan's citation of studies "which indicate that in childhood games girls tend to be less bound by abstract rules and more able to play it as it lays. . . . Girls are more tolerant of intruding realities, more willing to innovate, and less concerned with abstract codification" (p. 17). The relation of rules to innovation in play is worth investigating. Sennett, in *The Fall of Public Man*, uses the metaphor of self-distance rather than buoyancy to describe what happens in the play state because he wants to focus on the ways in which desire in play is transformed via rules. "The tools which permit children to delay, to remain in a state of play, are the rules," which act as a buffer against the burden of the "outside, non-play world" (p. 318). Through the self-distance that the rules of play make possible, the rules themselves become (potentially) light and transformable.

8. Emancipatory Strategies

1. In emphasizing these multiplying entrances I differ with Jehlen, who argues for the "integrity" of the text ("Archimedes and the Paradox of Feminist Criticism," p. 73). However, I do not want to revert to a simple-minded affirmation of the "free play" of the critic's "signifier," or to admit all readings and privilege none of them, but instead to consider how we can ask questions that release the text's emancipatory potential without ignoring its ideological limitations. To do this requires a multiplicity of paradigms, questions, entrances—but this variety, a version of Kolodny's "playful pluralism" in "Dancing Through the Minefield"—does not imply a "new critical" or poststructuralist affirmation of wanton reading. For extended discussions of the problematic relation of feminism and pluralism see Showalter, "Feminist Criticism in the Wilderness," Spender, *Man Made Language,* and Roberts, *Beyond Intellectual Sexism.*

2. Barthes, *S/Z,* pp. 12, 14. For a reading of S/Z that spells out the limitations of Barthes' "multiple entrances" see Johnson's "The Critical Difference."

3. Several other women poets have written a series of bee poems. See especially Sylvia Plath and H. D.

4. Dickinson, "I taste a liquor never brewed," from her *Complete Poems,* p. 214. Further references to *The Complete Poems* will be cited in the text as P followed by the poem number assigned by Johnson.

5. Marcuse, *Eros and Civilization,* p. 162. Further references to this work will be cited in the text.

6. Mary Oliver, "The Roses," in Oliver, *American Primitive,* p. 67.

7. Keats seems to be an exception to this rule—a poet who says, "let us not therefore go hurring about and collecting honey-bee like, buzzing here and there impatiently from a knowledge of what is to be arrived at: but let us open our leaves like a flower and be passive and receptive . . . taking hints from every novel insect that favors us with a visit" (*Selected Poems and Letters,* p. 266). Margaret Homans has explained the (male) Romantic bias of this passage in her unpublished English Institute paper, "Keats and Women Readers," delivered in Cambridge in August, 1986.

8. Kristeva, "Psychoanalysis of the Polis," p. 81. Discussions of women and delirium tend to focus on delirium as a psychodynamic rather than an epistemological process. Irigaray argues that women are made vulnerable by an inability to express delirium verbally; they experience it directly in the body. In her introduction to *The Newly Born Woman* Gilbert responds to Clement's use of "patriarchal" theory as if the woman writer's use of such theory must result in a negative delirium: "Clement herself inflicts, yet again, the ghostly bite of the tarantula—the invisible yet powerful insect of patriarchal lore, lure, and law. . . . And Cixous . . . does the dance, the tarantella of theory necessitated by the hideously potent yet phantasmic incision. . . . She transforms herself into the woman whose shrieks and steps mark her as pure desire, immediately outside all law" (Gilbert, xi; Clement, 117). Gilbert chooses not to emphasize the self-conscious uses of delirium we find in Cixous and Clement. But her own discussions of madwomen invite this leap into seeing delirium as a step toward some "other" kind of knowledge. In Gilbert and Gubar's *The Madwoman in the Attic* we see evidence not only of the woman writer as "split subject" who holds the mirror up to her nature and sees a mad countenance, but of a positive, aspiring delirium that moves the dialogue forward.

9. Kristeva, "Psychoanalysis and the Polis," pp. 81–82. We need, however, to discriminate among deliriums. In "Aristotle's Sister: A Poetics of Abandonment" Lipking

calls for a new feminist poetics. "In the absence of mothers, a father must raise the right issues." The poetics he describes are based on one of the dominant culture's favorite images: the stereotype of the abandoned woman. This eroticization of abandonment is a male ethic, a masculine form of delirium that refers back to a powerful fantasy of simultaneously possessing and rejecting the dangerous presence of the mother. If the "poetics of abandonment" is a male fantasy of what a woman's poetics should look like, my response to this delirium is to suggest that a more accurate (and thus more delirious?) basis for a woman's poetic could be discovered in woman's habitual response to this masculine fantasy, and I have proposed here a poetics not of woman's abandonment, but of her abandoning. Women writers have been actively engaged in abandoning and refashioning a literary tradition that has tried to abandon them.

10. Barthes, *The Pleasure of the Text*, pp. 40–41.

11. De Man, "Shelley Disfigured," p. 68.

12. *Ibid*.

13. Rossetti, "Goblin Market," ll. 554–55. Further references to this work will be cited by line numbers in the text. For a more skeptical reading of the sexual politics of Rossetti's poem, see Gilbert and Gubar, *Madwoman*, pp. 564–75.

14. Sartre, *What is Literature?* p. 39. Further references to this work will be cited in the text. My comparison of Sartre and Barthes is indebted to Susan Sontag's preface to Barthes' *Writing Degree Zero*.

15. Barthes, *Writing Degree Zero*, p. 9.

16. *Ibid*.

17. Lyotard, "Interview," p. 17.

18. *Ibid*., p. 18.

19. Lyotard, *Just Gaming*, pp. 98–99.

20. Barthes, *Writing Degree Zero*, pp. 11, 17.

21. Adorno, *Negative Dialectics*, p. 53. Further references to this work will be cited in the text.

22. Foucault, *The Archaeology of Knowledge*, pp. 199–200. Further references to this work will be cited in the text.

23. Lentricchia, *Criticism and Social Change*, p. 139. Further references to this work will be cited in the text.

24. Bernstein, *Beyond Objectivism and Relativism*, p. 162.

25. Gadamer, "The Universality of the Hermeneutical Problem," in Gadamer, *Philosophical Hermeneutics*, pp. 15–16.

26. Gadamer, *Truth and Method*, p. 341.

27. Scheman, "Anger and the Politics of Naming," p. 177.

28. *Ibid*., p. 181.

29. Bakhtin, "Discourse in the Novel," in Bakhtin, *The Dialogic Imagination*, p. 270. Further references to this work will be cited in the text.

30. Kristeva, *Revolution in Poetic Language*, p. 148. Further references to this work will be cited in the text.

31. Habermas, *Knowledge and Human Interests*, p. 313. While I do not always agree with Habermas' critics, Nancy Fraser's "What's Critical About Critical Theory? The Case of Habermas and Gender" provides an interesting critique of Habermas' theories from a feminist perspective.

32. *Ibid*., p. 168.

33. Habermas, *Knowledge and Human Interests*, p. 315. In "Scope and Function," in Gadamer, *Philsophical Hermeneutics*, Gadamer challenges Habermas' claim that "hermeneutical reflection must pass into a criticism of ideology." First, Gadamer questions whether "an emancipatory interest" can be "at work" in reflection that will "free us of outer and inner social forces and compulsions simply by making us aware of them" (p. 30). Second, Gadamer insists that "for Habermas, and for psychoanalysis, the life of society and the life of the individual consists of the interaction of intelligible motives and concrete compulsions." For Gadamer this intelligibility is fictive, the artefact of psychoanalytic "hermeneutics."

34. McCarthy, *The Critical Theory of Jürgen Habermas*, p. 192.

35. Habermas, *Reason and the Rationalization of Society*, p. 68.

36. Macherey, *A Theory of Literary Production*, p. 27. Further references to this work will be cited in the text.

37. Eagleton, *Marxism and Literary Criticism*, p. 90.

38. *Ibid.*, p. 91.

39. Sedgwick, *Between Men*, p. 160.

40. Jameson, *The Political Unconscious*, p. 85. Further references to this work will be cited in the text.

41. Wittig, "The Straight Mind," pp. 105–6.

42. Janeway, *The Powers of the Weak*, p. 203.

43. Spivak, "French Feminism in an International Frame," p. 167.

44. Singer, "Value, Power, and Gender."

45. Buck-Morss, "Walter Benjamin," p. 55. Further references to this work will be cited in the text. See also Benjamin's *One Way Street*, pp. 360–61.

46. See also Benjamin's *Illuminations:* "Thinking involves not only the flow of thoughts, but their arrest as well. Where thinking suddenly stops in a configuration pregnant with tensions, it gives that configuration a shock, by which it crystallizes into a monad" (pp. 262–63).

47. Arendt, *On Revolution*, p. 175. See also Bernstein's discussion of Arendt in *Beyond Objectivism and Relativism*, pp. 207–223.

48. Arendt, *The Human Condition*, p. 210. For a wider-ranging discussion of the concept of power, see the collection of essays edited by Steven Lukes, *Power*, which includes an essay by Habermas on "Hannah Arendt's Communications Concept of Power," pp. 75–93.

49. Kelly, *Women, History, and Theory*, pp. xiii–xiv.

50. Davis, *Life in the Iron Mills*, p. 36. Further references to this work will be cited in the text.

51. The phrase is from Habermas' *Reason and the Rationalization of Society*, p. 398.

52. Coward & Ellis, *Language and Materialism*, p. 147.

53. See, however, Kristeva's, "The Semiotic and the Symbolic," in *Revolution in Poetic Language*, pp. 19–106, in which she explains that while poetic language or mimesis "may appear as an argument complicitous with dogma . . . they may also set in motion what dogma represses . . . and become . . . protestors against its posturing. And thus, its complexity unfolded by its practices, the signifying process joins social revolution" (p. 61).

54. Smith, *Killers of the Dream*, p. 93.

55. Plath, "The Swarm." From *Ariel*, pp. 65–66.

56. Plath, "Stings." From *Ariel,* p. 62.
57. Plath, "The Arrival of the Bee Box." From Ariel, p. 60.
58. Derrida, "Women in the Beehive," p. 191.
59. Kristeva, *Revolution in Poetic Language,* p. 233.
60. Habermas, *Theory of Communicative Action,* p. 398.
61. Arendt, *The Human Condition,* pp. 198–99.
62. Spender, *Man Made Language,* p. 144.
63. Gilbert and Gubar, "Sexual Linguistics," p. 523.

Bibliography

Adorno, Theodor W. *Negative Dialectics*. E. B. Ashton, tr. New York: Continuum, 1983.

Anouilh, Jean. *Antigone: A Tragedy*. In *Five Plays*, vol. 1. Lewis Galantiere, tr. New York: Hill and Wang, 1958.

Arendt, Hannah. *The Human Condition*. Chicago: University of Chicago Press, 1958.

—— *On Revolution*. New York: Penguin, 1977.

Auerbach, Nina. *The Woman and the Demon: The Life of a Victorian Myth*. Cambridge: Harvard, 1982.

Austen, Jane. *Northanger Abbey*. New York: Signet, 1965.

Bakhtin, M. M. *The Dialogic Imagination*. Caryl Emerson and Michael Holquist, trs. Austin: University of Texas Press, 1981.

—— *Rabelais and His World*. Helene Iswolsky, tr. Cambridge: M.I.T. Press, 1968.

Barthes, Roland. "From Work to Text." In Josue V. Harari, ed., *Textual Strategies: Perspectives in Post-Structuralist Criticism*, pp. 73–81. Ithaca: Cornell University Press, 1979.

Barthes, Roland. *The Pleasure of the Text*. Richard Miller, tr. New York: Hill and Wang, 1975.

—— *Sade, Fourier, Loyola*. Richard Miller, tr. New York: Hill and Wang, 1976.

—— "The Spirit of the Letter." In Roland Barthes, *The Responsibility of Forms: Critical Essays on Music, Art, and Representation*, pp. 98–102. Richard Howard, tr. New York: Hill and Wang, 1985.

—— *S/Z*. Richard Miller, tr. New York: Hill and Wang, 1974.

—— *Writing Degree Zero*. Introduction by Susan Sontag. Annette Lavers and Colin Smith, trs. New York: Hill and Wang, 1968.

Baum, L. Frank. *The Land of Oz*. Chicago: Reilly and Lee, 1904.

Benjamin, Walter. *One Way Street and Other Writings*. Edmund Jephcott and Kingsley Shorter, trs. London: New Left Books, 1979.

—— *Illuminations*. Hannah Arendt, ed. Harry Zohn, tr. New York: Schocken, 1969.

Benveniste, Emile. *Problems in General Linguistics*. Mary Elizabeth Meek, tr. Miami: University of Miami Press, 1971.

Bernstein, Richard J. *Beyond Objectivism and Relativism: Science, Hermeneutics, and Praxis*. Philadelphia: University of Pennsylvania Press, 1983.

Bishop, Elizabeth. *Elizabeth Bishop: The Collected Prose*. Robert Giroux, ed. New York: Farrar, Straus, Giroux, 1984.

Black, Max. *Models and Metaphors: Studies in Language and Philosophy*, Ithaca: Cornell University Press, 1962.

Blake, William. *The Poetry and Prose of William Blake*. David V. Erdman, ed. Garden City, New York: Doubleday, 1970.

Bové, Paul. "Intellectuals at War: Michel Foucault and the Analytics of Power," *Substance* (1983), 11:36–55.

Brand, Gerd. *The Essential Wittgenstein*. Robert E. Innis, tr. New York: Basic Books, 1979.

Brontë, Emily. "The Philosopher's Conclusion." In *The Brontë Sisters: Selected Poems of Charlotte, Emily, and Anne Brontë*. Stevie Davies, ed. Cheadle, Cheshire: Carcanet Press, 1976, pp. 80–81.

Brontë, Charlotte. *Jane Eyre*. Q. D. Leavis, ed. New York: Penguin, 1966.

Brontë, Charlotte. *Villette*. New York: Dutton, 1978.

Brontë, Emily. *Wuthering Heights*. David Daiches, ed. New York: Penguin, 1965.

Brownstein, Rachel. *Becoming A Heroine: Reading About Women in Novels*. New York: Penguin, 1984.

Buck-Morss, Susan. "Walter Benjamin—Revolutionary Writer," parts 1 and 2. *New Left Review* (1981), 129:50–75, 130:77–95.

Burke, Kenneth. *Counter-Statement*. Berkeley: University of California Press, 1969.

Carby, Hazel. "It Jus Be's Dat Way Sometime: The Sexual Politics of Women's Blues." *Radical America* (1987), 20:9–22.

Chessman, Harriet. *The Public Is Invited to Dance: Representation, the Body, and Dialogue in Gertrude Stein*. Stanford: Stanford University Press, 1988.

Chomsky, Noam. *Cartesian Linguistics: A Chapter in the History of Rationalist Thought*. New York: Harper and Row, 1966.

Chopin, Kate. *The Awakening*. Margaret Culley, ed. New York: Norton, 1976.

Cixous, Hélène and Catherine Clement. *The Newly Born Woman*. Betsy Wing, tr. Minneapolis: University of Minnesota Press, 1986.

Cixous, Hélène, Madeleine Gagnon, and Annie Leclerc. *La Venue à l'écriture*. Paris: Union Générale d'Editions, "10/18," 1977.

Clark, Katerina and Michael Holquist. *Mikhail Bakhtin*. Cambridge: Harvard University Press, 1984.

Clifton, Lucille. *Good Times*. New York: Random House, 1969.

Coleridge, Samuel Taylor. *The Complete Poetical Works of Samuel Taylor Coleridge*, vol. 1. Ernest Hartley Coleridge, ed. Oxford: Clarendon Press, 1912.

Conley, Verna Andermatt. *Hélène Cixous: Writing the Feminine*. Lincoln: University of Nebraska Press, 1984.

Coward, Rosalind and John Ellis. *Language and Materialism*. Boston: Routledge, 1977.

Davis, Rebecca Harding. *Life in the Iron Mills or the Korl Woman*. Tillie Olsen, ed. Old Westbury, New York: Feminist Press, 1972.

de Beauvoir, Simone. *The Second Sex*. H. M. Parshley, tr. New York: Random House, 1974.

de Lauretis, Teresa. *Alice Doesn't: Feminism, Semiotics, Cinema*. Bloomington: Indiana University Press, 1984.

—— "Feminist Studies, Critical Studies: Issues, Terms, and Contexts. In de Lauretis, ed., *Feminist Studies/Critical Studies*. Bloomington: Indiana University Press, 1986.

de Man, Paul. "Shelley Disfigured." In Harold Bloom et al., eds., *Deconstructions and Criticism*, pp. 39–74. New York: Continuum, 1979.

Derrida, Jacques. *Dissemination*. Barbara Johnson, tr. Chicago: University of Chicago Press, 1981.

—— *Of Grammatology*, Gayatri Chakravorty Spivak, tr. Baltimore: Johns Hopkins, 1976.

—— *Writing and Difference*. Alan Bass, tr. Chicago: University of Chicago Press, 1978.

Dickinson, Emily. *The Complete Poems of Emily Dickinson*. Thomas H. Johnson, ed. Boston: Little Brown, 1960.

Dinnerstein, Dorothy. *The Mermaid and the Minotaur*. New York: Harper, 1976.

Dodgson, Charles. *Alice in Wonderland and Through the Looking Glass*. New York: Grosset and Dunlap, 1981.

Donovan, Josephine. *Feminist Theory: The Intellectual Traditions of American Feminism*. New York: Frederick Unger, 1985.

Duren, Brian. "Cixous's Exorbitant Texts." *SubStance* (1981), 32:39–51.

Eagleton, Terry. *Marxism and Literary Criticism*. Berkeley: University of California Press, 1976.

—— *Myths of Power: A Marxist Study of the Brontës*. London: Barnes and Noble, 1975.

—— *The Rape of Clarissa: Writing, Sexuality and Class Struggle in Samuel Richardson*. Minneapolis: University of Minnesota Press, 1982.

—— *Walter Benjamin or Towards a Revolutionary Criticism*. London: Verso, 1981.

Eliot, George. *The Mill on the Floss*. A. S. Byatt, ed. New York: Viking Penguin, 1979.

Empson, William. *Some Versions of Pastoral*. New York: New Directions, 1974.

Foucault, Michel. *The Archaeology of Knowledge and The Discourse on Language*. A. M. Sheridan Smith, tr. New York: Pantheon, 1972.

—— *The History of Sexuality*. Vol. 1: *An Introduction*. New York: Vintage, 1980.

—— *The Order of Things: An Archaeology of the Human Sciences*. New York: Vintage, 1973.

—— *Power/Knowledge: Selected Interviews and Other Writings 1972–1977*. Colin Gordon, Leo Merchall, John Mepham, and Kate Soper, trs. New York: Pantheon, 1980.

Fraser, Nancy. "What's Critical About Critical Theory? The Case of Habermas and Gender." *New German Critique* (1986), 12:97–131.

Freud, Sigmund. *Beyond the Pleasure Principle*. James Strachey, tr. New York: Norton, 1961.

Fuller, Margaret. *Woman in the Nineteenth Century*. New York: Norton, 1971.

Gadamer, Hans-Georg. *Philosophical Hermeneutics*. David E. Linge, ed. and tr. Berkeley: University of California Press, 1976.

—— *Truth and Method*. Garrett Barden and John Cumming, eds. and trs. New York: Crossroads, 1984.

Gallop, Jane. *The Daughter's Seduction: Feminism and Psychoanalysis*. Ithaca: Cornell University Press, 1982.

—— "*Quand nos lèvres s'écrivent:* Irigaray's Body Politic."*Romanic Review* (1983) 74:77–83.

Gaudin, Colette, et al. *Yale French Studies* (1981), vol. 62. *Special issue: Feminist Readings: French Texts, American Contexts*.

Geertz, Clifford. "Deep Play: Notes on the Balinese Cockfight." *Daedulus* (1972), 101:1–37.

Gilbert, Sandra M. "The Second Coming of Aphrodite: Kate Chopin's Fantasy of Desire." *Kenyon Review* (1983), 5:42–65.

Gilbert, Sandra and Susan Guber. *The Madwoman in the Attic: The Woman Writer and the Nineteenth-Century Literary Imagination*. New Haven: Yale University Press, 1979.

—— "Sexual Linguistics: Gender, Language, Sexuality." *New Literary History* (1985), 16:515–43.

Gubar, Susan. " 'The Blank Page' and Female Creativity." *Critical Inquiry* (1981), 8:243–64.

Habermas, Jürgen. *Knowledge and Human Interests*. Jeremy J. Shapiro, tr. Boston: Beacon Press, 1971.

—— *Theory and Practice*. John Viertel, tr. Boston: Beacon, 1973.

—— *Reason and the Rationalization of Society. The Theory of Communicative Action*. Vol. 1. Thomas McCarthy, tr. Boston: Beacon Press, 1984.

Hardy, Thomas. *Jude the Obscure*. Irving Howe, ed. Boston: Houghton Mifflin (Riverside), 1965.

Haraway, Donna. "A Manifesto for Cyborgs: Science, Technology, and Socialist Feminism in the 1980's." *Socialist Review* (1985), 15:65–105.

Hartman, Geoffrey. "Poem and Ideology," in Geoffrey Hartman, *The Fate of Reading and Other Essays*, pp. 124–46. Chicago: Chicago University Press, 1975.

—— "The Unremarkable Wordsworth." In Marshall Blonsky, ed., *On Signs*, pp. 321–33. Baltimore: Johns Hopkins University Press, 1985.

Heidegger, Martin. *An Introduction to Metaphysics*. Ralph Manheim, tr. Garden City, N.Y.: Anchor, 1961.

—— *Poetry, Language, Thought*. Albert Hofstadter, tr. New York: Harper, 1971.

Hegel, G. W. F. *On Art, Religion, Philosophy*. J. Glenn Gray, ed. New York: Harper, 1970.

Heilbrun, Carolyn G. *Reinventing Womanhood*. New York: Norton, 1979.

Heilbrun, Carolyn and Catherine Stimpson. "Theories of Feminist Criticism: A Dialogue." In Josephine Donovan, ed., *Feminist Literary Criticism: Explorations in Theory*. Lexington: University Press of Kentucky, 1975, pp. 61–73.

Homans, Margaret. " 'Her Very Own Howl': The Ambiguities of Representation in Recent Women's Fiction." *SIGNS* (1983), 9:186–205.

—— *Women Writers and Poetic Identity: Dorothy Wordsworth, Emily Brontë, and Emily Dickinson*. Princeton: Princeton University Press, 1980.

Howells, William D. *A Modern Instance*. William M. Gibson, ed. Boston: Houghton Mifflin (Riverside), 1957.

Huizinga, Johan. *Homo Ludens*. Boston: Beacon, 1955.

Hunter, Diane. "Hysteria, Psychoanalysis, and Feminism: The Case of Anna O." In Shirley Nelson Garner, Claire Kahane, and Madelon Sprengnether, eds., *The (M)other Tongue: Essays in Feminist Psychoanalytic Interpretation*. Ithaca: Cornell University Press, 1985.

Irigaray, Luce. "When Our Lips Speak Together." Tr. Carolyn Burke, tr. *SIGNS* (1980), 6:65–79.

Jabès, Edmond. *Le livre des questions*. Paris: Gallimard, 1963.

Jacobs, Lea. "*Now Voyager*: Some Problems of Enunciation and Sexual Difference." In *Camera Obscura* (1985), 7:88–109.

Jacobus, Mary. "The Buried Letter: Feminism and Romanticism in *Villette*." In Mary Jacobus, ed., *Women Writing and Writing About Women*, pp. 42–60. Totowa, N.J.: Barnes and Noble, 1979.

—— "The Question of Language: Men of Maxims and *The Mill on the Floss*." *Critical Inquiry* (1981), 8:207–22.

—— "Review of *The Madwoman in the Attic*." *SIGNS* (1981), 6:517–23.

Jacobus, Mary. *Romanticism, Writing, and Sexual Difference: Essays on the Prelude*. London: Oxford, 1988.

Jameson, Fredric. *The Political Unconscious: Narrative as Socially Symbolic Act*. Ithaca: Cornell University Press, 1981.

—— "Interview." *Diacritics* (1982), 12:72–91.

Janeway, Elizabeth. *Powers of the Weak.* New York: Morrow, 1981.

Jardine, Alice. "Gynesis." *Diacritics* (1982), 12:54–65.

—— "Pre-Texts for the Transatlantic Feminist." *Yale French Studies* (1981), 62:220–36.

Jehlen, Myra. "Archimedes and the Paradox of Feminist Criticism." In Elizabeth Abel and Emily K. Abel, eds., *The SIGNS Reader: Women, Gender, and Scholarship,* pp. 69–96. Chicago: University of Chicago Press, 1983.

Johnson, Barbara. "The Critical Difference: BartheS/BalZac." In Barbara Johnson, *The Critical Difference: Essays in the Contemporary Rhetoric of Reading,* pp. 3–12. Baltimore: Johns Hopkins University Press, 1980.

Jones, Ann Rosalind. "Assimilation with a Difference: Renaissance Women Poets and Literary Influence." *Yale French Studies* (1981), 62:135–53.

—— "Surprising Fame: Renaissance Gender Ideologies and Women's Lyric." In Nancy K. Miller, ed., *The Poetics of Gender,* pp. 74–95. New York: Columbia University Press, 1986.

Kamuf, Peggy. "Replacing Feminist Criticism." *Diacritics* (1982), 12:42–47.

Keats, John. *Selected Poems and Letters.* Douglas Bush, ed. Boston: Houghton Mifflin (Riverside), 1959.

Keats, John. *The Letters of John Keats.* Maurice Buxton Forman, ed. New York: Oxford University Press, 1952.

Kelly, Joan. *Women, History and Theory: The Essays of Joan Kelly.* Chicago: University of Chicago Press, 1984.

Kelly, Mary. *Postpartum Document.* London: Routledge, 1983.

Kofman, Sarah. *The Enigma of Woman: Woman in Freud's Writings.* Catherine Porter, tr. Ithaca: Cornell University Press, 1985.

Kolodny, Annette. "Dancing Through the Minefield: Some Observations on the Theory, Practice, and Politics of a Feminist Literary Criticism." In Elaine Showalter, ed., *The New Feminist Criticism: Essays on Women, Literature, and Theory.* New York: Pantheon, 1985.

Kristeva, Julia. *Desire in Language: A Semiotic Approach to Literature and Art.* Leon S. Goudiez, ed. New York: Columbia University Press, 1980.

—— "Interview" Claire Pajaczkowska, tr. *m/f* (1981), no. 5/6.

—— *Revolution in Poetic Language.* Margaret Waller, tr. New York: Columbia University Press, 1984.

—— "Psychoanalysis and the Polis." Margaret Wailer, tr. *Critical Inquiry* (Sept. 1982) *(The Politics of Interpretation),* 9(1):77–92.

Lacan, Jacques. *Écrits: A Selection.* Alan Sheridon, tr. New York: Norton, 1977.

Lemaire, Anika. *Jacques Lacan.* David Macey, tr. Boston: Routledge, Kegan Paul, 1977.

Lentricchia, Frank. *Criticism and Social Change.* Chicago: University of Chicago Press, 1983.

Lévi-Strauss, Claude. *From Honey to Ashes.* Vol. 3 of *Mythologiques.* John and Doreen Weightman, trs. New York: Harper and Row, 1973.

—— *The Origins of Table Manners.* Vol. 4 of *Mythologiques.* John and Doreen Weightman, trs. New York: Harper and Row, 1979.

Lipking, Lawrence. "Aristotle's Sister: A Poetics of Abandonment." *Critical Inquiry* (1983), 10:61–82.

Little, Malcolm. *The Autobiography of Malcolm X.* With the assistance of Alex Haley. New York: Grove, 1965.

Lukacs, Georg. *The Theory of the Novel: A Historico-Philosophical Essay on the Forms of Great Epic Literature.* Anna Bostock, tr. Cambridge: M.I.T. Press, 1971.

Lukes, Steven, ed. *Power.* New York: New York University Press, 1986.

Lyotard, Jean-Francois and Jean-Loup Thebaud. *Just Gaming.* Wlad Godzich, tr. Minneapolis: University of Minnesota Press, 1985.

—— "Interview." Geroges Van Den Abbeele, tr. *Diacritics* (1984), 14:16–21.

—— *The Post-Modern Condition: A Report on Knowledge.* Geoff Bennington and Brian Massumi, trs. Minneapolis: University of Minnesota Press, 1984.

McCarthy, Thomas. *The Critical Theory of Jürgen Habermas.* Cambridge: M.I.T. Press, 1981.

McClintock, Anne and Rob Nixon. "No Words Apart: The Separation of Word from History in Derrida's "Le Dernier Mot du Racisme." *Critical Inquiry* (1986), 13:140–154.

McCullers, Carson. *The Ballad of the Sad Cafe and Other Stories.* New York: Bantam, 1958.

McGann, Jerome J. *The Romantic Ideology: A Critical Investigation.* Chicago: University of Chicago Press, 1983.

Macherey, Pierre. *A Theory of Literary Production.* London: Routledge, 1978.

MacKinnon, Catherine. "Marxism, Feminism and the State." In Elizabeth Abel and Emily K. Abel, eds., *The SIGNS Reader: Women, Gender, and Scholarship.* Chicago: University of Chicago Press, 1983.

Marcuse, Herbert, *Eros and Civilization: A Philosophical Inquiry into Freud.* Boston: Beacon Press, 1955.

—— *Reason and Revolution: Hegel and the Rise of Social Theory.* Boston: Beacon Press, 1960.

Marks, Elaine and Isabel de Courtivron, eds. *New French Feminisms.* Amherst: University of Massachusetts Press, 1980.

Melville, Herman. *Moby-Dick or, the Whale.* Charles Feidelson, Jr., ed. Indianapolis: Bobbs-Merrill, 1964.

Michie, Helena. *The Flesh Made Word: Female Figures and Women's Bodies.* New York: Oxford University Press, 1987.

Miller, J. Hillis. *Fiction and Repetition.* Cambridge: Harvard, 1982.

Miller, Nancy K. "Emphasis Added: Plots and Plausibilities in Women's Fiction." *PMLA* (1981), 96:36–48.

—— "The Text's Heroine: A Feminist Critic and Her Fiction." *Diacritics* (1982), 12:48–53.

Milton, John. *Paradise Lost.* In *The Complete Poems and Major Prose.* Merritt Y. Hughes, ed. Indianapolis: Odyssey Press, 1957.

Minnich, Elizabeth Kamarck. "Hannah Arendt: Thinking as We Are." In Carol Ascher, Louise De Salvo, and Sara Ruddick, eds., *Between Women: Biographers, Novelists, Critics, Teachers and Artists Write about Their Work on Women,* pp. 171–86. Boston: Beacon, 1984.

Mitchell, Juliet. *Women: The Longest Revolution.* New York: Pantheon, 1984.

Moi, Toril. *Sexual/Textual Politics: Feminist Literary Theory.* London: Methuen, 1985.

Moss, Howard. "A Long Voyage Home." (Book review of *Elizabeth Bishop: The Collected Prose.*) *The New Yorker* (1985), 61:104–12.

Munich, Adrienne. "Notorious Signs, Feminist Criticism, and Literary Tradition." In Gayle Green and Coppelia Kahn, eds., *Making a Difference: Feminist Literary Criticism,* pp. 238–259. London: Methuen, 1986.

Nisbet, Robert A. *Social Change and History: Aspects of a Western Theory of Development.* London: Oxford University Press, 1969.

O'Brien, Mary. "Feminist Theory and Dialectical Logic." *SIGNS* (1981), 7:144–57. Boston: Beacon Press, 1986.

Oliver, Mary. *American Primitive.* Boston: Little, Brown, 1983.

—— *Twelve Moons.* Boston: Little, Brown, 1979.

Olsen, Tillie. *Silences.* New York: Delta, 1978.

Ostriker, Alicia. "Natural Facts." *The Nation* (1986), 243:148–50.

—— *Stealing the Language: The Emergence of Women's Poetry in America.*

Plath, Sylvia. *Ariel.* New York: Harper and Row, 1968.

Poovey, Mary. *The Proper Lady and the Woman Writer: Ideology as Style in the Works of Mary Wollstonecraft, Mary Shelley, and Jane Austen.* Chicago: University of Chicago Press, 1984.

Racevskis, Karlis. *Michel Foucault and the Subversion of Intellect.* Ithaca: Cornell University Press, 1983.

Rich, Adrienne. *The Dream of a Common Language: Poems 1974–1977.* New York: Norton, 1978.

—— *Adrienne Rich's Poetry.* New York: Norton, 1975.

Roberts, Joan. *Beyond Intellectual Sexism: A New Woman, a New Reality.* New York: David McKay, 1976.

Rorty, Richard. "Habermas and Lyotard on Postmodernity." In Richard J. Bernstein, ed., *Habermas and Modernity,* pp. 161–76. Cambridge: M.I.T. Press, 1985.

—— *Philosophy and the Mirror of Nature.* Princeton: Princeton University Press, 1979.

Rossetti, Christina. "Goblin Market." In Walter E. Houghton and G. Robert Stange, eds., *Victorian Poetry and Poetics,* pp. 602–8. New York: Houghton Mifflin, 1968.

Rousseau, Jean Jacques. *Emile.* Barbara Foxley, tr. London: Everyman, 1911.

Russo, Mary. "Female Grotesques: Carnival and Theory." Working Paper No. 1. Milwaukee: Center for Twentieth-Century Studies, 1985.

Sartre, Jean-Paul. *What Is Literature?* Bernard Frechtman, tr. New York: Harper, 1965.

Schiller, Friedrich von. *The Aesthetic Letters, Essays, and the Philosophical Letters.* J. Weiss, tr. Boston: Little, Brown, 1845.

Scholes, Robert and Robert Kellogg. *The Nature of Narrative.* London: Oxford University Press, 1966.

Sennett, Richard. *The Fall of Public Man: On the Social Psychology of Capitalism.* New York: Vintage, 1976.

Showalter, Elaine, ed., *The New Feminist Criticism: Essays on Women, Literature, and Theory.* New York: Pantheon, 1985.

Showalter, Elaine. "Feminist Criticism in the Wilderness," *Critical Inquiry* (1981), 8:179–206.

Silver, Brenda. "The Reflecting Reader in *Villette.*" In Elizabeth Abel, Marianne Hirsch, and Elizabeth Langland, eds., *The Voyage In: Fictions of Female Development.* Hanover, N.H.: University Press of New England, 1983.

Silverman, Kaja. "*Histoire d'O:* The Construction of a Female Subject." In Carole S. Vance, ed., *Pleasure and Danger: Exploring Female Sexuality,* pp. 320–49. Boston: Routledge, 1984.

Singer, Linda. "Value, Power, and Gender: Do We Need a Different Voice?" In Judith Genova, ed. *Power, Gender, Value.* Edmonton, Alberta: Academic Press, forthcoming.

Smith, Lillian. *Killers of the Dream.* New York: Norton, 1978.

Spender, Dale. *Man Made Language.* London: Routledge, 1980.

Spillers, Hortense, "Interstices: A Small Drama of Words." In Carole S. Vance, ed., *Pleasure and Danger: Exploring Female Sexuality.* Boston: Routledge and Kegan Paul, 1984.

Spivak, Gayatri. "French Feminism in an International Frame." *Yale French Studies* (1981), 62:154–84.

Stevens, Wallace. *The Collected Poems of Wallace Stevens.* London: Faber and Faber, 1955.

Todovov, Tzveton. *Mikhail Bakhtin: The Dialogic Principle.* Wlad Godzich, tr. Minneapolis: University of Minnesota Press, 1984.

Turner, Victor. *Dramas, Fields, and Metaphors: Symbolic Action in Human Society.* Ithaca: Cornell University Press, 1974.

Valéry, Paul. *Idée Fixe.* David Paul, tr. New York: Pantheon, 1965.

Van Ghent, Dorothy. *The English Novel: Form and Function.* New York: Harper, 1961.

Webster, Paula. "Pornography and Pleasure." *Heresies* (1981) (special issue on sex), 12:48–51.

Weiskel, Thomas. *The Romantic Sublime: Studies in the Structure and Psychology of Transcendence.* Baltimore: Johns Hopkins University Press, 1976.

Welty, Eudora. "A Piece of News." In Eudora Welty, A Curtain of Green. New York: Harcourt Brace (Harvest), 1979. pp. 21–31.

Williams, Raymond. Marxism and Literature. Oxford: Oxford University Press, 1977.

Winnicott, D. W. Playing and Reality. New York: Basic Books, 1971.

Wittig, Monique. Les Guérillères. Peter Owen, tr. New York: Avon, 1971.

——— "The Straight Mind." Feminist Studies (1980), 1:103–11.

Wollstonecraft, Mary. A Vindication of the Rights of Woman. Carol H. Poston, ed. New York: Norton, 1975.

Woolf, Virginia. A Room of One's Own. New York: Harcourt, Brace, Jovanovich, 1957.

Wordsworth, William. Selected Poems and Prefaces. Jack Stillinger, ed. Boston: Houghton Mifflin (Riverside), 1965.

Yaeger, Patricia. " 'Because a Fire Was in My Head': Eudora Welty and the Dialogic Imagination." PMLA (1984), 99:955–73.

——— "A Language Which Nobody Understood: Emancipatory Strategies in The Awakening." Novel, Spring 1987.

Index

Library of Congress Cataloging-in-Publication Data

Yaeger, Patricia.
Honey-mad women.

(Gender and culture)
Bibliography: p. 303
Includes index.
1. English literature—Women authors—History and
criticism. 2. American literature—Women authors—
History and criticism. 3. Women and literature.
4. Feminism and literature. 5. French literature—
Women authors—History and criticism. I. Title.
II. Series.
PR119.Y34 1988   820'.9'9287   87-10236
ISBN 0-231-06514-0